Language and the Internet

David Crystal investigates the nature of the impact which the Internet is making on language. There is already a widespread popular mythology that the Internet is going to be bad for the future of language – that technospeak will rule, standards be lost, and creativity diminished as globalization imposes sameness. The argument of this book is the reverse: that the Internet is in fact enabling a dramatic expansion to take place in the range and variety of language, and is providing unprecedented opportunities for personal creativity. The Internet has now been around long enough for us to 'take a view' about the way in which it is being shaped by and is shaping language and languages, and there is no one better placed than David Crystal to take that view. His book is written to be accessible to anyone who has used the Internet and who has an interest in language issues.

DAVID CRYSTAL is one of the world's foremost authorities on language, and as editor of the *Cambridge Encyclopedia* database he has used the Internet for research purposes from its earliest manifestations. His work for a high technology company involved him in the development of an information classification system with several Internet applications, and he has extensive professional experience of Web issues.

Professor Crystal is author of the hugely successful *Cambridge Encyclopedia of Language* (1987; second edition 1997), *Cambridge Encyclopedia of the English Language* (1995), *English as a Global Language* (1997), and *Language Death* (2000). An internationally renowned writer, journal editor, lecturer and broadcaster, he received an OBE in 1995 for his services to the English language. His edited books include *The Cambridge Encyclopedia* (1990; second edition 1994; third edition 1997; fourth edition 2000), *The Cambridge Paperback Encyclopedia* (1993; second edition 1995; third edition 1999), *The Cambridge Biographical Encyclopedia* (1994; second edition 1998) and *The Cambridge Factfinder* (1994; second edition 1997; third edition 1998; fourth edition 2000).

Language and the Internet

DAVID CRYSTAL

CAMBRIDGE
UNIVERSITY PRESS

PUBLISHED BY THE PRESS SYNDICATE OF THE UNIVERSITY OF CAMBRIDGE
The Pitt Building, Trumpington Street, Cambridge, United Kingdom

CAMBRIDGE UNIVERSITY PRESS
The Edinburgh Building, Cambridge CB2 2RU, UK
40 West 20th Street, New York NY 10011-4211, USA
10 Stamford Road, Oakleigh, VIC 3166, Australia
Ruiz de Alarcón 13, 28014 Madrid, Spain
Dock House, The Waterfront, Cape Town 8001, South Africa

http://www.cambridge.org

First published 2001

Printed in the United Kingdom at the University Press, Cambridge

Typeface Minion 11/14 pt.   *System* LATEX 2$_\varepsilon$ [TB]

A catalogue record for this book is available from the British Library.

Library of Congress Cataloguing in Publication data
Crystal, David, 1941–
Language and the Internet / David Crystal.
    p.   cm.
Includes bibliographical references and index.
ISBN 0 521 80212 1
1. Language and languages.   2. Internet (Computer network)   I. Title.
P107 .C78   2001
400′.2854678 – dc21   2001025792

ISBN 0 521 80212 1 hardback

November 16, 200?

Contents

Preface

In his book *A brief history of the future: the origins of the Internet*, John Naughton comments:[1]

> The Internet is one of the most remarkable things human beings have ever made. In terms of its impact on society, it ranks with print, the railways, the telegraph, the automobile, electric power and television. Some would equate it with print and television, the two earlier technologies which most transformed the communications environment in which people live. Yet it is potentially more powerful than both because it harnesses the intellectual leverage which print gave to mankind without being hobbled by the one-to-many nature of broadcast television.

In *Weaving the Web*, the World Wide Web's inventor, Tim Berners-Lee, quotes a speech made by the South African president, Thabo Mbeki:[2]

> on how people should seize the new technology to empower themselves; to keep themselves informed about the truth of their own economic, political and cultural circumstances; and to give themselves a voice that all the world could hear.

And he adds: 'I could not have written a better mission statement for the World Wide Web.' Later he comments:

> The Web is more a social creation than a technical one.

And again:

> the dream of people-to-people communication through shared knowledge must be possible for groups of all sizes, interacting electronically with as much ease as they do now in person.

[1] Naughton (1999: 21–2).
[2] Berners-Lee (1999: 110, 133, 169).

Remarks of this kind have grown since the mid-1990s. An emphasis, which formerly was on technology, has shifted to be on people and purposes. And as the Internet comes increasingly to be viewed from a social perspective, so the role of language becomes central. Indeed, notwithstanding the remarkable technological achievements and the visual panache of screen presentation, what is immediately obvious when engaging in any of the Internet's functions is its linguistic character. If the Internet is a revolution, therefore, it is likely to be a linguistic revolution.

I wrote this book because I wanted to find out about the role of language in the Internet and the effect of the Internet on language, and could find no account already written. In the last few years, people have been asking me what influence the Internet was having on language and I could give only impressionistic answers. At the same time, pundits have been making dire predictions about the future of language, as a result of the Internet's growth. The media would ask me for a comment, and I could not make an informed one; when they insisted, as media people do, I found myself waffling. It was time to sort out my ideas, and this book is the result. I do not think I could have written it five years ago, because of the lack of scholarly studies to provide some substance, and the general difficulty of obtaining large samples of data, partly because of the sensitivity surrounding the question of whether Internet data is public or private. Even now the task is not an easy one, and I have had to use constructed examples, from time to time, to fill out my exposition. Fortunately, a few books and anthologies dealing with Internet language in a substantial way appeared between 1996 and 2000, and focused journals, notably the online *Journal of Computer-Mediated Communication*, began to provide a useful range of illustrations, associated commentary, and an intellectual frame of reference. The extent to which I have relied on these sources will be apparent from the footnotes.

A single intuition about Internet language is next to useless, given the sheer scale of the phenomenon; and the generally youthful character of those using the medium hitherto has put my personal intuition under some strain, given that I fall just outside the peak age-range of Internet users (said to be 20-somethings). I am therefore very happy to acknowledge the assistance at various points of daughters Lucy and Suzanne – both professionally involved in the communications world – and son Ben for providing a bridge to the Internet as *they* know it to be, in their generation, and for providing extra data. I am also most grateful to Patricia Wallace, Simon Mitchell, and my editor at Cambridge University Press, Kevin Taylor, for further valuable comment, and to my wife, Hilary, for her invaluable critical reading of the screenscript. It is conventional for authors to express their sense of responsibility for any remaining infelicities, and this I willingly do – but of course excluding, in this case, those developments in the Internet revolution, predictable in their unpredictability, which will manifest themselves between now and publication, and make my topical illustrations seem dated. Nine months is a short time in terms of book production, but a very long time in the world of the Internet. Who knows how many of the Web sites I have used will still be around in a year's time? I hope nonetheless that my focus on general issues will enable *Language and the Internet* to outlast such changes, and provide a linguistic perspective which will be of relevance to any of the Internet's future incarnations.

David Crystal
Holyhead, January 2001

1   *A linguistic perspective*

> Will the English-dominated Internet
> spell the end of other tongues?
>
> Quite e-vil: the mobile phone
> whisperers
>
> A major risk for humanity

These quotations illustrate widely held anxieties about the effect
of the Internet on language and languages. The first is the sub-
heading of a magazine article on millennial issues.[1] The second is
the headline of an article on the rise of new forms of impoliteness in
communication among people using the short messaging service
on their mobile phones.[2] The third is a remark from the President of
France, Jacques Chirac, commenting on the impact of the Internet
on language, and especially on French.[3] My collection of press clip-
pings has dozens more in similar vein, all with a focus on language.
The authors are always ready to acknowledge the immense technological achievement, communicative power, and social potential
of the Internet; but within a few lines their tone changes, as they
express their concerns. It is a distinctive genre of worry. But unlike
sociologists, political commentators, economists, and others who
draw attention to the dangers of the Internet with respect to such
matters as pornography, intellectual property rights, privacy, security, libel, and crime, these authors are worried primarily about
linguistic issues. For them, it is language in general, and individual
languages in particular, which are going to end up as Internet

---

[1] Used in an article by Jim Erickson, 'Cyberspeak: the death of diversity', *Asiaweek*, 3 July 1998, 15.
[2] Lydia Slater, in *The Sunday Times*, 30 January 2000, 10.
[3] 'Language and electronics: the coming global tongue', *The Economist*, 21 December 1996, 37.

casualties, and their specific questions raise a profusion of spectres. Do the relaxed standards of e-mails augur the end of literacy and spelling as we know it? Will the Internet herald a new era of technobabble? Will linguistic creativity and flexibility be lost as globalization imposes sameness?

There is of course nothing new about fears accompanying the emergence of a new communications technology. In the fifteenth century, the arrival of printing was widely perceived by the Church as an invention of Satan, the hierarchy fearing that the dissemination of uncensored ideas would lead to a breakdown of social order and put innumerable souls at risk of damnation. Steps were quickly taken to limit its potentially evil effects. Within half a century of Gutenberg's first Bible (1455), Frankfurt had established a state censorship office to suppress unorthodox biblical translations and tracts (1486), and soon after, Pope Alexander VI extended censorship to secular books (1501). Around 400 years later, similar concerns about censorship and control were widespread when society began to cope with the political consequences of the arrival of the telegraph, the telephone, and broadcasting technology. The telegraph would destroy the family and promote crime.[4] The telephone would undermine society. Broadcasting would be the voice of propaganda. In each case, the anxiety generated specifically linguistic controversy. Printing enabled vernacular translations of the Bible to be placed before thousands, adding fuel to an argument about the use of local languages in religious settings which continues to resonate today. And when broadcasting enabled selected voices to be heard by millions, there was an immediate debate over which norms to use as correct pronunciation, how to achieve clarity and intelligibility, and whether to permit local accents and dialects, which remains as lively a debate in the twenty-first century as it was in the twentieth.

The Internet is an association of computer networks with common standards which enable messages to be sent from any central

---

[4] The parallels between the arrival of the Internet and the arrival of the telegraph are explored in Standage (1999).

computer (or *host*) on one network to any host on any other. It developed in the 1960s in the USA as an experimental network which quickly grew to include military, federal, regional, university, business, and personal users. It is now the world's largest computer network, with over 100 million hosts connected by the year 2000, providing an increasing range of services and enabling unprecedented numbers of people to be in touch with each other through electronic mail (*e-mail*), discussion groups, and the provision of digital 'pages' on any topic. Functional information, such as electronic shopping, business data, advertisements, and bulletins, can be found alongside creative works, such as poems and scripts, with the availability of movies, TV programmes, and other kinds of entertainment steadily growing. Some commentators have likened the Internet to an amalgam of television, telephone, and conventional publishing, and the term *cyberspace* has been coined to capture the notion of a world of information present or possible in digital form (the *information superhighway*). The potential of the Internet is currently limited by relatively slow data-transmission speeds, and by the problems of management and retrieval posed by the existence of such a vast amount of information (see chapter 7); but there is no denying the unprecedented scale and significance of the Net, as a global medium. The extra significance is even reflected in the spelling, in languages which use capital letters: this is the first such technology to be conventionally identified with an initial capital. We do not give typographical enhancement to such developments as 'Printing', 'Publishing', 'Broadcasting', 'Radio', or 'Television', but we do write 'Internet' and 'Net'.[5]

What is it like to be a regular citizen of the Internet, a *netizen*? Those who already spend appreciable amounts of time online need

---

[5] In its sense as a global network of computers. When the term is used to refer to a local network, or some local set of connected networks, it is usually given a lower-case initial – though usage is uncertain in both contexts. The abbreviated form, Net, is generally capitalized. Private networks within organizations, or *intranets*, are always lower-case. It is important to note that other networks exist. A chatgroup system, such as the Usenet newsgroups (pp. 131–3), may be carried by other networks than the Internet (such as UUCP). Although the focus of this book is the Internet, its conclusions apply just as much to these other nets.

only self-reflect; for those who do not, the self-descriptions of a 'day in a netizen's life' are informative. Here is Shawn Wilbur's, as he describes what a 'virtual community' means to him:[6]

> For me it is the work of a few hours a day, carved up into minutes and carried on from before dawn until long after dark. I venture out onto the Net when I wake in the night, while coffee water boils, or bath water runs, between manuscript sections or student appointments. Or I keep a network connection open in the background while I do other work. Once or twice a day, I log on for longer periods of time, mostly to engage in more demanding realtime communication, but I find that is not enough. My friends and colleagues express similar needs for frequent connection, either in conversation or through the covetous looks they cast at occupied terminals in the office. Virtual community is this work, this immersion, and also the connections it represents. Sometimes it is realtime communication. More often it is asynchronous and mostly solitary, a sort of textual flirtation that only occasionally aims at any direct confrontation of voices or bodies.

And there are now several sites which will advise you of the symptoms to look out for if you want to know whether you are Internet-driven. Here is a short selection from various pages headed 'addicted to the Internet':

> You wake up at 3 a.m. to go to the bathroom and stop to check your e-mail on the way back to bed.
> You sign off and your screen says you were on for 3 days and 45 minutes.
> You placed the refrigerator beside your computer.
> You say 'scroll up' when someone asks what it was you said.
> All of your friends have an @ in their names.
> You tell the cab driver you live at
>   http://123.elm.street/house/bluetrim.html
> You check your mail. It says 'no new messages'. So you check it again.
> Your phone bill comes to your doorstep in a box.

[6] Wilbur (1996: 13–14). See also Naughton's account (1999: 143ff.).

It is not the aim of this book to reflect on the consequences for individuals or for society of lives that are lived largely in cyberspace. My aim is much more modest: it is to explore the ways in which the nature of the electronic medium as such, along with the Internet's global scale and intensity of use, is having an effect on language in general, and on individual languages in particular. It seems likely that these effects will be as pervasive and momentous as in the case of the previous communication technologies, mentioned above, which gave language printed and broadcast dimensions that generated many new distinctive varieties and usages, from the telegrammatic graphic prominence of newspaper headlines to the hyperverbal sonic prominence of sports commentaries. The electronic medium, to begin with, presents us with a channel which facilitates and constrains our ability to communicate in ways that are fundamentally different from those found in other semiotic situations. Many of the expectations and practices which we associate with spoken and written language, as we shall see (chapter 2), no longer obtain. The first task is therefore to investigate the linguistic properties of the so-called 'electronic revolution', and to take a view on whether the way in which we use language on the Internet is becoming so different from our previous linguistic behaviour that it might genuinely be described as revolutionary.

The linguistic consequences of evolving a medium in which the whole world participates – at least in principle, once their countries' infrastructure and internal economy allow them to gain access – are also bound to be far-reaching. We must not overstate the global nature of the Internet: it is still largely in the hands of the better-off citizens of the developed countries. But it is the principle which matters. What happens, linguistically, when the members of the human race use a technology enabling any of them to be in routine contact with anyone else? There has been much talk of the notion of a 'global village', which is at first sight a persuasive metaphor. Yet such a concept raises all kinds of linguistic questions. A village is a close-knit community, traditionally identified by a local dialect or language which distinguishes its members from those elsewhere: 'That's not how we say things round here.' If there is to be a genuine global village,[7] then we need to ask 'What is its dialect?', 'What are the shared features of language which give the world community of users their sense of identity?' And, if we cannot discern any unifying dialect or language, or a trend towards such a unity, we need to ask ourselves if this 'global village' is anything more than a media fiction. Similar questions might be asked of related notions, such as 'digital citizens', 'the virtual community', and the 'Net generation'. The linguistic perspective is a critical part of this debate. As Derek Foster puts it, reflecting on the notion of a virtual community, 'the fullest understanding of the term is gained by grounding it in the communicative act itself'.[8] So the second task is to investigate whether the Internet is emerging as a homogenous linguistic medium, whether it is a collection of distinct dialects, reflecting the different backgrounds, needs, purposes, and attitudes of its users, or whether it is an aggregation of trends and idiosyncratic usages which as yet defy classification.

Internet situations

In a setting where linguistic differences are likely to loom large, the concept of a *language variety* will be helpful. A variety of language is a system of linguistic expression whose use is governed by situational factors.[9] In its broadest sense, the notion includes speech and writing, regional and class dialects, occupational genres (such as legal and scientific language), creative linguistic expression (as

---

[7] McLuhan (1962: 31), and elsewhere.
[8] Foster (1996: 35).
[9] Within linguistics, several terms have been used, over the years, for talking about language which varies according to situation, such as *speech community*, *register*, *genre*, *text*, and *discourse type*, each of which operates in its own theoretical frame of reference (see Crystal and Davy, 1969). As Internet linguistics develops, more sophisticated models will be needed to capture all elements of the variation found. For the present book, which is only a 'first approximation', I have avoided a more complex terminological system, and used the term *variety* without further qualification for all kinds of situationally influenced language. I also sometimes refer to *genres* within a variety. Within the Internet literature, terminology also varies a great deal when discussing the different kinds of Internet situation, such as *environment*, *interactive setting*, and *virtual space*.

in literature), and a wide range of other styles of expression. Varieties are, in principle, systematic and predictable. It is possible to say, with some degree of certainty in a given language, how people from a particular region will speak, how lawyers will write, or how television commentators will present a type of sport. Notions such as 'British English' or 'Liverpool English', 'legal French', and 'sports commentary' are the result. To change an important element in any situation is to motivate a change in the language people use there, if they wish to behave conventionally – whether the change is from one region to another, from law court to the street, from home to pub, from one listener to many, or from face-to-face to distant conversation. Sometimes the features of a variety are highly constrained by the situation: there are strict rules governing the kind of language we may use in court, for example, and if we break them we are likely to be criticized or even charged with contempt. In other situations there may be an element of choice in what we say or write, as when we choose to adopt a formal or an informal tone in an after-dinner speech, or a combination of the two. But all language-using situations present us with constraints which we must be aware of and must obey if our contribution is to be judged acceptable. Factors such as politeness, interest, and intelligibility govern what we dare to introduce into an after-dinner speech, and such criteria apply in all situations. 'Anything goes' is never an option – or, at least, if people do decide to speak or write without paying any attention to the sociolinguistic expectations and mores of their interlocutors, and of the community as a whole, they must expect to be judged accordingly.[10]

The distinctive features of a language variety are of several kinds. Many stylistic approaches recognize five main types, for written language.[11]

- *graphic* features: the general presentation and organization of the written language, defined in terms of such factors as

---

[10] Allowances can sometimes be made – as with some kinds of psychiatric disturbance and linguistic pathology, or the utterances of very young children.
[11] For the application of a model of this kind to several varieties of English, see Crystal and Davy (1969).

distinctive typography, page design, spacing, use of illustrations, and colour; for example, the variety of newspaper
English would be chiefly identified at this level through the
use of such notions as headlines, columns, and captions.

- *orthographic* (or *graphological*) features: the writing system
  of an individual language, defined in terms of such factors as
  distinctive use of the alphabet, capital letters, spelling, punctuation, and ways of expressing emphasis (italics, boldface,
  etc.); for example, American and British English are distinguished by many spelling differences (e.g. *colour* vs. *color*),
  and advertising English allows spelling modifications that
  would be excluded from most other varieties (e.g. *Beanz
  Meanz Heinz*).

- *grammatical* features: the many possibilities of syntax and
  morphology, defined in terms of such factors as the distinctive
  use of sentence structure, word order, and word inflections;
  for example, religious English makes use of an unusual
  vocative construction (*O God, who knows...*) and allows a
  second-person singular set of pronouns (*thou, thee, thine*).

- *lexical* features: the vocabulary of a language, defined in terms
  of the set of words and idioms given distinctive use within a
  variety; for example, legal English employs such expressions
  as *heretofore, easement,* and *alleged,* as well as such phrases as
  signed sealed and delivered and Latin expressions such as *ex
  post facto.*

- *discourse* features: the structural organization of a text,
  defined in terms of such factors as coherence, relevance,
  paragraph structure, and the logical progression of ideas;
  for example, a journal paper within scientific English typically consists of a fixed sequence of sections including the
  abstract, introduction, methodology, results, discussion, and
  conclusion.

'Whatever else Internet culture may be, it is still largely a text-based
affair.'[12] Spoken language currently has only a limited presence on

---

[12] Wilbur (1996: 6).

the Internet, through the use of sound clips, films, and video; but the use of speech will undoubtedly grow as technology develops, and it will not be long before we see the routine use of interactive voice (and video) dialogues, speech synthesis to provide a spoken representation of what is on a screen or to give vocal support to a graphic presentation, and automatic speech recognition to enable users to interact verbally with sites (see further, chapter 8). In addition to the above five types, therefore, we need to recognize two more:

- *phonetic* features: the general auditory characteristics of spoken language, defined in terms of such factors as the distinctive use of voice quality, vocal register (e.g. tenor vs. bass), and voice modality (e.g. speaking, singing, chanting); for example, in TV commentary, different sports make use of different vocal norms (e.g. the loud enthusiastic crescendos of football vs. the hushed monastic tones of snooker).
- *phonological* features: the sound system of an individual language, defined in terms of such factors as the distinctive use of vowels, consonants, intonation, stress, and pause; for example, regional accents are defined by the way they make different use of sounds, and distinctive pronunciation is also a notable feature of such varieties as newsreading, preaching, and television advertising.

Grammatical, lexical, and discourse features of course play a distinctive role in all spoken varieties of a language, as they do in the written. A television commentary is not distinctive solely in its pronunciation, but in its use of grammar, vocabulary, and general organization as well.

So the initial question for the person interested in Internet linguistics to ask is: is the Net a homogenous language-using electronic situation, likely to generate a single variety of language, defined using such variables as those listed above? Will all users of the Internet present themselves, through their messages, contributions, and pages, with the same kind of graphic, orthographic, grammatical, lexical, and discourse features? To answer these questions we need first to establish how many different situations the Internet contains. We then need to describe the salient linguistic features of each situation, and to identify variations in the way they are used. This will help us talk more precisely about the strategies that people employ and the linguistic attitudes they hold, and thus enable us to begin evaluating their beliefs and concerns about Internet language. Some of these situations are easy to identify, because they have been around a relatively long time and have begun to settle down. Some are still in their infancy, with their situational status totally bound up with emerging technology, and therefore subject to rapid change: an example is the linking of the Internet to mobile phone technology, where the small screen size immediately motivated a fresh range of linguistic expression (see p. 228). Given the speed of technological change, doubtless new situational variables will emerge which will make any attempt at classification quickly outdated. But, as of the beginning of 2001, it is possible to identify five broad Internet-using situations which are sufficiently different to mean that the language they contain is likely to be significantly distinctive.

Electronic mail (e-mail)

E-mail is the use of computer systems to transfer messages between users – now chiefly used to refer to messages sent between private mailboxes (as opposed to those posted to a chatgroup). Although it takes up only a relatively small domain of Internet 'space', by comparison with the billions of pages on the World Wide Web, it far exceeds the Web in terms of the number of daily individual transactions made. As John Naughton says, 'The Net was built on electronic mail. . . . It's the oil which lubricates the system.'[13] Today, for example, I called up pages on the Web three times but sent twenty e-mails. My contacts included family, friends, and colleagues, as well as a range of new and long-standing business associates. My incoming e-mails included several of these, along with a sporadic sampling of 'junk' mail from organizations that had got hold of

---

[13] Naughton (1999: 150).

my e-address, some of which had attachments that were indistinguishable from a Web page in their linguistic character. Many of the messages, incoming and outgoing, varied greatly in length and style. The diversity of e-mail contexts is immediately apparent. So here, too, the chief issue must be to determine the linguistic coherence of the situation. Do the requirements of immediate and rapid e-messaging promote the use of certain linguistic features which transcend its many variations in audience and purpose? Indeed, can we generalize about the language of e-mail at all? This question is addressed in chapter 4.

Chatgroups

Chatgroups are continuous discussions on a particular topic, organized in 'rooms' at particular Internet sites, in which computer users interested in the topic can participate. There are two situations here, depending on whether the interaction takes place in real time (*synchronous*) or in postponed time (*asynchronous*).

- In a synchronous situation, a user enters a chat room and joins an ongoing conversation in real time, sending named contributions which are inserted into a permanently scrolling screen along with the contributions from other participants. Internet Relay Chat (IRC) is an example of one of the main systems available to users, consisting of thousands of rooms dealing with different topics. Although most people enter just one room at a time, there is nothing to stop them opening more than one chat window and engaging in two or more conversations simultaneously, if they have the requisite cognitive and linguistic skills.
- In an asynchronous situation, the interactions are stored in some format, and made available to users upon demand, so that they can catch up with the discussion, or add to it, at any time – even after an appreciable period has passed. The *bulletin boards*, a popular feature of 1980s computer-mediated communication, are one example. The thousands

of *newsgroups* on Usenet, covering a vast number of topics, provide another. Another is the *mailing list*, such as LIST-SERV®, to which users subscribe, knowing that all messages sent in to the list will reach everyone on that list.

Some chatgroups are global, receiving contributions from any geographical location; some are local, restricted to a particular country or region. Some are moderated, in the hands of an owner or editor; others are uncontrolled, other than by internal forces (see p. 146). Although the chatgroup situation would seem, at first sight, to promote the use of a highly distinctive and consistent language variety, the different factors involved – especially the factor of synchronicity – make it likely that it will contain significant diversity. This question is addressed in chapter 5.

Virtual worlds

Virtual worlds are imaginary environments which people can enter to engage in text-based fantasy social interaction. From the early notion of a *MUD* (originally 'multi-user dungeon', a derivation from the 1970s role-playing adventure game 'Dungeons and Dragons'), several adventure genres developed, offering players the opportunity to experience imaginary and vividly described environments in which they adopt new identities, explore fantasy worlds, engage in novel exploits, and use their guises to interact with other participants. Many MUDs, while reliant on the use of a shared virtual space and role-playing identities, move away from the creation of adventure worlds – for example, constructing worlds within education or business contexts, or using them for elaborate chat sessions. As a result, the acronym is also glossed as 'multi-user domain' or 'multi-user dimension'. Later technological developments enabled multimedia elements to be added to this genre, sound and video functions supplementing or replacing text to enable participants to take up an on-screen visual presence as avatars (a term from Hindu mythology, referring to an incarnation of a deity in earthly form) in what some commentators have called *metaworlds*.[14] A range of sub-genres, with differing emphases, technical options, and of course acronym-like names, now exists, such as MOOs (MUD, Object-Orientated), MUSHes, MUCKs, MUSEs, and TinyMUDs (p. 173). The linguistic possibilities, in such imagination-governed worlds, are plainly immense, but – as with all games – there need to be constraints guiding the play, without which the interactions would be chaotic. These will be addressed in chapter 6.

World Wide Web (WWW)

The World Wide Web is the full collection of all the computers linked to the Internet which hold documents that are mutually accessible through the use of a standard protocol (the HyperText Transfer Protocol, or HTTP),[15] usually abbreviated to *Web* or *W3* and, in site addresses, presented as the acronym *www*. The creator of the Web, computer scientist Tim Berners-Lee, has defined it as 'the universe of network-accessible information, an embodiment of human knowledge'.[16] It was devised in 1990 as a means of enabling high-energy physicists in different institutions to share information within their field, but it rapidly spread to other fields, and is now all-inclusive in subject-matter, and designed for multimedia interaction between computer users anywhere in the world. Its many functions include encyclopedic reference, archiving, cataloguing, 'Yellow Pages' listing, advertising, self-publishing, games, news reporting, creative writing, and commercial transactions of all kinds, with movies and other types of entertainment becoming increasingly available. With such an enormous range of topic and purpose, the chief linguistic issues

---

[14] For example, Wallace (1999: 8).

[15] A protocol is a set of rules which enables computers to communicate with each other or other devices; the Transmission Control Protocol / Internet Protocol, TCI/IP, was made the Internet standard in 1985; *Wired Style* calls it 'the mother tongue of the Internet' (Hale and Scanlon, 1999: 159).

[16] Berners-Lee (1999). It should be evident that the popular practice of using the terms *Internet* and *Web* interchangeably is very misleading. The Web is one of several Internet situations.

here must be whether the Web can be said to have any coherence, as a linguistic variety, and whether it is possible to make useful or valid generalizations about its use of language at all. This question is addressed in chapter 7.

These five situations are not entirely mutually exclusive. It is possible to find sites in which all elements are combined, or where one situation is used within another. For example, many Web sites contain discussion groups and e-mail links; e-mails often contain Web attachments; and some MUDs include asynchronous chatgroups and permit participants to contact each other via e-mail. The Internet world is an extremely fluid one, with users exploring its possibilities of expression, introducing fresh combinations of elements, and reacting to technological developments. It seems to be in a permanent state of transition, lacking precedent, struggling for standards, and searching for direction. About the only thing that is clear is that people are unclear about what is going to happen. As John Naughton puts it, at the end of his book, *A brief history of the future*, 'The openness of the Net also applies to its future. The protocols which govern it leave the course of its evolution open.'[17] For example, it is likely that my five situations will need to be supplemented very soon by a sixth, as interactive voice dialogue becomes increasingly available, and conversationalists make decisions about what kind of spoken language to use to exploit the new medium. But there is no way of predicting whether this new language-using situation will make use of old conversational norms or invent fresh stylistic techniques to facilitate interaction, or what particular combination of new and old will prove to be most effective. This will doubtless add an extra chapter to some later edition of this book.

For each of the five situations outlined above, it is evident that people are still getting to grips with the communicative potential made available to them. They are in a learning situation of a rather special kind. They are having to acquire the rules (of how

---

[17] Naughton (1999: 271).

to communicate via e-mail, of how to talk in chatgroups, of how to construct an effective Web page, of how to socialize in fantasy roles), and yet there are no rules, in the sense of universally agreed modes of behaviour established by generations of usage. There is a clear contrast with the world of paper-based communication. Letter-writing, for instance, is routinely taught in school; and because there is widespread agreement on how letters are to be written, supported by the recommendations of usage manuals, we feel secure in that knowledge. We know such conventions as how to use opening and closing formulae (*Dear Sir/Madam, Yours faithfully*), where to put the address and date, and how to break up the text into paragraphs. Adults make use of this knowledge almost without thinking, and on occasion, as in informal letter-writing, they dare to break the rules with confidence. But with the Internet equivalent of letter-writing – e-mails – there is no such long tradition. Most people have been using e-mails for less than a decade, and they are unaware of the factors which have to be respected if their messages are not to be misunderstood. Often, the first indication that they have misconstructed a message comes when they receive an unpalatable response from the recipient.

Nobody knows all the communicative problems which lurk within e-discourses of all five kinds. Recommendations about approach and style are only beginning to be formulated, and many are tentative (see chapter 2). Market research companies are investing a great deal to discover how people react to different Web page configurations. Psychologists are beginning to probe the kinds of problem which affect individuals who engage in unconstrained fantasy play. There is an enormous amount of idiosyncrasy and variation seen in e-encounters. At the same time, the detailed studies which have taken place have begun to identify levels of shared usage within individual e-situations. Lynn Cherny, for example, having studied the language found in one kind of MUD (ElseMOO, p. 174), concludes that 'the linguistic interactions in ElseMOO are most amenable to description in terms of register', and Boyd Davis and Jeutonne Brewer, in their study of a chatgroup, although initially tentative, conclude that it 'may come to be seen as a

register...[an] emergent register'.[18] Certainly the participants
themselves seem to be aware that their language is distinctive.
Cherny in fact reports an attempt by ElseMOO in 1994 to document its distinctive language.[19] Although it did not get very far –
being criticized by some members as going against the 'insider'
ethos of the community – the argument suggests some clear intuitions about the status of its usage as a variety.

The language of Internet users is plainly in a state of transition.
As Patricia Wallace puts it, in her discussion of the false impressions
Net participants gain about each other during encounters: 'On the
Internet we are struggling with a very odd set of tools and pushing
them as hard as we can. Homo sapiens are both set in their ways
and amazingly adaptable, and right now, all of us are learning some
painful and awkward lessons about impression formation online.'
And she adds: 'I look forward to the time when the kinds of "interaction rituals" that Goffman described will stabilize on the net
and the business of forming impressions will be more predictable,
reliable, and familiar, and much less prone to those hazardous
misperceptions.'[20] The need for greater predictability, reliability,
and familiarity is something which affects all Internet situations,
and also the language which is found there. It is a world where
individuals have tried to solve the problem of an electronically
constrained communications medium (see chapter 2) in countless
idiosyncratic ways. It is also a world where many of the participants are highly motivated individualists, intent on exploring the
potential of a new medium, knowledgeable about its procedures,
and holding firm views about the way it should be used. The most
informed of this population are routinely referred to as *geeks* –
defined by *Wired Style*, an influential Internet manual, as 'someone
who codes for fun, speaks Unix among friends, and reads Slashdot
daily'.[21] We might expect a great deal of linguistic innovation and

---

[18] Cherny (1999: 27), Davis and Brewer (1997: 28–9, 157).
[19] Cherny (1999: 85). She introduces the relevant chapter with an epigraph from a character
called Damon, who says, 'anyone who doesn't think we speak some strange separate dialect
has been smoking crack'.
[20] Wallace (1999: 36); see, also, Goffman (1959).
[21] Hale and Scanlon (1999: 88). Slashdot is a Website created in 1997 to provide 'News

ingenuity in their usage, accordingly. At the same time, everyone is aware that too much idiosyncrasy causes problems of intelligibility. Also, the pressure towards conformity is strong in those participatory activities to which the label 'community' has often been applied. As one contributor to a discussion about aggressive language (*flaming*, p. 55) said: 'You and I can talk any way we want on Internet; the question is what kind of conversation are we looking for.'[22] So, what kind of conversations are there, online, and how does one participate in them? Do we have to learn a new kind of language – 'Netspeak', as I shall call it – in order to be a netizen?

Netspeak

The term 'Netspeak' is an alternative to 'Netlish', 'Weblish', 'Internet language', 'cyberspeak', 'electronic discourse', 'electronic language', 'interactive written discourse', 'computer-mediated communication' (CMC), and other more cumbersome locutions. Each term has a different implication: 'Netlish', for example, is plainly derived from 'English', and is of decreasing usefulness as the Net becomes more multilingual (p. 216); 'electronic discourse' emphasizes the interactive and dialogue elements; 'CMC' focuses on the medium itself. It is perhaps unsurprising to see 'Netspeak', as a term, being given some popular currency – following the Orwellian introduction of *Newspeak* and *Oldspeak* in *1984*, later developments such as *Doublespeak* and *Seaspeak*, and media labels such as *Royalspeak* and *Blairspeak*. From the perspective of this book, it is broader than *Webspeak*, which has also had some use. As a name, *Netspeak* is succinct, and functional enough, as long as we remember that 'speak' here involves writing as well as talking, and that any 'speak'

---

for Nerds. Stuff that Matters': <http://www.slashdot.com>. If you have just learned something from this footnote, you are not a geek.

[22] Millard (1996: 154–5). Other references which focus on the linguistic identity of various e-situations include: Ferrara, Brunner, and Whittemore (1991), Baym (1993), Maynor (1994), Collot and Belmore (1996), and Baron (1998b). The notion of 'virtual speech community' is encountered in various forms, such as 'discourse community' (Gurak, 1997).

suffix also has a receptive element, including 'listening and reading'. The first of these points hardly seems worth the reminder, given that the Internet is so clearly a predominantly written medium (for its spoken dimension, see chapter 8), and yet, as we shall see, the question of how speech is related to writing is at the heart of the matter. But the second point is sometimes ignored, so its acknowledgement is salutary. On the Internet, as with traditional[23] speaking and writing, the language that individuals produce is far exceeded by the language they receive; and as the Internet is a medium almost entirely dependent on reactions to written messages, awareness of audience must hold a primary place in any discussion. The core feature of the Internet is its real or potential interactivity.

There is a widely held intuition that some sort of Netspeak exists – a type of language displaying features that are unique to the Internet, and encountered in all the above situations, arising out of its character as a medium which is electronic, global, and interactive. The linguistic basis for this intuition is examined in detail in chapters 2 and 3; but the fact that people are conscious of something 'out there' is demonstrated by the way other varieties of language are being affected by it. It is always a sure sign that a new variety has 'arrived' when people in other linguistic situations start alluding to it. For example, a comic courtroom sketch on television will borrow freely from legal language, assuming that viewers will recognize the linguistic allusions; and individuals can introduce references to legal language into their speech even if they have never been inside a courtroom in their lives – 'the tooth, the whole tooth, and nothing but the tooth' was one particularly bad dental pun I encountered recently. It is therefore of considerable

---

[23] The terms 'traditional' and 'conventional' are often used to refer to non-electronically mediated linguistic communication – old-style speech and writing – but there is no standard usage. More generally, there is no standard terminology for the distinction between the electronic and non-electronic worlds – though commonly used is the opposition *VR* ('virtual reality') and *RL* ('real life') or the adverbial *IRL* ('in real life'), the 'physical world', and other such locutions. Ihnatko (1997: 160) defines 'real world' as 'That which cannot be accessed via a keyboard. A nice place to visit, a good place to swing by when you're out of Coke, but you wouldn't want to live there.'

interest to note the way in which salient features of Netspeak, taken from one or other of its situational manifestations, have already begun to be used outside of the situation of computer-mediated communication, even though the medium has become available to most people only in the past decade or so. The influence is mainly on vocabulary, with graphology affected in some written varieties.[24]

In everyday conversation, terms from the underlying computer technology are given a new application among people who want their talk to have a cool cutting-edge. Examples from recent over-heard conversations include:

> It's my turn to download now (i.e. I've heard all your gossip, now hear mine)
> I need more bandwidth to handle that point (i.e. I can't take it all in at once)
> She's multitasking (said of someone doing two things at once)
> Let's go offline for a few minutes (i.e. let's talk in private)
> Give me a brain dump on that (i.e. tell me all you know)
> I'll ping you later (i.e. get in touch to see if you're around)
> He's 404 (i.e. he's not around; see p. 82)
> He started flaming me for no reason at all (i.e. shouting at me; see p. 55)
> That's an alt.dot way of looking at things (i.e. a cool way; see p. 83)
> Are you wired? (i.e. ready to handle this)
> Get with the programme (i.e. keep up)
> I got a pile of spam in the post today (i.e. junk-mail; see p. 53)
> He's living in hypertext (i.e. he's got a lot to hide; see p. 202)
> E you later (said as a farewell)

Programmers have long needed special vocabulary to talk about their lines of code, and some of this has now spilled over into

---

[24] An interesting influence occurs in those languages, such as Spanish and Portuguese, which lack the letter *w*, and where the existence of *WWW* in effect adds an extra letter to their alphabet. The influence of English on the vocabulary of other languages is also growing, such as *hack* and *scroll* (as verbs in Dutch), *scrollare* and *deletare* (Italian), *debugear* and *lockear* (Spanish).

everyday speech, especially to handle the punctuation present in an electronic address. For example, radio and television presenters commonly add e-addresses when telling listeners and viewers how they might write in to a programme, using *at*, *dot*, and *forward slash* to punctuate their utterance. *Dot com* is now a commonly heard phrase, as well as appearing ubiquitously in writing in all kinds of advertising and promotional material.

In fact, written English shows developments well beyond the stage of the literal use of *.com*. This suffix is one of several domain names (with some US/UK variation) showing what kind of organization an electronic address belongs to:[25] *.com* (commercial), *.edu* or *.ac* (educational), *.gov* (governmental), *.mil* (military), *.net* (network organizations), and *.org* or *.co* (everything else). *Dotcom* has come to be used as a general adjective (with or without the period, and sometimes hyphenated), as in *dotcom organizations* and *dotcom crisis*. It has, however, come to be used in a variety of ludic ways, especially in those varieties where language play is a dominant motif – newspaper headlines and advertising.[26] It has been expanded into other words: a computer hardware store advertises itself as *SHOPNAME.computer*. Similarly, *www* became *web without worry* in a British Telecom advertising campaign. The similarity of *com* to *come* has been noticed, and doubtless there are similar links made in other languages. An offer to win a car on the Internet is headed *.com and get it*. A headline in the *Independent Graduate* on openings still available on the Web is headed: *Dot.com all ye faithful*. A phonetic similarity motivated a food-outlet advertisement: *lunch@Boots.yum*. The 'dot' element is now introduced into all kinds of phrases: *Learnhow.to* and *launch.anything*, are names of sites. The phrase *un.complicated* introduced an ad for personal finance. One company uses the slogan *Get around the www.orld*; another has the slogan *www.alk this way*.

---

[25] As of 2000. Other domain names are under consideration, such as .rec and .shop, allocated by such organizations as Network Solutions in the USA until 2000 and Nominet in the UK; the US role was taken over by Internet Corporation for Assigned Names and Numbers, established in 1998.

[26] Crystal (1998). Interestingly, when *dot.com* is written with a period, as here, the punctuation mark is never spoken aloud: we do not say 'dot dot com'.

A similar ludic trend applies to the symbol @, now the universal link between recipient and address. It was chosen pragmatically by a computer engineer, Ray Tomlinson, who sent the first network e-mail in 1972. He needed a character which did not occur in names, and this typewriter keyboard symbol stood out, with the bonus of having an appropriate meaning (of someone being 'at' somewhere).[27] A subsequent irony is that many firms and organizations have replaced the letter *a* or *at* in their name by an @: *@llgood*, *@tractions*, *@cafe*, *@Home*, *@pex*. And it has been seen turning up in other settings where traditionally the word *at* would be used: *This is where it's @* is one slogan; Bill Gates' 1999 book is called *Business @ the speed of thought*; and an academic article concludes a review of the interaction between literary and everyday language through the device *language @ literature* and *literature @ language*.[28] It has even been added to text where the word *at* would not normally appear – a postcard to my house read: *Crystals @ . . .* followed by the address.

By now the *e*-prefix must have been used in hundreds of expressions. *The Oxford dictionary of new words* (1997)[29] had already noted *e-text*, *e-zine*, *e-cash*, and *e-money*, and in 1998 the American Dialect Society named *e-* 'Word [*sic*] of the Year' as well as 'Most Useful and Most Likely to Succeed'. Examples since noted include *e-tailing* and *e-tailers* ['retailing on the Internet'], *e-lance* ['electronic free-lance'] and *e-lancers*, *e-therapy* and *e-therapists*, *e-management* and *e-managers*, *e-government*, *e-bandwagon*, *e-books*, *e-conferences*, *e-voting*, *e-loan*, *e-newsletters*, *e-security*, *e-cards*, *e-pinions*, *e-shop*, *e-list*, *e-rage*, *e-crap*, and (Spanish) *e-moción*. Awareness of the form, though in the reverse direction, appeared on the side of a London taxi: *Watrloo No Problm* – glossed beneath by *no-e.anything*. A bookmaker developing a Net presence called the firm *e-we go*. Journalistic headlines and captions often

---

[27] Though some languages have borrowed the English word 'at' for this symbol, several have their own name for it: for example, @ is a 'snail' in Italian, a 'little mouse' in Chinese, an 'elephant's trunk' in Swedish, a 'worm' in Hungarian, and a 'spider monkey' in German.
[28] Crystal (1999).
[29] Knowles (1997).

play with terms in search of eye-catching effects, so it is not surprising to find e-motivated lexical formations in specialist newspapers and magazines, as well as in the general press. Examples include:

MAJOR BREAKTHROUGH IN SEARCHITIS
STOP INTERNET CLICKTOSIS
Dealing with the dot.com Brain Drain
The Geekicon (headline of an *Economist* review of a computer
  dictionary)

How many of these developments will become a permanent feature of the language it is impossible to say. We can never predict language change, only recognize it once it has happened. There are already signs of a reaction against some of the above usages. The authors of *Wired Style*, for example, beg, in relation to the use of *e-*: 'Please, resist the urge to use this vowel-as-cliche', citing such 'too-facile coinages' as *e-lapse*, *e-merge*, and *e-quip*.[30] A Silicon Valley company, Persistence Software, is reported to have established The Society for the Preservation of the Other 25 Letters of the Alphabet, in order to campaign against the proliferation of e-words. There have been similar complaints about the use of *dot.com* in advertising. A United States company-names specialist, Neil Cohen, is quoted as saying (in mid-2000), 'Using "e", "i", and ".com" will make the company seem like a dinosaur even five years from now.'[31] But this only makes the general hypothesis more compelling, that a notion of Netspeak has begun to evolve which is rapidly becoming a part of popular linguistic consciousness, and evoking strong language attitudes. The next step, accordingly, is to determine what its chief linguistic properties are. If Netspeak exists, the above examples will prove to be pointing to the tip of a large iceberg. Moreover, there will prove to be more fundamental linguistic strategies at work than these anecdotal illustrations suggest. If, then, people are worried about the effect of the Internet

---

[30] Hale and Scanlon (1999: 76).
[31] In *Language International*, 12 (4), August 2000, 48. See also Koizumi (2000), who reports that in 1999 the Japanese Patent Bureau accepted 50 names starting with *i-* (prompted by such names as *iMac* and *ipaq*) and 190 with *e-*.

on language in general and on their own language in particular –
as the quotations at the beginning of this chapter suggest – a first
step is to explore Netspeak in its various situational manifestations
to see what actually happens there. As John Paolillo puts it, in his
introduction to a paper on the virtual speech community:[32] 'If we
are to understand truly how the Internet might shape our language,
then it is essential that we seek to understand how different varieties
of language are used on the Internet.' Chapters 4–7, accordingly,
investigate the kind of language used in each of the five situations
described above. But all five have certain linguistic properties in
common, and these form the subject-matter of chapters 2 and 3.

[32] Paolillo (1999).

2   *The medium of Netspeak*

The Internet is an electronic, global, and interactive medium, and each of these properties has consequences for the kind of language found there. The most fundamental influence arises out of the electronic character of the channel. Most obviously, a user's communicative options are constrained by the nature of the hardware needed in order to gain Internet access. Thus, a set of characters on a keyboard determines productive linguistic capacity (the type of information that can be sent); and the size and configuration of the screen determines receptive linguistic capacity (the type of information that can be seen). Both sender and receiver are additionally constrained linguistically by the properties of the Internet software and hardware linking them. There are, accordingly, certain traditional linguistic activities that this medium can facilitate very well, and others that it cannot handle at all. There are also certain linguistic activities which an electronic medium allows that no other medium can achieve. How do users respond to these new pressures, and compensate linguistically?

It is important to know what the various limitations and facilitations are. A well-established axiom of communication states that users should know the strengths as well as the restrictions of their chosen medium, in relation to the uses they subject it to and the purposes they have in mind. People have strong expectations of the Internet, and established users evidently have strong feelings about how it should be used to achieve its purposes. However, it is not a straightforward relationship. The evolution of Netspeak illustrates a real tension which exists between the nature of the medium and the aims and expectations of its users. The heart of the matter seems to be its relationship to spoken and written language. Several writers have called Internet language 'written speech';[1] and *Wired Style* advises: 'Write the way people talk.'[2] The authors of a detailed study of an asynchronous chatgroup, Davis and Brewer, say that 'electronic discourse is writing that very often reads as if it were being spoken – that is, as if the sender were writing talking'.[3] But to what extent is it possible to 'write speech', given a keyboard restricted to the letters of the alphabet, numerals, and a sprinkling of other symbols, and a medium which – as we shall see – disallows some critical features of conversational speech?[4] Moreover, as the world is composed of many different types of people who talk in many different ways, what kind of speech is it, exactly, that the new style guides want us to be writing down? The language of geeks (p. 16) has had a strong influence on Netspeak hitherto, its jargon appealing to a relatively young and computer-literate population. But what will happen to Netspeak as the user-base broadens, and people with a wider range of language preferences come online? 'Write the way people talk' sounds sensible enough, until we have to answer the question: which people?

Before we can answer these questions, we need to be clear about the nature of spoken and written language, and of the factors which differentiate them – factors which have received a great deal of attention in linguistics. Table 2.1 is a summary of the chief differences, derived from one general source, *The Cambridge encyclopedia of the English language.*[5] Speech is typically time-bound,

---

[1] For example, Elmer-Dewitt (1994).

[2] In full: *Wired style: principles of English usage in the digital age* (Hale and Scanlon, 1999). The quotation is part of Principle 5: 'Capture the colloquial' (see p. 75 below).

[3] Davis and Brewer (1997: 2). Ferrara, Brunner, and Whittemore (1991) talk of 'interactive written discourse', and similar locutions can be found, such as 'textual conversation' and 'electronic dialogue'.

[4] The reduced communicative system has been called 'metacommunicative minimalism' by Millard (1996: 147).

[5] Crystal (1995: 291). Other characteristics of speech and writing have been noted, recognizing the differentiating role of more specific linguistic features, such as personal pronouns and formulaic expression. The word 'typically' is crucial: it has long been known that there is no absolute difference between spoken and written language (Crystal and Davy, 1969); even the notion of a continuum is an oversimplification of the way the variables intertwine (Biber, 1988; and see also the use of this model by Collot and Belmore, 1996). But it proves illuminating, nonetheless, to set typical features in contrast, as a heuristic.

Table 2.1. *Differences between speech and writing (after Crystal, 1995)*

Speech	Writing
1. Speech is time-bound, dynamic, transient. It is part of an interaction in which both participants are usually present, and the speaker has a particular addressee (or several addressees) in mind.	Writing is space-bound, static, permanent. It is the result of a situation in which the writer is usually distant from the reader, and often does not know who the reader is going to be (except in a very vague sense, as in poetry).
2. There is no time-lag between production and reception, unless one is deliberately introduced by the recipient (and thus, is available for further reaction on the part of the speaker). The spontaneity and speed of most speech exchanges make it difficult to engage in complex advance planning. The pressure to think while talking promotes looser construction, repetition, rephrasing, and comment clauses (e.g. *you know, you see, mind you*). Intonation and pause divide long utterances into manageable chunks, but sentence boundaries are often unclear.	There is always a time-lag between production and reception. Writers must anticipate its effects, as well as the problems posed by having their language read and interpreted by many recipients in diverse settings. Writing allows repeated reading and close analysis, and promotes the development of careful organization and compact expression, with often intricate sentence structure. Units of discourse (sentences, paragraphs) are usually easy to identify through punctuation and layout.
3. Because participants are typically in face-to-face interaction, they can rely on such extralinguistic cues as facial expression and gesture to aid meaning (feedback). The lexicon of speech is often characteristically vague, using words which refer directly to the situation (deictic expressions, such as *that one, in here, right now*).	Lack of visual contact means that participants cannot rely on context to make their meaning clear; nor is there any immediate feedback. Most writing therefore avoids the use of deictic expressions, which are likely to be ambiguous.

Table 2.1. (*cont.*)

Speech	Writing
4. Many words and constructions are characteristic of (especially informal) speech, such as contracted forms (*isn't, he's*). Lengthy co-ordinate sentences are normal, and are often of considerable complexity. There is nonsense vocabulary (e.g. *thingamajig*), obscenity, and slang, some of which does not appear in writing, or occurs only as graphic euphemism (e.g. *f****).	Some words and constructions are characteristic of writing, such as multiple instances of subordination in the same sentence, elaborately balanced syntactic patterns, and the long (often multi-page) sentences found in some legal documents. Certain items of vocabulary are never spoken, such as the longer names of chemical compounds.
5. Speech is very suited to social or 'phatic' functions, such as passing the time of day, or any situation where casual and unplanned discourse is desirable. It is also good at expressing social relationships, and personal opinions and attitudes, due to the vast range of nuances which can be expressed by the prosody and accompanying non-verbal features.	Writing is very suited to the recording of facts and the communication of ideas, and to tasks of memory and learning. Written records are easier to keep and scan, tables demonstrate relationships between things, notes and lists provide mnemonics, and text can be read at speeds which suit a person's ability to learn.
6. There is an opportunity to rethink an utterance while the other person is listening (starting again, adding a qualification). However, errors, once spoken, cannot be withdrawn; the speaker must live with the consequences. Interruptions and overlapping speech are normal and highly audible.	Errors and other perceived inadequacies in our writing can be eliminated in later drafts without the reader ever knowing they were there. Interruptions, if they have occurred while writing, are also invisible in the final product.

(*Continued*)

Table 2.1. (*cont.*)

Speech	Writing
7. Unique features of speech include most of the prosody. The many nuances of intonation, as well as contrasts of loudness, tempo, rhythm, pause, and other tones of voice cannot be written down with much efficiency.	Unique features of writing include pages, lines, capitalization, spatial organization, and several aspects of punctuation. Only a very few graphic conventions relate to prosody, such as question marks and italics (for emphasis). Several written genres (e.g. timetables, graphs, complex formulae) cannot be read aloud efficiently, but have to be assimilated visually.

spontaneous, face-to-face, socially interactive, loosely structured, immediately revisable, and prosodically rich. Writing is typically space-bound, contrived, visually decontextualized, factually communicative, elaborately structured, repeatedly revisable, and graphically rich. How does Netspeak stand, with reference to these characteristics?

Speech or writing?

What makes Netspeak so interesting, as a form of communication, is the way it relies on characteristics belonging to both sides of the speech/writing divide. At one extreme is the Web, which in many of its functions (e.g. databasing, reference publishing, archiving, advertising) is no different from traditional situations which use writing; indeed, most varieties of written language can now be found on the Web with little stylistic change other than an adaptation to the electronic medium (see chapter 7). Legal, religious, literary, scientific, journalistic, and other texts will all be found there, just as they would in their non-electronic form. Any attempt to identify the stylistic distinctiveness of Web pages will need to deal with the same sort of visual and graphic matters as any other variety of written expression. Here therefore we find a use of language which displays the general properties of writing as described in Table 2.1: for example, Web page-writers typically have no idea who their readers are going to be, and in their guessing, targeting, and feedback-requesting they display the same behaviour as any paper-bound author or organization might. At the same time, some of the Web's functions (e.g. e-sales) do bring it much closer to the kind of interaction more typical of speech, with a consequential effect on the kind of language used, and many sites now have interactive facilities attached, in the form of e-mail and chatgroup facilities.

In contrast to the Web, the situations of e-mail, chatgroups, and virtual worlds, though expressed through the medium of writing, display several of the core properties of speech. They are time-governed, expecting or demanding an immediate response; they are transient, in the sense that messages may be immediately deleted (as in e-mails) or be lost to attention as they scroll off the screen (as in chatgroups); and their utterances display much of the urgency and energetic force which is characteristic of face-to-face conversation.[6] The situations are not all equally 'spoken' in character. We 'write' e-mails, not 'speak' them. But chatgroups are for 'chat', and people certainly 'speak' to each other there – as do people involved in virtual worlds. Player X 'says' something to player Y, as in this sequence from one study:[7]

> Plate raises his hand and shouts . . .
> Fork sighs loudly. . . .
> Plate says 'Nope'

These are 'speech acts', in a literal sense. The whole thrust of the metalanguage in these situations is spoken in character.

But there are several major differences between Netspeak and face-to-face conversation, even in those electronic situations which

---

[6] Face-to-face interaction is regularly abbreviated to *f2f* in Netspeak. It is also referred to as *facetime* (i.e. time spent offline) or *facemail* (i.e. the process of talking f2f). Ihnatko (1997: 69) defines *f2f* as 'Time spent physically standing in the room with someone and talking with them. Most netters intend to try this out some time.'
[7] Marvin (1996: 10).

are most speech-like.[8] The first is a function of the technology – the lack of simultaneous feedback. Messages sent via a computer are complete and unidirectional. When we send a message to someone, we type it a keystroke at a time, but it does not arrive on that person's screen a keystroke at a time – in the manner of the old teleprinters (an exception is described on p. 201). The message does not leave our computer until we 'send' it, and that means the whole of a message is transmitted at once, and arrives on the recipient's screen at once. There is no way that a recipient can react to our message while it is being typed, for the obvious reason that recipients do not know they are getting any messages at all until the text arrives on their screens.[9] Correspondingly, there is no way for a participant to get a sense of how successful a message is, while it is being written – whether it has been understood, or whether it needs repair. There is no technical way (currently: see chapter 8) of allowing the receiver to send the electronic equivalent of a simultaneous nod, an *uh-uh*, or any of the other audio-visual reactions which play such a critical role in face-to-face interaction. Messages cannot overlap. As a result, recipients are committed to experiencing a waiting period before the text appears – on their screen there is nothing, and then there is something, an 'off–on' system which well suits the binary computer world but which is far removed from the complex realities of everyday conversation.[10] The same circumstances apply even in two-way protocols, such as the systems which split a screen to allow the messages from two participants to be seen side-by-side;

---

[8] The notion of a continuum between different types of communication is presented by Baron (1984: 120; 2000: 22): emphasizing spatial and temporal factors, she identifies a serial relationship between: face-to-face conversation – videophones/teleconferencing – telephones – computers/word-processing – writing. Her approach rejects a dichotomous view of 'speech vs. writing', arguing that spoken language often has some characteristics of written language, and vice versa. No stylistician would deny this, while recognizing that a presentation such as Table 2.1 nonetheless has expository usefulness.

[9] This is an especial problem in an electronic conversation when one of the participants wants to send a long message; as Marvin (1996: 6) notes, 'In face-to-face conversations, a listener waits for an ending to a speaker's long statement, and stays alert for opportunities to speak, perhaps inwardly thinking, "When will this person *stop?*" In typed conversations of the MOOs [p. 174], a long statement requires a long wait on the part of the reader, during which the reader wonders, "When will this person *start?*"'

[10] Nonetheless, participants in chatgroups and virtual worlds interactions have become adept at minimizing this problem: see chapters 5 and 6.

it may appear from the layout as if such dialogues are providing simultaneous feedback, but it is not really there, because of the temporal delay.

The second big difference between Netspeak and face-to-face conversation also results from the technology: the rhythm of an Internet interaction is very much slower than that found in a speech situation, and disallows some of conversation's most salient properties. With e-mails and asynchronous chatgroups, a response to a stimulus may take anything from seconds to months, the rhythm of the exchange very much depending on such factors as the recipient's computer (e.g. whether it announces the instant arrival of a message), the user's personality and habits (e.g. whether messages are replied to at regular times or randomly), and the circumstances of the interlocutors (e.g. their computer access). The time-delay (usually referred to as *lag*) is a central factor in many situations: there is an inherent uncertainty in knowing the length of the gap between the moment of posting a message and the moment of receiving a reaction. Because of lag, the rhythm of an interaction – even in the fastest Netspeak encounters, in synchronous chatgroups and virtual worlds – lacks the pace and predictability of that found in telephonic or face-to-face conversation (see chapters 5 and 6). Even if a participant types a reply immediately, there may be a delay before that message reaches the other members' screens, due to several factors, such as bandwidth processing problems, traffic density on the host computer, or some problem in the sender's or receiver's equipment.[11]

All lags cause problems, but some are much worse than others. A low lag is of the order of 2–3 seconds, a delay which most participants tolerate – though even here some people find their tolerances tested, for 2–3 seconds is significantly greater than that found in most conversational exchanges. Anything over 5 seconds will certainly generate frustration, often prompting people to make remarks about the lag itself – references might be made to the 'lag

---

[11] For a discussion of theoretical approaches to the effects of limited bandwidth on communication, reducing the number of available cues, see Cherny (1999: 21).

monster' or to 'lag wars'. The frustration is on both sides of the communication chain. From the sender's point of view, the right moment to speak may be missed, as the point to which the intended contribution related may have scrolled off the screen and be fast receding from the group's communal memory. And from the recipient's point of view, the lack of an expected reaction is ambiguous, as there is no way of knowing whether the delay is due to transmission problems or to some 'attitude' on the sender's part. Unexpected silence in a telephone conversation carries a similar ambiguity, but at least there we have well-established turn-taking manoeuvres which can bring immediate clarification ('Hello?', 'Are you still there?'). The linguistic strategies which underpin our conversational exchanges are much less reliable in chatgroups. Colin may never get a reaction to his reply to Jane because Jane may never have received it (for technical reasons), may not have noticed it (because there are so many other remarks coming in at the same time), may have been distracted by some other conversation (real or online), may not have been present at her terminal to see the message (for all kinds of reasons), or simply decided not to respond. Equally, she may have replied, and it is *her* message which has got delayed or lost. When responses are disrupted by delays, there is little anyone can do to sort such things out.

The larger the number of participants involved in an interaction, the worse the situation becomes.[12] Delays in a conversation between two people are annoying and ambiguous, but the level of disruption is usually manageable, because each person has only one interlocutor to worry about. If a simple e-mail situation is affected by serious delay, feedback via phone or fax is easily providable. But when an electronic interaction involves several people, such as in chatgroups, virtual worlds, and e-mails which are copied repeatedly, lag produces a very different situation, because it interferes with another core feature of traditional face-to-face

---

[12] Also, the wider the spread of participants, culturally speaking, the worse the problem becomes. Some cultures are more used to silence as a communicative force, and are more tolerant of delays (e.g. Japanese); others operate on a very short fuse (e.g. American and British). See Tannen and Saville-Troike (1985).

interaction, the conversational *turn*. Turn-taking is so fundamental to conversation that most people are not conscious of its significance as a means of enabling interactions to be successful. But it is a conversational fact of life that people follow the routine of taking turns, when they talk, and avoid talking at once or interrupting each other randomly or excessively. Moreover, they expect certain 'adjacency-pairs' to take place: questions to be followed by answers, and not the other way round; similarly, a piece of information to be followed by an acknowledgement, or a complaint to be followed by an excuse or apology.[13] These elementary strategies, learned at a very early age, provide a normal conversation with its skeleton.

When there are long lags, the conversational situation becomes so unusual that its ability to cope with a topic can be destroyed. This is because the turn-taking, as seen on a screen, is dictated by the software, and not by the participants:[14] in a chatgroup, for instance, even if one did start to send a reaction to someone else's utterance before it was finished, the reaction would take its turn in a non-overlapping series of utterances on the screen, dependent only on the point at which the send signal was received at the host server. Messages are posted to a receiver's screen linearly, in the order in which they are received by the system. In a multi-user environment, messages are coming in from various sources all the time, and with different lags. Because of the way packets of information are sent electronically through different global routes, between sender and receiver, it is even possible for turn-taking reversals to take place, and all kinds of unpredictable overlaps. The time-frames of the participants do not coincide. Lucy asks a question; Sue receives it and sends an answer, but on Ben's screen the answer is received before the question. Or, Lucy sends a question, Sue replies, and Lucy sends another question; but on Ben's screen the second question arrives before Sue's reply to the first. Or Lucy, not yet having received Sue's reply, reformulates her question and sends it again;

---

[13] For an introduction to conversational exchanges in discourse analysis, see Stubbs (1983).
[14] See Murray (1989).

Sue replies to both; Ben then receives the sequence in the order Q1, R2, Q2, R1. The situation may be further complicated if Sue (or anyone) decides to give answers to two questions from different participants, sending them together. The possibilities for confusion, once orderly turn-taking is so disruptable and adjacency-pairs are so interruptable, are enormous. The number of overlapping interactions that a screen may display at any one time increases depending on the number of participants and the random nature of the lags. In a typical scenario, the situation is at best confusing to an outsider, as the extracts in chapter 5 illustrate (p. 157), it being extremely difficult to keep track of a topic (a *thread*). What is surprising is that practised participants seem to tolerate (indeed revel in) the anarchy which ensues. (The reasons for this are discussed at the end of chapter 5.)

Issues of feedback and turn-taking are ways in which Netspeak interaction differs from conversational speech. But Netspeak is unlike speech also with respect to the formal properties of the medium – properties that are so basic that it becomes extremely difficult for people to live up to the recommendation that they should 'write as they talk'. Chief among these properties is the domain of *prosody* and *paralanguage*[15] – phonological terms which capture the notion of 'it ain't what you say but the way that you say it' – as expressed through vocal variations in pitch (intonation), loudness (stress), speed, rhythm, pause, and tone of voice. As with traditional writing, there have been somewhat desperate efforts to replace it in the form of an exaggerated use of spelling and punctuation, and the use of capitals, spacing, and special symbols for emphasis. Examples include repeated letters (*aaaaahhhhh, hiiiiiii, ooops, soooo*), repeated punctuation marks (*no more!!!!!, whohe????,*

---

[15] Crystal and Quirk (1964), Crystal (1969). Emoticons have been called 'the paralanguage of the Internet' (Dery, 1993), but they are not the same, in that they have to be consciously added to a text. Their absence does not mean that the user lacks the emotion conveyed. In face-to-face communication, someone may grin over several utterances, and the effect be noted. In Netspeak, a 'grin' emoticon might be added to just one utterance, although the speaker may continue to 'feel' the relevant emotion over several turns. There is also no guarantee that the person who sends a 'grin' is actually grinning at all – a point which also applies to abbreviations used: how many people are actually 'laughing out loud' when they send *LOL*?

hey!!!!!!!!!, see what you started???????????????????), and the following range of emphatic conventions:

all capitals for 'shouting':	I SAID NO
letter spacing for 'loud and clear':	W H Y N O T, w h y n o t
word/phrase emphasis by asterisks:	the *real* answer

(Underbars are also sometimes used for emphasis, as in 'the _ real _ answer', but are less widespread, as they have other functions, such as their use as space-fillers in addresses to ensure that a compound name is a single electronic string (*David_Crystal*).) These features are indeed capable of a certain expressiveness, but the range of meanings they signal is small, and restricted to gross notions such as extra emphasis, surprise, and puzzlement. Less exaggerated nuances are not capable of being handled in this way, and there is no system in the use of the marks – it seems likely that the number of question-marks or exclamation-marks reflects only the length of time the relevant key is held down. There are signs of other characters or character combinations being used in order to express shades of meaning (e.g. *sure/*, *\so*), but in the absence of agreed conventions it is difficult to know how to read such symbols, or what the user means by them. As a result, it is no surprise to find participants in chatgroups falling back on literary expressions in an attempt to capture the range of effects and emotions involved, using a graphic convention to distinguish the text from the rest of the conversation, as in these examples:[16]

<Hoppy giggles quietly to himself>
<Jake squeals insistently>
<Henry eyes Jane warily>

In virtual worlds, there are commands which allow people to express textually the emotion they feel, often with the addition of synthesized sounds and visual effects. Despite these innovations, users are aware of the ever-present ambiguity when the prosody

---

[16] Angle brackets have several other functions in Netspeak: they identify commands in HTML, surround e-mail addresses, and indicate speaker responses in e-mail dialogues.

of speech is lacking, as can be seen in the regular injunctions in usage guides to be careful, especially when engaging in humour or irony.

Related to this is the way Netspeak lacks the facial expressions, gestures, and conventions of body posture and distance (the *kinesics* and *proxemics*)[17] which are so critical in expressing personal opinions and attitudes and in moderating social relationships. The limitation was noted early in the development of Netspeak, and led to the introduction of *smileys* or *emoticons* (a name deriving from Emote, used in MUDs to convey actions: p. 180).[18] These are combinations of keyboard characters designed to show an emotional facial expression: they are typed in sequence on a single line, and placed after the final punctuation mark of a sentence. Almost all of them are read sideways. The two basic types express positive attitudes and negative attitudes respectively (the omission of the 'nose' element seems to be solely a function of typing speed or personal taste):

> :-) or :)   :-(or : (

Table 2.2 illustrates the most commonly used forms, along with a few of the hundreds of ludic shapes and sequences which have been invented and collected in smiley dictionaries. It is plain that they are a potentially helpful but extremely crude way of capturing some of the basic features of facial expression, but their semantic role is limited. They can forestall a gross misperception of a speaker's intent, but an individual smiley still allows a huge number of readings (happiness, joke, sympathy, good mood, delight, amusement, etc.) which can only be disambiguated by referring to the verbal context. Some commentators have even described them as 'futile'.[19] Without care, moreover, they can lead to their own misunderstanding:

[17] See Sebeok, Hayes, and Bateson (1964), Hall (1959).
[18] See the collection in Sanderson (1993).
[19] Dery (1997: 2), quoting an anonymous correspondent: 'Shit happens, especially on the Net, where everyone speaks with flattened affect. I think the attempt to signal authorial intent with little smileys is interesting but futile. They're subject to slippage like any other kind of sign.'

Table 2.2. *Examples of smileys (after Sanderson, 1993)*

Basic smileys		
:-)		pleasure, humour, etc.
:-(		sadness, dissatisfaction, etc.
;-)		winking (in any of its meanings)
;-(	:~-(	crying
%-(	%-)	confused
:-o	8-o	shocked, amazed
:-]	:-[	sarcastic

Joke smileys	
[:-)	User is wearing a walkman
8-)	User is wearing sunglasses
B:-)	User is wearing sunglasses on head
:-{)	User has a moustache
:*)	User is drunk
:-[	User is a vampire
:-E	User is a bucktoothed vampire
:-F	User is a bucktoothed vampire with one tooth missing
:-~	User has a cold
:-@	User is screaming
-:-)	User is a punk
-:-(	Real punks don't smile
+-:-)	User holds a Christian religious office
0 :-)	User is an angel at heart

Smiley stories

:-)   8-)   8-{)
A smiley to disguise himself gets glasses and a fake moustache.
C:-)   >[]   C8-)
A smart smiley left watching too much TV

adding a smile to an utterance which is plainly angry can increase rather than decrease the force of the 'flame'. It is a common experience that a smile can go down the wrong way: 'And you can wipe that smile off your face, as well!' Those who get into the habit of routinely using smileys can also find themselves in the position of having their unmarked utterances misinterpreted precisely because they have no smiley attached to them.[20] Usage guides warn against overuse. However, they are not especially frequent; in one study, only 13.4% of 3,000 posts contained them – and some people did not use them at all.[21] Most participants, moreover, made no use of most of the formal possibilities, restricting themselves to just one or two basic types, especially variants of the 'positive' smiley, as in:

> dont be silly :)   hi :))   that's a pain :)))))

It should be noted, too, that smileys have other roles than disambiguation. Sometimes they seem to be doing little more than expressing rapport. Often, their presence seems to have purely pragmatic force – acting as a warning to the recipient(s) that the sender is worried about the effect a sentence might have. David Sanderson makes this point in his dictionary, when he recommends:[22]

> You might include a smiley as a reminder of the ongoing context of the conversation, to indicate that your words don't stand on their own. A smiley can point out to the other participants of the conversation that they need to understand you and your personality in order to understand what you've said.

What is interesting to the linguist, of course, is why these novelties have turned up now. Written language has always been ambiguous, in its omission of facial expression, and in its inability to express all the intonational and other prosodic features of speech. Why did no one ever introduce smileys there? The answer must be something to do with the immediacy of Net interaction, its closeness to speech. In traditional writing, there is time to develop phrasing which makes personal attitudes clear; that is why the formal

---

[20] Brian Connery (1996: 175) makes a similar point in relation to other softening devices. Talking about people who avoid flaming by using such abbreviations as *IMHO* ('In My Humble Opinion') and *my $0.02* ('my two cents worth'), he comments: 'Ironically, because of the innately authoritative nature of writing, within such anti-authoritarian conversations, the absence of such cues may trigger flames because of the suspicion that the author is claiming to put forward the definitive response which will end the discussion.'

[21] Witmer and Katzman (1997). Baron (2000) also notes the paucity of smileys in e-mails, other than among youngsters; in her view, adults have the communicative skills to make their messages sufficiently clear to avoid the need for the crude signals that smileys can provide.

[22] Sanderson (1993: 25).

conventions of letter-writing developed. And when they are missing, something needs to replace them. A rapidly constructed Net
message, lacking the usual courtesies, can easily appear abrupt
or rude. A smiley defuses the situation. (Incidentally, the same
problems can arise with faxes, especially quickly handwritten ones,
though as yet smiley-type conventions have not made an impact
there.)

Whatever their function, and despite their limited use, smileys
are one of the most distinctive features of e-mail and chatgroup
language. But they are not the only mechanism devised to get round
the absence of kinesic and proxemic features. Verbal glosses are
also used, often within angle brackets, as in the prosodic examples
above:

> <Eagle smiles sympathetically at Gunner>
> <Spoon nods in greeting>

This convention is widely used in virtual worlds for all kinds of
kinesic effects, such as <smirk> and <laugh>. Abbreviated words
are also found in some groups, notably <g> = 'grin', used to react
to a message thought to be funny, or to convey teasing. The convention has developed a small system of its own: bigger smiles are
symbolized by <gg>, <ggg>, etc., and a range of acronyms based
on the letter <g> have been devised, such as <vbg> = 'very big
grin', <gd&r> = 'grinning, ducking and running' (as a music-hall
performer might do after a bad joke).

These features of Netspeak have evolved as a way of avoiding
the ambiguities and misperceptions which come when written language is made to carry the burden of speech. They are brave efforts,
but on the whole Netspeak lacks any true ability to signal meaning through kinesic and proxemic features, and this, along with
the unavailability of prosodic features, places it at a considerable
remove from spoken language.[23] Absent also are other linguistic

---

[23] This gap is probably the chief reason why, as Wallace puts it in her discussion of Internet
anonymity, 'it is so easy to lie and get away with it' (1999: 51). In face-to-face interaction,
only the most skilled liars can keep their deceptions out of their facial expression and
tone of voice. In Netspeak, nothing could be easier – though participants can still give
the game away by their unconscious use of other linguistic features (see p. 166).

features typical of conversational speech, and these make it even
more difficult for language to be used on the Internet in a truly
conversational way. These limitations arise out of the current dependence of the medium on typing speed and ability (see chapter 8
for future possibilities). The fact of the matter is that even the fastest
typist comes nowhere near the spontaneity and speed of speech,
which in conversation routinely runs at 5 or 6 syllables a second.
Even apparently spontaneous Internet messages can involve elements of preplanning, pausing to think while writing, and mental
checking before sending, which are simply not options in most everyday conversation. Some features of spoken language are often
present in Internet writing, as we shall see below, such as short
constructions, phrasal repetition, and a looser sentence construction. But studies of e-mail and chatgroup interactions have shown
that they generally lack the very features of spoken language which
indicate most spontaneity – notably, the use of reaction signals
(*m, mhm, uh-huh, yeah*...) and comment clauses (*you know, you
see, mind you*...). Indeed, some writers have identified the lack of
these features as one of the reasons why so many Internet interactions are misperceived as abrupt, cold, distant, or antagonistic.[24]
In face-to-face conversation, rapport, warmth, and agreement are
regularly conveyed by subtle reaction signals which are injected at
salient points by the listener; and the speaker adds softness, sympathy, friendliness, and solidarity by introducing such items as *you
know* – there is a world of difference, stylistically, between *I think
you're wrong* and *Y'know, I think you're wrong*. But because immediate reaction signals are not possible (see above, p. 32), and
comment clauses are not a natural part of typing (most people are
unaware they use them, or how frequently they use them, in everyday speech), these cues are missing from Netspeak. It is possible
to do something about comment clauses, and Patricia Wallace (see
fn. 23) is one who recommends their increased use, as a means
of improving e-rapport. Also, informality, and thus warmth, can

---

[24] For example, Wallace (1999: 16), who devotes a whole chapter to the social psychological
implications.

be improved through the use of colloquial grammar and vocabulary (especially 'cool' abbreviations, see p. 85) and a readiness
to introduce language play. But there is nothing one can do about
reaction signals. Addressing someone on the Internet is a bit like
having a telephone conversation in which a listener is giving you
no reactions at all: it is an uncomfortable and unnatural situation,
and in the absence of such feedback one's own language becomes
more awkward than it might otherwise be.

Although Netspeak tries to be like speech, in its e-mail, chatgroup, and virtual world incarnations, it remains some distance
from it, in respect of several of spoken language's most fundamental properties. One commentator has called it 'metacommunicative
minimalism', which he characterizes in this way:[25]

> Textual cyberspace filters away all qualities of a personal self save
> the highly mediated, acutely self-conscious elements that appear
> in written language. Phatic or metacommunicative cues, the
> linguistic and paralinguistic signs that maintain cognizance of the
> social relation between the sender and receiver of a message, are
> drastically reduced in this medium.

Table 2.3 is a summary of the seven characteristics of speech outlined in Table 2.1, applied to the Internet situations described in
my opening chapter. Notwithstanding the way netizens routinely
talk about their domain in terms which derive from everyday conversation, in my estimation the actual amount that Netspeak has
in common with speech is very limited. The Web is furthest away
from it; chatgroup and virtual world interactions are somewhat
closer to it; and e-mails sit uncertainly in the middle. The latter
three categories are certainly more speech-like than any other variety of traditional writing; but the similarities are balanced, if not
outweighed, by the differences. So, if Netspeak does not display the
properties we would expect of speech, does it instead display the
properties we expect of writing?

Here too, the situation is not straightforward, as can be seen
from the analogous summary in Table 2.4. Let us consider first the

---

[25] Millard (1996: 147).

Table 2.3. *Spoken language criteria (see Table 2.1) applied to Netspeak*

	Web	e-mail	Chatgroups	Virtual worlds
1 time-bound	no	yes, but in different ways	yes, but in different ways	yes, but in different ways
2 spontaneous	no	variable	yes, but with restrictions	yes, but with restrictions
3 face-to-face	no	no	no	no
4 loosely structured	variable	variable	yes	yes
5 socially interactive	no, with increasing options	variable	yes, but with restrictions	yes, but with restrictions
6 immediately revisable	no	no	no	no
7 prosodically rich	no	no	no	no

Table 2.4. *Written language criteria (see Table 2.1) applied to Netspeak*

	Web	e-mail	Chatgroups	Virtual worlds
1 space-bound	yes, with extra options	yes, but routinely deleted	yes, but with restrictions	yes, but with restrictions
2 contrived	yes	variable	no, but with some adaptation	no, but with some adaptation
3 visually decontextualized	yes, but with considerable adaptation	yes	yes	yes, but with some adaptation
4 elaborately structured	yes	variable	no	no
5 factually communicative	yes	yes	variable	yes, but with some adaptation
6 repeatedly revisable	yes	variable	no	no
7 graphically rich	yes, but in different ways	no	no	yes, but in different ways

space-bound character of traditional writing – the fact that a piece of text is static and permanent on the page. If something is written down, repeated reference to it will be an encounter with an unchanged text. We would be surprised if, upon returning to a particular page, it had altered its graphic character in some way. Putting it like this, we can see immediately that Netspeak is not by any means like conventional writing. A 'page' on the Web often varies from encounter to encounter (and all have the option of varying, even if page-owners choose not to take it) for several possible reasons: its factual content might have been updated, its advertising sponsor might have changed, or its graphic designer might have added new features. Nor is the writing that you see necessarily static, given the technical options available which allow text to move around the screen, disappear/reappear, change colour, and so on. From a user point of view, there are opportunities to 'interfere' with the text in all kinds of ways that are not possible in traditional writing. A page, once downloaded to the user's screen, may have its text cut, added to, revised, annotated, even totally restructured, in ways that nonetheless retain the character of the original. The possibilities are causing not a little anxiety among those concerned about issues of ownership, copyright, and forgery (see chapter 7).

The other Internet situations also display differences from traditional writing, with respect to their space-bound presence. E-mails are in principle static and permanent, but routine textual deletion is expected procedure (it is a prominent option in the management system), and it is possible to alter messages electronically with an ease and undetectability which is not possible when people try to alter a traditionally written text. Messages in asynchronic chatgroups tend to be long-term in character; but those in synchronic groups and in virtual worlds are not. In the literature on computer-mediated communication, reference is often made to the *persistence* of a conversational message – the fact that it stays on the screen for a period of time (before the arrival of other messages replaces it or makes it scroll out of sight).[26] This certainly introduces

---

[26] For example, Thomas Erickson (1999).

certain properties to the conversation which are not available in speech. It means, for example, that someone who enters a conversation a couple of turns after an utterance has been made can still see the utterance, reflect upon it, and react to it; the persistence is relatively short-lived, however, compared with that routinely encountered in traditional writing. It also means, for those systems that provide an archiving log of all messages, in the order in which they were received by the server, that it is possible in principle to browse a past conversation, or search for a particular topic, in ways that spontaneous (unrecorded) conversation does not permit; however, in practice none of the systems currently available enable this to be done with ease, time-lags and the other factors described above making it extremely difficult to follow a topical thread in a recorded log (see chapter 5). There are well-established means of finding one's way through a traditional written text: they are called indexes, and they are carefully compiled by indexers, who select and organize relevant information. Indexes of this kind are not likely in interactive Netspeak, because there is so much of it and the subject-matter does not usually warrant it. There has been little research into the question of whether automatic indexing could be adapted so as to provide useful end-products (see chapter 7).

The other characteristics of traditional written language also display an uncertain relationship to Netspeak. Is Netspeak contrived, elaborate in its construction, and repeatedly revisable (items 2, 4, and 6 in Table 2.4)? For the Web, the answer has to be yes, allowing the same range of structural complexity as would be seen elsewhere. For chatgroups and virtual worlds, where the pressure is strong to communicate rapidly, the answer has to be no, though the fact that smileys and other graphic conventions have been devised illustrates a certain degree of contrivance. E-mails vary enormously: some people are happy to send messages with no revision at all, not caring if typing errors, spelling mistakes, and other anomalies are included in their messages; others take as many pains to revise their messages as they would in non-Internet settings – or even more, if there is some sensitivity over flaming (p. 55). Is Netspeak visually decontextualized (item 3 in Table 2.4)? Immediate visual feedback is always absent, as discussed above, so in this respect Netspeak is just like traditional writing. But Web pages often provide visual aids to support text, in the form of photographs, maps, diagrams, animations, and the like; and many virtual-world settings have a visual component built in, with signs of adaptation even in text-only worlds (such as instructions to 'move North' or 'leave through the East door' on a game screen; see p. 177). Is Netspeak factually communicative (item 5 in Table 2.4)? For the Web and e-mails, the answer is a strong yes. The other two situations are less clear. Within the reality parameters established by a virtual world, factual information is certainly routinely transmitted, but there is a strong social element always present which greatly affects the kind of language used. Chatgroups vary enormously: the more academic and professional they are, the more likely they are to be factual in aim (though often not in achievement, if reports of the amount of flaming are to be believed); the more social and ludic chatgroups, on the other hand, routinely contain sequences which have negligible factual content.

Finally, is Netspeak graphically rich? Once again, for the Web the answer is yes, its richness having increased along with technological progress, putting into the hands of the ordinary user a range of typographic and colour variation that far exceeds the pen, the typewriter, and the early word processor, and allowing further options not available to conventional publishing, such as animated text, hypertext links, and multimedia support (sound, video, film). On the other hand, as typographers and graphic designers have repeatedly pointed out, just because a new visual language is available to everyone does not mean that everyone can use it well. Despite the provision of a wide range of guides to Internet design and desk-top publishing,[27] examples of illegibility, visual confusion, over-ornamentation, and other inadequacies abound. They are compounded by the limitations of the medium, which cause

---

[27] For example, Pring (1999).

no problem if respected, but which are often ignored, as we encounter screenfuls of unbroken text, paragraphs which downwards interminably, or text which scrolls awkwardly of right-hand side of the screen. The problems of *graphic transla bility* are only beginning to be appreciated – that it is not possible to take a paper-based text and put it on a screen without rethinking the graphic presentation and even, sometimes, the content of the message.[28] Add to all this the limitations of the technology. The time it takes to download pages which contain 'fancy graphics' and multimedia elements is a routine cause of frustration, and in interactive situations can exacerbate communicative lag (p. 31).

Disregarding the differences between Internet situations, in Tables 2.3 and 2.4, and looking solely at the cells in terms of 'yes', 'variable', and 'no', it is plain that Netspeak has far more properties linking it to writing than to speech. Of the 28 cells in the speech summary in Table 2.3, only 9 are 'yes', 4 are 'variable', and 15 are 'no'. The situation for the writing summary in Table 2.4, as we would expect, is almost exactly the reverse: 16 are 'yes', 4 are 'variable', and 8 are 'no'. Once we take the different Internet situations into account, then the Web is seen to be by far the closest to written language, with chatgroups furthest away, and the other two situations in between. The differences are striking, as later chapters will further illustrate. But on the whole, Netspeak is better seen as written language which has been pulled some way in the direction of speech than as spoken language which has been written down. However, expressing the question in terms of the traditional dichotomy is itself misleading. Netspeak is identical to neither speech nor writing, but selectively and adaptively displays properties of both. Davis and Brewer see it thus, as an eclectic resource: 'Writing in the electronic medium, people adopt conventions of oral and written discourse to their own, individual communicative needs'.[29]

Netspeak is more than an aggregate of spoken and written features. As we shall see in later chapters, it does things that neither

---

[28] For graphic translatability, see Twyman (1982).   [29] Davis and Brewer (1997: 19).

of these other mediums do, and must accordingly be seen as a new species of communication. Baron, in a metaphor which takes up the species theme, calls it an 'emerging language centaur – part speech, part writing'.[30] I would have to adopt an aliens metaphor to capture my own vision of Netspeak as something genuinely different in kind – 'speech + writing + electronically mediated properties'.[31] It is more than just a hybrid of speech and writing, or the result of contact between two long-standing mediums.[32] Electronic texts, of whatever kind, are simply not the same as other kinds of texts. According to Marilyn Deegan,[33] they display fluidity, simultaneity (being available on an indefinite number of machines), and non-degradability in copying; they transcend the traditional limitations on textual dissemination; and they have permeable boundaries (because of the way one text may be integrated within others or display links to others). Several of these properties have consequences for language, and these combine with those associated with speech and writing to make Netspeak a genuine 'third medium'.

Netspeak maxims

How should we further characterize Netspeak, viewed as a novel medium combining spoken, written, and electronic properties? One method is to continue with the comparative approach used above. Several linguists and philosophers of language have investigated what counts as a 'normal' kind of conversation. The philosopher H. P. Grice is one, well known in pragmatics research for his

[30] Baron (2000: 248), and see below, p. 128. Baron also sees the relationship between speech and writing as continuum-like, though she makes a different set of distinctions. From one extreme, which she labels 'writing (as product)', she recognizes 'joint composition > anonymous dialogue > 1–many dialogue (not anonymous) > 1–1 dialogue (not anonymous)' before arriving at 'speech (as process)' (p. 158).

[31] Sociolinguist Celso Alvarez-Caccamo (in Cumming, 1995: 6) also seems to sense a uniqueness in the nature of computer-mediated communication, when he talks of an observing alien characterizing it in terms of 'its fundamental "weirdness"' – by which he means the speed, invisibility, distribution, and anonymity of electronic interaction (in which the choice of a particular language is incidental).

[32] The view of e-mail as a contact language is argued by Baron (2000: ch. 9).

[33] Deegan (2000).

four maxims of conversation that underlie the efficient co-operative use of language.[34] They can be expressed as follows:

> *The maxim of Quality*
> Try to make your contribution one that is true, specifically:
> Do not say what you believe to be false.
> Do not say that for which you lack adequate evidence.
> *The maxim of Relevance*
> Make your contributions relevant.
> *The maxim of Quantity*
> Make your contribution as informative as is required for the
> current purposes of the exchange.
> Do not make your contribution more informative than is required.
> *The maxim of Manner*
> Be perspicuous, and specifically:
> Avoid obscurity.
> Avoid ambiguity.
> Be brief.
> Be orderly.

The point of an analysis of this kind is not to suggest that we always behave exactly according to the principles; common experience shows that we do not. But we do seem to tacitly recognize their role as a perspective or orientation within which actual utterances can be judged. For example, people who tell lies or make false claims can be challenged; if they talk too much they can be told (in so many words) to shut up; if they say something irrelevant, they can be asked to stick to the point; and if they fail to make themselves clear, they can be requested to say it again. The fact that we do all of these things indicates that we are bearing these maxims in mind. Moreover, if someone makes a remark that seems to flout these maxims, we instinctively look for ways to make sense of what has been said. If Joe asks 'Where's Uncle Kevin?' and Jill replies 'I expect there's a dilapidated blue bicycle outside The Swan', we do not criticize her for breaking all four maxims at once. Rather, we take it for granted that she is co-operating in the conversation, and that (a) she has good grounds from past experience for knowing

---

[34] Grice (1975). For a general discussion, see Levinson (1983: ch. 3).

that a bicycle will be outside The Swan at this time; (b) she knows the mention of a bicycle is relevant, because Uncle Kevin rides one; (c) she knows its attributes include being dilapidated and blue, and feels that the mention of both makes for a more vivid or jocular sentence than one which uses just one adjective or no adjective at all; and (d) she knows that Joe knows all this, so that her answer will be perfectly clear. In such ways, and by making such assumptions, we are able to make sense of all kinds of superficially bizarre contributions to conversations.

It is not so easy to work out what is going on in the Internet world. Part of the difficulty arises out of the anonymity inherent in the electronic medium. This is not the first medium to allow spoken interaction between individuals who wish to remain anonymous, of course, as we know from the history of telephone and amateur radio; but it is certainly unprecedented in the scale and range of situations in which people can hide their identity, especially in chatgroups and virtual worlds.[35] These situations routinely contain individuals who are talking to each other under nicknames (*nicks*), which may be an assumed first-name, a fantasy description (*top-dude, sexstar*), or a mythical character or role (*rockman, elfslayer*) (see further, chapter 5). In e-mails, the personal identity element (the part of the address found before the @) may be any of these, or simply a number or code, it then being up to the sender to decide what authentic signature the text of the e-mail will contain. The lexical structure and character of the names themselves is an important feature of Netspeak, of course; but there are other consequences for the type of language used. Operating behind a false

---

[35] The electronic traceability of messages, through server records, backups, and other monitoring procedures, might be thought enough to make anonymity impossible. As several commentators have said: never write anything that you wouldn't want to see read out in court (e.g. Durusau, 1996) – see further below, p. 127. But tracing can be made extremely difficult in various ways, such as through using 'anonymizers' – services that combine encryption, pseudonyms, and proxy servers to let you browse and send messages anonymously, 'remailer' services which disguise where a message comes from, or free e-mail services which do not check the user's personal details. There is no real way of knowing if an e-mail has been interfered with. Although the system is sufficiently abused (e.g. false or insulting messages sent out under someone's name) that some organizations impose e-mail controls, the general problem does not seem to have affected the vast majority of users, who operate unconcernedly with their online personae.

persona seems to make people less inhibited: they may feel emboldened to talk more and in different ways from their real-world linguistic repertoire. They must also expect to receive messages from others who are likewise less inhibited, and be prepared for negative outcomes. There are obviously inherent risks in talking to someone we do not know, and instances of harassment, insulting or aggressive language, and subterfuge are legion. Questions about identity – of a kind which would be totally redundant in face-to-face settings – are also a feature of initial chatgroup encounters. Certain kinds of information are asked for and given, notably about location, age, and gender (not usually about race or socio-economic status). Gender is so sensitive an issue that it has given rise to the terms *Morf* (= 'male or female'), an online query addressed to someone who uses a gender-ambiguous name (e.g. *Chris, Hilary, Jan*) and *Sorg* (= 'straight or gay'). People seem to become particularly anxious if they do not know the sex and sexual preference of the person they are talking to.

Multiple and often conflicting notions of truth therefore co-exist in Internet situations, ranging from outright lying through mutually aware pretence to playful trickery. As Patricia Wallace puts it, referring to the absence of prosodic and kinesic clues in Netspeak: 'The fact that it is so easy to lie and get away with it – as long as we can live with our own deceptions and the harm they may cause others – is a significant feature of the Internet.'[36] It is of course possible to live out a lie or fantasy logically and consistently, and it is on this principle that the games in virtual worlds operate and the nicknamed people in chatgroups interact. But it is by no means easy to maintain a consistent presence through language in a world where multiple interactions are taking place under pressure, where participants are often changing their names and identities, and where the co-operative principle can be arbitrarily jettisoned. Putting this another way, when you see an Internet utterance, you often do not know how to take it, because you do not know what set of conversational principles it is obeying. Here are

[36] Wallace (1999: 51).

two such circumstances, both of which undermine the maxim of quality.

A *spoof* is any message whose origin is suspect; the sending of such messages, *spoofing*, is commonplace in some Internet situations. Unattributed utterances may be introduced into a virtual-worlds conversation, for example. Normally, each conversational turn is preceded by the name of the player, along the lines of *Mole says, 'I'm hungry.'* But it is possible for a player to interpolate an utterance with no name preceding, such as: *An angry lion appears in the doorway.* Spoof utterances may also be inserted by the software, and not by any of the participants. When a spoof is noticed, the players may condemn it, question it, or play about with it. The result can be a fresh element of fun injected into a game which is palling, with everybody knowing what is going on and willingly participating. Equally, because spoofing can confuse other players, and severely disrupt a game which is proceeding well, the various guides to manners in virtual worlds tend to be critical of it, and discourage it. Some groups insist on displaying the identity of the spoofer, such as by making the sender add his/her nick afterwards: *1,000 linguists have converged on Parliament – Doc.*[37] Because there is no way of knowing whether the content of a spoof is going to be true (with reference to the rest of the conversation) or false, such utterances introduce an element of anarchy into the co-operative ethos of conversation.

A similar problem arises with *trolling*, the sending of a message (a *troll*) specifically intended to cause irritation to others, such as the members of a chatgroup. It is an innocent-sounding question or statement, delivered deadpan, and usually short, though some trolls are verbose in their apparent cluelessness. For example, somebody who wanted to troll a linguistics group might send the message *I've heard that the Eskimo language has 1,000 words for snow* – then sit back to enjoy the resulting explosions.[38] The term derives from fishing (the trailing of a baited hook to see what bites), though it also

---

[37] This is the procedure followed in Cherny's group (Cherny 1999: 115).
[38] For the reason, see Pullum and McCawley (1991).

captures the resonance of the trolls of Scandinavian mythology – the bridge-guarders who would let people pass only if they answered a question correctly. On the Internet, the bait is false information, deliberately introduced into a conversation to see who falls for it. People who respond, and correct the misinformation, show that they do not belong to the group, or are newcomers to it (*newbies*); old hands will simply ignore it, or – if they can be bothered – laconically send the response 'nice troll' to the originator, or *YHBT* (= 'you have been trolled') to the responder. Not all chatgroups troll; some insert clues to the existence of a troll into a message that only the cognoscenti recognize; some are very much against the whole process, conscious of the communicative disruption that can result.

The maxim of quantity is also often undermined in Internet situations. At one extreme there is *lurking* – a refusal to communicate. *Lurkers* are people who access a chatgroup and read its messages but do not contribute to the discussion. The motives include newbie reluctance to be involved, academic curiosity (researching some aspect of Internet culture), or voyeurism. Some manuals refer to lurking as 'spying'.[39] *Spamming* refers to the sending of usually unwanted messages of excessive size. The origin of the term lies in a 1970 *Monty Python* sketch in which a cafe waitress describes the available dishes to two customers, and culinary variation is introduced by an increasing reliance on spam – 'Well, there's egg and bacon; egg sausage and bacon; egg and spam; egg bacon and spam; egg bacon sausage and spam; spam bacon sausage and spam; spam egg spam spam bacon and spam; spam sausage spam spam bacon spam tomato and spam . . .' – the whole interchange being accompanied, as one would expect, by the chanting of the same word from a passing group of Vikings.[40] In one of those semantic shifts which makes etymology such a fascinating subject, the

---

[39] Lurking is not the same as *idling*, which is not an active attempt to hide one's presence from the other members of a group – as when a participant decides to do something else while staying connected, or simply has nothing to say. A further label identifies *smurfs* and *smurfettes* – people who post messages to a group but without saying anything much.

[40] *Monty Python's Flying Circus*, BBC, 2nd series, episode 25 (15 December 1970).

term was first applied to cases where a single message would be sent to many recipients, as when a company sends out an ad to everyone on a mailing list, producing electronic 'junk-mail'. It later came to be used for the complementary situation – the sending of many messages to one user, as when a group of people electronically lobby a politician or attack a company's policy.[41] Either way, people find themselves having to deal with quantities of unwanted text.

Not all spam is the same, either in intention or effect. Charles Stivale identifies three types common in virtual worlds: playful, pernicious, and ambiguous.[42] *Playful* spamming occurs when visual or audio effects (such as a duck quacking) have been programmed to turn up in the text, unasked-for, at intervals within the game situation. It can also be found when one character does something aggressively playful to another (a *bonk* – but not in the UK sense, please note),[43] thereby eliciting a vociferous response. In some game situations (especially MOOs), several participants may simultaneously respond to a playful stimulus, producing a sequence of text messages on screen which come in so fast that they can hardly be read. *Pernicious* spamming refers to the Internet equivalent of real-life harassment, often involving sexually explicit language and description of actions, and usually prompting the introduction of control measures of some kind by the group moderators. Lengthy aggressive utterances (*flaming* – see below) are often involved. *Ambiguous* spamming falls between these extremes. A participant might repeatedly send a message which irritates other players, or cause another player to do something unlooked-for (e.g. *Sting throws Moog out of the plane*) or be sent to another 'room' in the game (such as 'Prison'). The ambiguity lies in the fact that the intention behind the spam may be unclear, and the effect variously unpredictable. What counts as spam is often a matter of taste; as Marvin

---

[41] A further distinction is the sending of many messages to a server in an attempt to shut it down – what is usually referred to as a *mailbomb*. The automatic deletion of spam mail is known as *blackholing*.

[42] Stivale (1996).

[43] As *The New Penguin English Dictionary* (2000) intriguingly puts it: '**bonk,** *verb trans informal* **2** *Brit* to have sexual intercourse with (somebody)'.

puts it: 'one participant's spam is another's entertainment'.[44] But in all cases, spamming is a gratuitous addition to the communicative exchange, and thus breaks the maxim of quantity.

Flaming differs from spamming, in that messages (*flames*) are always aggressive, related to a specific topic, and directed at an individual recipient (spamming, by contrast, is often ludic or emotionally neutral, unspecific in content, and aimed at anyone within 'earshot'). It is similar in some ways to the ritual verbal duelling encountered between rival gangs and opposing army generals.[45] However, there is considerable dispute over what counts as a flame, and why people do it. People's sensitivities, tastes, communicative preferences, and styles differ – as they do in everyday conversation, indeed, where it is also not always agreed between two parties whether they are 'arguing' or 'having a discussion', or why an argument has blown up. Curiously, the two chatgroup parties involved in a flame often do not see their interchange as flaming, though other participants in the group do. Parties who have had their flaming pointed out to them are often surprised at the level of their linguistic aggressiveness – a function, presumably, of flamers finding themselves at a safe and often anonymous electronic distance from each other.[46] Cultural differences intervene, especially when messages are being exchanged internationally, so that an observation which might seem totally innocent to a sender in country A might seem inexplicably rude to a receiver in country B. Also, it often takes time for a series of exchanges to develop from a mild disagreement into an antagonistic interchange, and it can be difficult to identify the point when this happens. Plainly, an exchange in which participants have stopped talking about their topic and are simply exchanging verbal abuse would be a clear flame; but it is more debatable whether aggressive argument (of the kind common enough in much academic and political debate),

---

[44] Marvin (1996: 9). The subjectivity of the notion is also noted by Cherny (1999: 75) who refers to Marvin and observes, 'party conversation that appears witty and fun to one person is annoying spam to another'.
[45] For examples, see Crystal (1997a: 60).
[46] In one study, the members of anonymous groups made six times more hostile remarks than the members of non-anonymous ones: Wallace (1999: 125).

continuing to focus on the topic, albeit rudely, is flaming or not. The point has attracted considerable discussion within chatgroups (where flaming behaviour is common, at least by comparison with e-mail).[47] William Millard reports a case where a discussion moved to a different level, involving a dispute over whether a message was a flame or not, thereby attracting the attention of the list moderator, who attempted to control the way the interaction was going:[48]

> The message below is not a flame, although the poster claims it is. I have noticed on lists that when anyone uses the word 'flame' in a post hitherto dormant netters gather for the kill from all parts of the known electronic universe. Don't overreact here . . .

Ironically, such interventions can lead to a further discussion of what constitutes flaming, in which people take strong positions, and end up flaming each other about the topic of flaming – what Millard calls *metaflaming*.

Flaming behaviour, arising as it does out of frustration over the way a conversation is going, would seem more to contravene Grice's maxim of manner than of quantity. Its presence in Netspeak should not be underestimated. Millard, focusing on academic lists, identifies several factors in Internet writing which account for it. In addition to the metacommunicative minimalism of the medium, referred to above (p. 41), there is also:

> the customary economic constraints on connection time (and thus on personal patience), the delayed response of the audience, or the uncertainties ensuing from the consciousness that Internet communities are new enough to lack clear social protocols – as well as the general underlying tension between conceptions of language as a transparent medium for serious work or a dense material for ludic performance

– all of which, he concludes, 'implies that online academic writing as a genre is conducive to anxiety, wrath, and vendetta'.[49] The point

---

[47] Baron (2000: 239) finds a diminution in e-mail flaming, and suggests that the behaviour may have been an early symptom of the novelty of the medium.
[48] Millard (1996: 152–3).   [49] Millard (1996: 147).

goes well beyond the academic. Some groups have even gone so far as to experiment with flame filters, which search a message for potential inflammatory words or phrases (e.g. *get* + *lost/real/with it/life; you* + *noun*) and automatically exclude them. But the investigation of the formal linguistic equivalents of this particular genre of communicative competence is too rudimentary for such procedures to be reliable – both in what they exclude and fail to exclude. Rather more useful are such features as the 'scribble' command (used on the virtual community known as The Well = 'Whole Earth 'Lectronic Link': p. 130), which allows senders to delete what they have sent, inserting <scribbled> in its place.

The maxim of manner is also seriously challenged by the way some Internet situations operate. Will contributions be orderly and brief, avoiding obscurity and ambiguity? Brevity is certainly a recognized desideratum in all Netspeak interactions, in terms of sentence length, the number of sentences in a turn, or the amount of text on a screen. Style manuals repeatedly exhort users to be brief (p. 74); and while there are several signs of brevity in the different Internet situations, it takes only a short exposure to the Web to find many instances where the principle is honoured more in the breach than the observance. Also, Web page designers constantly talk about the importance of 'clear navigation' around a page, between pages in a site, and between sites, with the aim of providing unproblematic access to sites, clear screen layouts, and smoothly functioning selection options (for searching, help, further information, etc). But the inevitable amateurishness of many Web pages (the cost of designing a high-quality Web site can be considerable) means that the manner maxim is repeatedly broken. In synchronous chatgroups, the challenge is much more fundamental; there is an extraordinary degree of disorder, chiefly due to the number of participants all speaking at once, which makes a transcript of an interaction extremely difficult to follow. An interesting question is the extent to which obscurity and ambiguity is more likely in Netspeak because of the dependency of the medium upon typed input. Typing, not a natural behaviour, imposes a strong pressure on the sender to be selective in what is said, especially if one is not a very fast or competent typist. And selectivity in expression must lead to all kinds of inclarity.

Fourthly, the maxim of relevance – that contributions should clearly relate to the purpose of the exchange – is also undermined in some Internet situations. What is the purpose of an Internet exchange, one might well ask? In some cases, it is possible to define the purpose quite easily – a search for information on a specific topic on the Web, for example, or the desire to score points in a fantasy game. In others, several purposes can be present simultaneously, such as an e-mail which combines informational, social, and ludic functions. But in many cases, it is not easy to work out what the purpose of the exchange is. People often seem to post messages not in a spirit of real communication but just to demonstrate their electronic presence to other members of a group, to 'leave their mark' for the world to see (in the spirit of graffiti), or to use the medium to help themselves think something out.[50] The extreme situation is found in many chatgroups, where from the amount of topic-shifting we might well conclude that no subject-matter could ever be irrelevant. Informal conversation has long been recognized for its relative randomness of subject-matter;[51] but identifying the threads of subject-matter in a spoken dialogue is simplicity itself compared with the nature of the exchanges in such chatgroups, where several topics are being discussed at once, participants are interpolating comments about the way the conversation is going, and irrelevant utterances are being routinely introduced (as in the case of spoofing) for ludic or other reasons. The notion of relevance is usually related to an ideational or content-based function of language; but here we seem to have a situation where content is not privileged, and where factors of a social kind are given precedence.

The social function of much Internet communication has been a major theme of the literature in recent years, especially with

---

[50] This enhancing feature of the medium is illustrated by the finding that electronic group brainstorming seems to work better than its face-to-face counterpart: Wallace (1999: 84).

[51] Crystal and Davy (1969: ch. 1).

reference to the concept of a 'virtual community'. This notion has been not a little contentious, with some considering it an empty phrase, and others trying to give it a meaningful definition. Certainly, the mere fact of having engaged in an Internet activity does not produce in a user the sort of sense of identity and belonging which accompanies the term *community*. On the other hand, some Internet situations do promote such a sense of belonging, which comes from 'the experience of sharing with unseen others a space of communication'.[52] Underlying this view is a broader issue, to do with the way the Internet has come to be used in practice. To summarize a complex debate (in a netshell, perhaps): the Internet is not as global a medium as it might at first appear to be. While in principle much has been made of its ability to transcend the limitations of physical environments, cultural differences, and time-zones, thereby allowing people from anywhere to communicate with people anywhere else about anything at all, in practice the types of communication which take place are much more restricted and parochial. Most Internet interactions are not global in character; we are not talking to millions when we construct our Web pages, send an e-mail, join a chatgroup, or enter a virtual world. Derek Foster, summarizing a paper on computer-mediated communication (CMC) by Garth Graham, comments: 'The interactivity of CMC is about human connections. It is about talking. It serves individuals and communities, not mass audiences.'[53] Howard Rheingold describes the Internet as an 'ecosystem' of subcultures.[54] And Patricia Wallace identifies purpose as much more important than geography:[55]

> Though I like the 'global village' metaphor, the Internet is not really like that most of the time. With respect to human interaction, it is more like a huge collection of distinct neighborhoods where people with common interests can share information, work together, tell stories, joke around, debate politics, help each other out, or play games.

[52] Wilbur (1996: 13).   [53] Foster (1996: 29).
[54] Rheingold (1993: 3).   [55] Wallace (1999: 9).

Internet users are evidently wanting to talk to others who belong to their interest group (subculture, elite, niche...) or whom they would like to influence so that they become part of their interest group. Indicative is the way group members typically use such labels as 'guests', 'outsiders', and 'foreigners' when referring to visitors to their forum. The more light-hearted accounts go even further. Andy Ihnatko, for example, characterizes the situation in this way: 'the true purpose of language is to reenforce the divisions between society's tribes, or at least to make things difficult enough to understand so that the riff-raff keeps out. The new language of the Internet, spoken by a great number of rather insular types who like to keep interpersonal contact to a bare minimum to begin with, is no exception.'[56] Sociological analysis now seems to be moving away from the view that the kind of reduced social cues described earlier disallow the development of complex social and personal relationships on the Net. Just because we use a restricted set of graphic characters does not stop people constructing a new social world, and some have argued that cyberspace in certain conditions permits considerable levels of sophistication.[57]

Interesting linguistic questions follow. If real Internet communities are relatively small-scale, they will demonstrate their solidarity by evolving (consciously or unconsciously) measures of identity, some of which will be nonlinguistic (e.g. shared knowledge, a particular morality) and some linguistic in character. The linguistic features will take time to evolve, especially in a medium where technological facilities change so quickly and where some degree of nonconformity is commonplace among users, but eventually they will provide the community with an occupational dialect which newcomers will have to learn if they wish to join it. Linguistic idiosyncrasies belonging to individual chatgroups and MUDs have often been noted, at least as anecdotal observations. One of the aims of what one day might be called Internet sociolinguistics (or dialectology) will be to determine just how systematic such

---

[56] Ihnatko (1997: iii).   [57] See the review in Paccagnella (1997).

features are and how many such dialects can be distinguished. An initial enquiry into each of the main Internet situations provides the subject-matter of chapters 4–7. However, it is also likely, given the constraints that come from everyone using a broadly similar computer technology and having a broadly similar set of motivations, that there will be a set of shared linguistic features, found regardless of the Internet situation. The extent to which such a 'common core' exists is the subject of chapter 3.

3   *Finding an identity*

The uncertain linguistic identity of Netspeak, in its various Internet manifestations, is presumably why so many usage dictionaries, guides, and rule books have appeared in recent years. People seem to have begun to sense that they are dealing with something new, as far as their linguistic intuitions are concerned. They are realizing that their established knowledge, which has enabled them to survive and succeed in spoken and written linguistic encounters hitherto, is no longer enough to guarantee survival and success on the Internet. Perhaps they have encountered the 'painful and awkward lessons' in social interaction which Patricia Wallace talked about (p. 16). Perhaps they have been misunderstood, misperceived, or attacked (flamed) because they have failed to notice the differences between this new medium of communication and the old. David Porter sums it up this way:[1]

> There are words, but they often seem to be words stripped of
> context, words desperately burdened by the lack of the other
> familiar markers of identity in this strange, ethereal realm. It is no
> wonder that these digitalized words, flung about among strangers
> and strained beyond the limits of what written language in other
> contexts is called upon to do, are given to frequent misreading, or
> that they erupt as often they do into antagonistic 'flames'. In a
> medium of disembodied voices and decontextualized points of
> view, a medium, furthermore, beholden to the fetishization of
> speed, the experience of ambiguity and misreading is bound to be
> less an exception than the norm.

Whatever the reason, people seem to want guidance, and those with a track-record in using the Internet have not been slow to supply

---

[1] Porter (1996a: xi–xii).

it. An interesting kind of semi-prescriptivism has begun to emerge, as a result.

The distinction between prescriptive and descriptive approaches to language study has been a source of controversy since Classical times.[2] *Prescriptivism* is the view that one variety of language has an inherently higher value than others, and that this ought to be imposed on the whole of the speech community. It is an authoritarian view, espoused for English in the middle decades of the eighteenth century, and propounded especially in relation to usage in grammar, vocabulary, and pronunciation. The favoured variety is usually a version of the standard written language which most closely reflects literary style. Those who speak or write in this variety are said to be using language 'correctly'; those who do not are said to be using it 'incorrectly'. (Some analysts distinguish *prescriptive rules*, recommending what should be done, from *proscriptive rules*, recommending what should not be done.) Examples in English are (for grammar) 'Never begin a sentence with *and*', (for vocabulary) 'Always use *decimate* to mean "kill a tenth"', (for pronunciation) 'Avoid pronouncing an /r/ between vowels, as in *law(r) and order*', and (for spelling) 'There must always be an *ae* in *encyclopaedia*.' Quite plainly, the prescriptive approach ignores the realities of everyday usage, where most people (including many famous authors) do begin sentences with *and*, do use *decimate* to mean 'kill a large number', do link adjacent vowels with /r/, and do not put the *a* of *encyclopedia* in.

The descriptive approach, by contrast, does not condemn usages that do not follow the rules thought up by prescriptively minded authors. Rather, it describes the variations in usage found within a language, and explains why variant forms exist. American usage favours *encyclopedia*, traditional British usage *encyclopaedia*; but as the dominant influence during the twentieth century was from the US to the UK, the American spelling was increasingly found in British publications. Or again, both *This is the lady I was talking*

---

[2] For the issue of prescriptivism and descriptivism, see Milroy and Milroy (1991), and Crystal (1984).

to and *This is the lady to whom I was talking* co-exist. Prescriptive writers favour the latter and condemn the former ('Never end a sentence with a preposition'). Descriptive writers point out that both usages are widespread, traditional (used in English since the Middle Ages), and important, for they allow people to make a difference in the formality of their expression: the former is more colloquial than the latter. To condemn one version as 'bad grammar' is to deny English users the stylistic option of switching styles, when it is appropriate to do so, and thus reduces the versatility and richness of the language.

Descriptivists do not like the narrow-minded intolerance and misinformed purism of prescriptivists. Prescriptivists, correspondingly, do not like the all-inclusiveness and egalitarian philosophy of descriptivists, which they interpret as a lack of responsibility towards what is best in a language. The controversy shows no sign of going away, even after 250 years, with the arguments being recycled by each generation, and refuelled by new developments in society, such as broadcasting and, now, the Internet. What is of interest, in the burgeoning Internet literature, is to see the way writers are struggling to maintain a bent which is naturally descriptive and egalitarian in character while recognizing a prescriptive urge to impose regularity and consistency on a world which otherwise might spiral out of control. The situation is very reminiscent of the one Samuel Johnson encountered when he began work on his *Dictionary*:[3]

> When I took the first survey of my undertaking, I found our speech copious without order, and energetick without rules; wherever I turned my view, there was perplexity to be disentangled, and confusion to be regulated; choice was to be made out of boundless variety, without any established principle of selection; adulterations were to be detected, without a settled test of purity; and modes of expression to be rejected or received, without the suffrages of any writers of classical reputation or acknowledged authority.

---

[3] The two Johnson quotations are from his Preface to *A Dictionary of the English language* (1755).

He might have been talking about the early years of the Internet. Similar uncertainties underlie the series of questions which open the pages of *Wired Style*:[4]

> Writers today must navigate the shifting verbal currents of the post-Gutenberg era. When does jargon end and a new vernacular begin? Where's the line between neologism and hype? What's the language of the global village? How can we keep pace with technology without getting bogged down in buzzwords?

Johnson soon found that his prescriptive urges, fostered by the attitudes of his acquaintances, were absurd:

> Those who have been persuaded to think well of my design, will require that it should fix our language, and put a stop to those alterations which time and chance have hitherto been suffered to make in it without opposition. With this consequence I will confess that I flattered myself for a while; but now begin to fear that I have indulged expectation which neither reason nor experience can justify.... [no lexicographer] shall imagine that his dictionary can embalm his language, and secure it from corruption and decay, and that it is in his power to change sublunary nature, and clear the world at once from folly, vanity, and affectation.

It is a conclusion that prescriptively minded Internet writers need to bear in mind.

Most of the Netspeak authors are aware of the importance of grounding their work in descriptive reality. The authors of *Wired Style*, for example, are anxious to show that their ear is to the electronic equivalent of the ground:

> You might call *Wired Style* an experiment in nonlinear, networked editing. When a new technical term, a bullshit buzzword, or an especially gnarly acronym hits our screens, we send emails to various editors and style divas. *Wired Style* is the result of these online discussions, which are guided by actual usage rather than rigid rules.... Like new media, *Wired Style* is dynamic and rule-averse.

[4] Hale and Scanlon (1999: 2), for both quotations.

The approach is not quite as experimental as the authors think. It is standard lexicographical practice to check observed neologisms against a corpus of data, however it is derived. Some dictionaries, such as the *American Heritage*, have long used panels of advisers to judge the acceptability of contentious points, and in the late 1990s the pages of *English Today* provided precisely such a forum for a new style guide.[5] But it is good linguistics to make the effort to supplement one's own intuition with the intuitions of others. Obtaining opinions about usage does not imply an abdication of editorial responsibility, of course. Once the expert reactions have come in, the editors have still to impose order on what is always a miscellany of reactions, and make decisions over coverage and treatment. This is where intuitions about 'actual usage' are sorely tested, and where it is easy to allow decisions about what to include to be influenced by such considerations as personal taste, personality, and marketing. The lack of consensus can be easily seen from a comparison of the coverage of any two Internet dictionaries. *Cyberspeak* also claims to be a guide to common usage:[6]

> The lingo you'll find here is all in common currency, I assure you, and you'll find none of the faux-hipsterisms which would only have marked you as a hapless wannabe. I've also skipped over the mountains of slang which, while absolutely authentic, aren't in common use outside of a few specific research labs.

But it turns out that less than 25% of the headwords are shared by *Cyberspeak* and *Wired Style*. Dictionaries are never identical in their coverage, but when three-quarters of the words in one are different from the other – yet both claim to be surveying the same phenomenon, at more or less the same time (mid-1990s) – it is plain that factors other than frequency of use are very much involved. There would seem to be some difference of opinion, even among the experts, as to what counts as acceptable Netspeak. And the way manuals do not shirk condemning certain usages as unacceptable suggests that the spirit of prescriptivism is more strongly present

---

[5] See Peters (1998) and subsequent issues of *English Today*.   [6] Ihnatko (1997: iv).

than editorial denials suggest. It is very much present, in an intrusive and arbitrary form, in the spell-check and grammar-check aids provided by software packages (see p. 212).

A strong personal, creative spirit imbues Netspeak, as an emerging variety. Internet users are continually searching for vocabulary to describe their experiences, to capture the character of the electronic world, and to overcome the communicative limitations of its technology. The rate at which they have been coining new terms and introducing playful variations into established ones has no parallel in contemporary language use. Doubtless it will all slow down in due course; but as we begin the new millennium the editors who have set up sites to monitor new usages report no diminution in the rate at which proposals for fresh jargon are made. The *Jargon File*, which records 'the language hackers use among themselves for fun, social communication, and technical debate', is quite clear about its innovative, ludic, dynamic properties:[7]

> Hackers ... regard slang formation and use as a game to be played for conscious pleasure. Their inventions thus display an almost unique combination of the neotenous enjoyment of language-play with the discrimination of educated and powerful intelligence. Further, the electronic media which knit them together are fluid, 'hot' connections, well adapted to both the dissemination of new slang and the ruthless culling of weak and superannuated specimens.

Gareth Branwyn's *Jargon watch* is also illustrative, and his method of handling the flood instructive:[8]

> When someone submits a term, we're not overly concerned about its origins (although we prefer words that have established usage).

---

[7] The introduction to the *Jargon File* (<http://www.tuxedo.org/~esr/jargon/html/>), a work which as of August 2000 contained over 2,100 entries. The File has several senses for *hacker*, of which the first one is: 'A person who enjoys exploring the details of programmable systems and how to stretch their capabilities, as opposed to most users, who prefer to learn only the minimum necessary'. In general English usage, *hacker* has developed a pejorative sense: 'A malicious meddler who tries to discover sensitive information by poking around'. This usage is deprecated by true hackers, who refer to such individuals as *crackers*. Another online dictionary can be found at <www.netlingo.com>.
[8] Branwyn (1997: Introduction).

f it strikes my fancy, I pass it down the editorial food chain. If after
assing through all the editor's [*sic*] hands it hasn't been given the
, I assume it's interesting and useful enough to get a shot in the
magazine. I fancy myself a sort of slang impresario. If a term
passes the editorial audition, I push it out onto the stage provided
by the magazine. If it bombs, it gets the hook and its career is
finished . . . If it's a big success, it ends up making the rounds of
email boxes, water coolers, and office cubicles, from Silicon Valley
to Silicon Alley[9] and beyond. The words that made it into the
column and this book are just a fraction of the terms submitted.

And he lists some of what he calls the 'scarier' submissions, by way
of illustration: *e-gasm, javangelist, pornetgraphy,* and *Webference.*
These he does not include. But there is no way of knowing, of
course, whether they will eventually enter the Internet lexicon
through some other door, or whether they will be included in some
other word-book edited by someone with different linguistic tastes.

Internet situations display a surprisingly large number of guidelines, principles, rules, and regulations relating to the way people
should linguistically behave once they engage in computer-
mediated communication. These are both prescriptive and proscriptive in character – helpful and informative insofar as they reflect real usage preferences, but needing to be viewed with caution
insofar as they represent a partial or prejudiced view of the online
userworld. Prejudices are widespread, in fact. Those who espouse
a particular technology, or a particular chatgroup or virtual world,
may scorn the terms belonging to another. And all hackers scorn
non-hackers:[10]

As usual with slang, the special vocabulary of hackers helps hold
their culture together – it helps hackers recognize each other's
places in the community and expresses shared values and
experiences. Also as usual, *not* knowing the slang (or using it
inappropriately) defines one as an outsider, a mundane, or (worst
of all in hackish vocabulary) possibly even a *suit.*

[9] 'An area of lower Manhattan that has a high concentration of computer and multimedia
firms. [entry from the dictionary]'.
[10] Introduction to the *Jargon File* (see fn.7).

A *suit*, according to the *Jargon File*, is 'ugly and uncomfortable "business clothing" often worn by non-hackers'; and the *Wired Style* definition is explicit:[11]

> Not a techie. Someone in management or bizdev (business development) or marcom (marketing/communications). Someone who thinks in profits rather than programs and cares more about the bottom line than lines of code.

Hackers are plainly very aware of their identity as members of an Internet culture (more precisely, a collection of subcultures), dating from the earliest days, proud of their common background and values, and conscious of their expertise. Most of the style manuals include a characterization of the hacker mindset and skills. The 'hacker ethic' has two main principles, according to the *Jargon File*: 'the belief that information-sharing is a powerful positive good, and that it is an ethical duty of hackers to share their expertise by writing open-source and facilitating access to information and to computing resources wherever possible', and (more controversially) 'the belief that system-cracking for fun and exploration is ethically OK as long as the cracker commits no theft, vandalism, or breach of confidentiality'. Hackers have to have certain skills – such as a knowledge of programming and an ability to write HTML (p. 205). But the hacker mindset is just as important. There are five characteristics of the 'hacker attitude' noted by the *Jargon File*:

- The world is full of fascinating problems waiting to be solved.
- Nobody should ever have to solve a problem twice.
- Boredom and drudgery are evil.
- Freedom is good.
- Attitude is no substitute for competence.

And a further five recommendations for aspiring hackers:

- Learn to write your native language well.
- Read science fiction.
- Study Zen, and/or take up martial arts.

[11] Hale and Scanlon (1999: 157).

- Develop an analytical ear for music.
- Develop your appreciation of puns and wordplay.

These characteristics will obviously bias the recommendations of the style guides. We respond to 'the voice of the quirky, individualist writer', say the authors of *Wired Style*, in expounding one of their principles (see below), and they recommend: 'play with voice'.

As hackers built the Internet and gave physical presence to its various situations, they have naturally developed a sense of ownership of Netspeak which is reflected in the attitudes of the current generation of dictionaries and style guides. But the beast they have created is now so large that it is beyond ownership. The hacker community is but a tiny part of the online population, and the linguistic intuitions and preferences of such vast numbers are immensely variable and impossible to control. Quirky, individualist writers there will be among them; but there will also be huge numbers of non-quirky, conservative writers, who don't read science fiction, study Zen, or go in for wordplay. For every one hacker, there are probably a thousand suits – and suits of many different linguistic fabrics. The future of Netspeak, then, is very much bound up with the extent to which hacker-originated language and style has developed a sufficiently stable and powerful identity to motivate new Internet users to use it, or whether these users will introduce fresh linguistic directions, evolving norms of stylistic usage which owe nothing to hacker origins, and which avoid the playful and esoteric features so much in evidence now. Although the linguistic features described below are those which are currently in widespread use, several of them figuring largely in Internet guides, any of them could have a limited future.

Making the rules explicit

But this is to be looking well ahead. For the moment, the guides and dictionaries have an important role introducing newbies to the Internet, giving advice and instruction about how to behave if they want their communications to be successful. Several general expositions about netiquette are available, and the topic turns up regularly in the press.[12] Certain behaviours are universally open to correction. An example would be the linguistic consequences of using the technology incorrectly – such as an e-mail which had a subject heading but no content, or a multiply repeated signature, or the inadvertent repeated sending of a single message. Also universally condemned are ethical violations, such as forwarding private mail without permission, or editing someone else's message without permission. Inappropriate language, such as flaming, is also widely criticised. Many sites provide advice which users are encouraged to read before they enter. Chatgroups usually provide FAQs (Frequently Asked Questions) which explain the basic rules that new participants should follow – for example, which topics are disallowed, how to refer to others' messages, and what sort of behaviour is banned.

People who fail to conform to these guidelines risk sanctions, such as explicit correction by other participants (from a jocular chiding to a severe flaming) or, the ultimate penalty, being excluded from the group (by the group moderator, or, sometimes, through an automatic filter) or having an account cancelled by the offender's service-provider. In virtual worlds, players who are seriously nonconformist can be *gagged* or *toaded* (their fantasy character is altered to appear ugly: see p. 176). The presence of *moderators* in chatgroups or *wizards* in games is itself an interesting convention – the recognition by participants that some kind of external presence is needed to avoid anarchy and to resolve internal disputes, even at the expense of the personal freedom which is supposed to be a feature of Internet presence. Without them, it would be easy for flaming exchanges to spiral out of control or for lengthy off-topic discussions to intrude. A degree of linguistic control is sometimes imposed automatically, as in those programmes which replace expletives by asterisks or euphemisms. The controls can also lead to second-order discussions (*metadiscussions*), in which participants debate the rules themselves and how they have been

---

[12] For example, Shea (1994). On standards of conduct generally, see McLaughlin, Osborne, and Smith (1994).

applied, in individual instances. It can take a chatgroup away from its theme for days.

Such explicit guidance is unusual in the real world. We do not expect to see, as we move around, directions about how we should behave, other than in a few specific circumstances, as in the case of road signs and keeping off the grass. Linguistic directions are only provided in specialist settings (e.g. the use of correct forms of address in a military context or in law courts), form-filling (e.g. whether to use capital letters, where to sign), and a few other situations. We are not usually instructed, as we enter a shop, about how the staff should be addressed, acknowledged, and thanked; nor would we expect any such instruction. The reason is obvious: we have a lifetime of experience behind us from which we have learned the conventions of interaction. Our parents or caretakers spent unremembered hours teaching us the pragmatic rules of the language ('Say ta', 'I haven't heard that little word yet' (viz. *please*), 'Don't talk like that to the vicar', 'I won't have language like that in here'), and our schoolteachers followed this up with more advanced lessons in formal politeness, letter-writing, report writing, and a range of other linguistic skills. Usage guides and style manuals are available for those who, having come through the educational system, remain uncertain of what counts as appropriate language; but these tend to deal only with contentious points of usage variation (such as those illustrated on p. 63), and not with broad issues of interaction, which are assumed to be known. This is a reasonable assumption. In everyday conversation, we do not expect to find moderators who tell us whether we are off-topic, saying something unacceptable, or going too far (though there are always self-appointed ones). That is for an Orwellian (*1984*) kind of world.

But with the Internet, explicit linguistic guidance is routine, varying from popular advice to detailed manuals of behaviour. One newspaper article on e-mail etiquette[13] provides a series

---

[13] David Thomas (2000). At the same time, some popular accounts of the Internet give the impression that new users will encounter no problems: 'If you're new to the Internet, the important thing to remember is that going online doesn't require any special techy skills or knowhow' ('This is the Internet', series produced by the *Independent* and the

of specific guidelines. There are parent-like instructions: 'Don't techno bully' (by being rude if someone is technically inept); 'Say something nice' (by sending thank-you notes); 'Mind your manners' (by keeping a check on what you write). There are teacher-like directions (on how to address someone; on thinking about a message's content before sending it; on not mass mailing). And there is common-sensical advice: 'Always check your messages'; 'Never e-dump lovers.' The article displays the characteristics of the genre. It is experience-driven, showing awareness of a range of problems arising in daily Internet use: 'Never write messages in capital letters – it's the e-mail equivalent of shouting.' At the same time there is an element of prescriptivism: 'When writing to someone called Bob, don't use the fuddy-duddy "Dear Bob", but simply "Bob".' And there is a strong element of personal taste: 'Some etiquette experts feel that invitations, acceptances and messages of thanks should always be sent via old-fashioned post, rather than e-mail, but I disagree.'

The ideal guide to Netspeak would be one grounded in systematic empirical observation, providing a representative corpus of material which would reflect the frequency with which Internet situations use and vary particular structures. But it takes a long time to carry out such descriptive linguistic surveys.[14] No e-corpus of this kind yet exists, and so it is inevitable that guides, whether in article or book form, will contain a great deal that is subjective, expressing personal or institutional taste. There is nothing wrong with impressionistic accounts, of course, in the early stages of getting to grips with a subject; indeed, they have their value in suggesting hypotheses about the nature of its language, which can guide research. The problem comes when impressionistic statements are cast as prescriptions, explicitly or implicitly. There is then a real risk that a biased account of Internet language will emerge, reflecting only the interests and background of the individual author, publication, or organization which produced it. If such accounts

---

Independent on Sunday, no date, but early 2000, Part 1). It all depends on what is meant by 'techy', of course, but the spirit of this statement does not match the linguistic reality.
[14] For example, Biber, Johansson, Leech, Conrad, and Finegan (1999).

are then taken or promoted as guides to the Internet in general, an unhelpful prescriptivism can be the result, similar in its naivety, unreality, and oversimplification to that encountered in the grammar books of old.

All these dangers can be seen in the newspaper article summarized above; and they are present in more sophisticated, book-length accounts too. For example, the editors of *Wired* magazine make ten recommendations in their handbook *Wired Style*, five to do with writing prose online, and five to do with ensuring consistency in spelling and punctuation.[15] The principles seem to have been compiled with a *Wired* readership in mind; but, as the quotation on p. 65 suggests, and as the book's blurb makes clear, the exposition is being offered to a wider world as '*the* guide for navigating the informal waters of digital prose'. The principles themselves are uncontentious, to my mind, and are summarized in Table 3.1. Several are well grounded in linguistic thinking; others are no different from those which inform the corresponding discussions of copy-editing in conventional publishing.[16] But when they are interpreted as being applicable to an audience that goes beyond that of *Wired*, there are grounds for concern, as can be seen from a discussion of the first two.

The first principle, headed 'The medium matters', requires the language to suit the technology: 'we need to craft our messages to suit the medium and its audience'. The linguistic recommendations which follow are: for e-mail, 'Think blunt bursts and sentence fragments. Writing that is on-the-fly – even frantic.' 'Pith and punch also define posting on the Web, The Well, wherever.' And they amplify this accordingly:

> Look to the Web not for embroidered prose, but for the sudden
> narrative, the dramatic story told in 150 words. Text must be
> complemented by clever interface design and clear graphics.
> Think brilliant ad copy, not long-form literature. Think pert,
> breezy pieces almost too ephemeral for print. Think turned-up
> volume – cut lines that are looser, grabbier, more tabloidy. Think
> distinctive voice or attitude.

[15] Hale and Scanlon (1999). Quotations are from pp. 3–24.
[16] For example, Butcher (1992).

Table 3.1. Wired Style's *ten usage principles, with some explanatory comment (after Hale and Scanlon, 1999). References are to pages.*

1 'The medium matters'	'In a world of scarce bandwidth, small screens, and evermore media sources competing for our attention, every word and sentence must score a high signal-to-noise ratio.' (p. 3)
2 'Play with voice'	There should be linguistic inventiveness, creativity, play, in the form of new words and odd constructions. 'Celebrate subjectivity. Write with attitude. Play with voice.' (p. 9)
3 'Flaunt your subcultural literacy'	Most Net audiences are relatively small groups who have their own identity and behaviour, and will share a certain background and style. 'Consider your own context. Narrowcast. Talk to your audience. Speak the culture.' (p. 9)
4 'Transcend the technical'	'Grasp the technologies, then describe them with vivid language and clear metaphors.' (p. 11). True jargon 'is lucid language and can be as elegant as it is meaningful. It's denotation: concrete, specific, direct, and necessary.' (p. 10)
5 'Capture the colloquial'	'At Wired, we write geek and we write street. We insist on accuracy and literacy, but we celebrate the colloquial.' (p. 11)
6 'Anticipate the future'	'Language moves in one predictable direction: forward.' (p. 12) 'We say, "Grow the language."' (p. 13) This involves welcoming neologisms, simplifying spellings, avoiding capitals, and removing hyphens from compound words.
7 'Be irreverent'	'Know your audiences well enough to violate journalism's cardinal rules and to toy with conventions.' The recommendation: 'Welcome inconsistency, especially in the interest of voice and cadence. Treat the institutions and players in your world with a dose of irreverence. Play with grammar and syntax. Appreciate unruliness.' (p. 15)

(Continued)

Table 3.1. (*cont.*)

8	'Brave the new world of new media'	This is a fairly orthodox account of the need to maintain typographical conventions (italics, quotes, capitals) to separate title from plaintext. *Wired* makes its distinctions (for names of films, songs, albums, Web sites, Internet services, etc.) just like any other publisher would.
9	'Go global'	'Yes, we write in English, but in these Webbed times, writing from a US-centric perspective is hopelessly outdated.' (p. 21) Style shifts may be necessary, for such things as date-expression, phone number style, and prices. For foreign words, 'don't be lazy or xenophobic – take the time to figure out correct spellings and accent marks.' (p. 21) 'Writing with a global perspective means being cosmopolitan: enjoying the best of other cultures and tongues, and resisting the impulse to put foreign ideas and phrases through a bottom-feeder filter.' (p. 21)
10	'Play with dots and dashes and slashes'	They draw attention to the clash between copy-editors and coders, in writing on or about the Net. 'Online, publishing meets programming – and punctuation leads a double life.' (p. 22)

The message is clear about what the editors would like Netspeak to be, and doubtless readers of *Wired* find this style congenial. But generalizing the point is problematic, for a great deal of apparently successful Internet communication does not conform to it. I receive innumerable e-mails which are anything but fragmented sentences; I read innumerable Web sites where the content demands longer and more sophisticated exposition. It is unlikely that a single principle of economy could ever explain the variety of uses, intentions, tastes, and effects which give the Internet its character. 'Tabloidy' might appeal to one type of readership, but it will appal others. And it is because the Internet copes with both extremes of user, allowing a broad spectrum of users in between, that it is becoming so universal.

Any style guide which promotes one variety of language at the expense of another is prescriptive. Traditional prescriptivism privileged writing over speech, formality over informality. Internet manuals are doing the reverse. It is prescriptivism nonetheless. And it is a worrying kind of prescriptivism because it is doing precisely what the old grammars did – reducing the potential richness and versatility of a medium of communication. It should be possible to make use of the Internet for formal as well as for informal purposes, to express elaborate as well as succinct messages. The more we can express stylistic contrasts and nuances in Netspeak, the more powerful a linguistic medium it will be. I have no problem at all with the many e-mails I receive which begin 'Dear David' (contravening the newspaper advice above). I can see immediately that such messages are more formal than those which begin 'Dave baby', or whatever. And I can also see a functional contrast with those which begin with no name at all, such as this morning's junk-mail which tells me directly, and without naming me at all, that I can be a millionaire by the weekend and have my sex-drive improved at the same time. Other address variations exist, such as the location of the addressee's name at the top or integrated within the first sentence, and these convey further expressive nuances. Internet guides need to recognize the presence of all these options, which help to make Netspeak a more powerful and expressive medium, rather than to go for one and reject the others. The relevant *Wired Style* section concludes: 'On the web, you forget your audience at your peril', which is wise advice, linguistically well-grounded. But no single stylistic recommendation can suit the expectations of the range of audiences that the Internet is now reaching. And to advocate one (albeit unintentionally) is to be unhelpfully prescriptive.

Wired Style's second principle leads to a similar conclusion. It is headed 'Play with voice', a phrase repeated in its summary: 'Celebrate subjectivity. Write with attitude. Play with voice.' Voice here refers to the personal element in communication:

> We respond to voice. Not the clear-but-oh-so-conventional voice of Standard Written English. Not the data-drowned voice of computer trade journals. And not the puréed voice of the mainstream press. The voice of the quirky, individualist writer.

The authors go on to describe how voice 'captures the way people talk' and 'adds attitude and authenticity'. They illustrate this by a science-fiction example, from which we may deduce that the desired style privileges the use of linguistic inventiveness, creativity, and play, in the form of new words and odd constructions. 'Writing with voice', they say, 'might mean going for the unexpected, the rough-edged, the over-the-top'. It is reinforced by their principle (7), 'Be irreverent', which translates into linguistic recommendations as follows:

> Welcome inconsistency, especially in the interest of voice and cadence. Treat the institutions and players in your world with a dose of irreverence. Play with grammar and syntax. Appreciate unruliness.

As with principle (1), there is nothing wrong with the appeal to a personal element in linguistic expression and the promotion of the ludic, creative function of language. Indeed, I am on record myself as advocating a greater attention to language play in our appreciation of linguistic interaction.[17] And any periodical has the right to do what it likes, by way of formulating a ludic language policy. But as soon as this policy is extended to the Internet as a whole, we encounter problems.

It is plainly unreal to think of restricting the Internet only to quirky, individualist writers, or to exclude writers of a more conventional or reverent leaning. The Internet is a home to all kinds of writing, including the trade journals and the newspapers, and these all have a right to their own style, too. Indeed, it is precisely these styles which provide the norms of usage to which writers of a more idiosyncratic bent can react. Norms – standard written English norms – are critical, if personal effects are to be appreciated; for if everybody breaks the rules, rule-breaking ceases to be novel. The antagonism to standard written English (or standard written French, or German...) is misplaced, therefore, for it will

[17] Crystal (1998).

maintain its place on the Internet as it does everywhere else in society. Indeed, it is unusual to see material on the Net written in non-standard English – such as regional dialect.[18] The vast majority of Web pages are in standard English. Most of my e-mails are in standard English – some very colloquial, but nonetheless respecting the conventions of the standard written language. Notwithstanding the idiosyncrasy of chatgroup and virtual worlds language, a great deal of it is written in standard English. And if we add up all the non-standard English (or perhaps I should say, not-yet-standard English) which is described in chapters 4–7, it is still only a small part of the language used on the Internet as a whole. In which case, principle (2), if used to fuel a general recommendation about Netspeak usage, hides another manifestation of prescriptivism. One style of language is being advocated as a norm, to the apparent exclusion of others, and apparently flying in the face of the bulk of Internet usage.

Similar arguments could be adduced about other recommendations in Table 3.1. 'Celebrate the colloquial' (principle 5) is a fine principle, but there are many occasions where it proves equally necessary to 'celebrate the formal'. It is an axiom of linguistics that all varieties of language must be celebrated, for each contributes a dimension to the rich mosaic of expressive effects that constitutes a language. It is understandable that, as the new medium grows, with all its exciting possibilities, the stylistic pendulum should swing away from the traditions of formal written language. In chapter 2, I reviewed some of the factors which have made this inevitable. But only an inclusive view of Netspeak will represent the reality of what is actually 'out there' in Internet situations. The same point applies to principle (4), 'Transcend the technical', which appeals to vividness and clarity. Clarity is crucial; indeed, it is a conversational maxim (p. 58). But one person's lucidity is another person's nightmare, and vice versa. *Wired Style* condemns

---

[18] The Dialectizer, with a straight face, converts standard English sentences into a number of 'equivalent' dialect forms: <http://www.rinkworks.com/dialect/>.

(*inter alia*) *turnkey*, *interoperability*, and *ease of use*, on the grounds that they are 'overused', along with 'anything starting with *e-*, *cyber-*, or *techno-*'. But the only result of using proscriptions of this kind is to distance the proscriber from the facts of online usage. They may not like the words, but the recognition that they are 'overused' reflects a usage reality that currently exists. Individuals have always tried to stop words coming into a language, and they have always failed.

Publications such as *Wired Style* have their place as part of a climate of opinion which will eventually help to shape Netspeak. The principles are important statements, as they make explicit a set of intuitions about language which are likely to be influential. Under principle (6), for example, 'Anticipate the future', they include such 'style commandments' as 'Save a keystroke' and 'When in doubt, close it up.' The former is illustrated by the replacement of initial capital letters by lower-case letters – as in *webmaster* and *telnet*. The latter refers to the trend for originally spaced compound words to become hyphenated and then written solid (as in such everyday examples as *flower pot*, *flower-pot*, and *flowerpot*). The authors are well aware that this is a regular feature of linguistic change, and they are keen to hasten the process: 'Go there now.' They recommend *startup*, *homepage*, and *email*, and solid setting for some syntactic constructions too, such as *logon* and *whois*. 'The way of the Net is just not a hyphenated way.' Comments of this kind are bound to influence people (such as myself) who have no idea what is normal usage, in Internet situations. I have always spelled *e-mail* with a hyphen, and have done so in this book. Whether I change to *email* in due course will depend on whether a consensus emerges. The problem is that, at present, the books I have been referring to vary in their recommendations: Branwyn uses *email*; but Ihnatko and almost all the manuals I discuss in chapter 4 use *e-mail*. I have no aesthetic axe to grind, and the presence of the additional keystroke is not going to have a serious effect upon my life. Eventually, one standard of usage will prevail, and it may well be the solid form. In the meantime, it is important to recognize the fact that there is a great deal of divided usage in Netspeak, and to treat with caution those guides which come down on one side or the other.

A systematic description of the features of Netspeak, as encountered in different Internet situations, is a new goal of descriptive linguistic research. At present, the distinct purposes and procedures involved in e-mailing, chatgroups, virtual worlds, and the Web make for significant differences between them (these are reviewed in chapters 4–7). At the same time, there is considerable overlap, because elements of one situation are now routinely incorporated within another (p. 14) – such as e-mails at a Web site, or Web attachments to an e-mail. And there seems to be a considerable mutual influence between situations. For example, the kind of abbreviations illustrated below may have historically originated in one situation (such as a particular chatgroup) but they have since spread to others. Chatgroup acronyms – words made from the initial letters of other words – such as *LOL* ('Laughing Out Loud') are now encountered in the other situations. It is therefore possible to begin making some observations about the kind of language which seems to be typical of the Internet domain as a whole. It is not yet possible to make judgements about frequency or preferences; the examples below are illustrative, not comprehensive. But they do make a strong case for the emergence of a new kind of English.

Some features of Netspeak

One of the most obvious – but not thereby less significant – features is the lexicon that belongs exclusively to the Internet, and which is encountered when someone enters any of its situations (see chapter 1). This lexicon does not include the terminology associated with computer science, programming, electronics, and other relevant subjects. Terms such as *cable, disk, bit, binary,* and *computer* form part of the jargon of science and technology which extends well beyond the Net. By contrast, a large number of words and phrases have emerged which are needed to talk about Internet-restricted situations, operations, activities, and personnel, making this one of the most creative lexical domains in contemporary English, involving all major lexical processes.[19]

Many terms are associated with the software which enables people to use the Internet, and which routinely appear on screen. Some have a permanent presence (albeit in hidden menus), in the form of the labels used to designate screen areas and functions, and to specify user options and commands: *file, edit, view, insert, paste, format, tools, window, help, search, refresh, address, history, stop, contact, top, back, forward, home, send, save, open, close, select, toolbars, fonts, options.* Some terms appear only at intervals on a screen, depending on circumstances – usually, when things are going wrong, in the form of error messages (there seem to be no positive messages to tell us that everything is going right): *forbidden, illegal operation, error, not found, 404 error* ['a page or site is no longer in service']. Several terms are associated with the use of computer hardware: *freeze, lock, down, hang, crash, bomb, client* (the machine, not the user). And terms have emerged for the population of Internet users themselves: *netizens, netters, netties, netheads, cybersurfers, nerds, bozos, newbies, surfers, digiterati, wizards, lusers* ['users who are losers'], *wannabees* ['aspiring hackers who can't hack']. Most of these words are everyday terms which have been given a fresh sense in an Internet context.

A popular method of creating Internet neologisms is to combine two separate words to make a new word, or *compound.* Some elements turn up repeatedly: *mouse* in such forms as *mouseclick, mousepad, mouseover* and also as a phrasal verb (*mouse across, mouse over*); *click* in *click-and-buy, one-click, cost-per-click, double-click, click-and-mortar* [an e-commerce strategy, from *bricks-and-mortar*], *clickthrough rate* ['measure of pageviews']; *ware* in *firmware, freeware, groupware, shareware, shovelware, wetware* ['brain']; *web* in *webcam, webcast, webmail, webliography, webmaster, webonomics, webster, webzine, webhead* ['Web addict']; *net*

---

[19] On types of word-formation, see Bauer (1983).

in *netlag, netdead, netnews, hypernet, Usenet, Netspeak, EcoNet, PeaceNet,* and many other organizational names; *hot* in *hotlist, hotspot, hotlink, Hotmail, HotBot, HotJava,* and other trade names; and *bug* ['software error'] in *bug fix, bugtracker, bug bash* ['hunt for bugs'], *BugNet.* Similar in function are the use of *cyber-* and *hyper-* as prefixes or combining forms (*cyberspace, cyberculture, cyberlawyer, cybersex, cybersquatter, cyberian, cyber rights; hypertext, hyperlink, hyperfiction, hyperzine*) and the suffixal use of *-bot* [an artificial intelligence program, from *robot*], as in *annoybot, chatterbot, knowbot, cancelbot, softbot, mailbot, spybot.* Other prefixes include *e-* (influential in the language as a whole, p. 21); *V-* ['virtual'], as in *V-chat*; and *E* [for a number raised to a power, from mathematics], as in *ThanksE6* ['Thanks a million']. The word *at*, often shown as @ (p. 21), also has an increasingly prefixal function: *atcommand, atsign, @-party, @-address, @Home*; this too has come to be influential in non-Internet settings. And a productive future may be in store for the suffix *-icon*, as people derive words based on *emoticon* – such as *assicon*. Blends (in which part of one word is joined to part of another) are illustrated by *netiquette, netizen, infonet, cybercide* ['the killing of a persona in a virtual worlds game'], *datagram, infobahn, Internaut, Bugzilla* ['a bug-tracking agency']. An innovation is the replacement of a word-element by a similar sounding item, as in *ecruiting* ['electronic recruiting'], *ecruiter,* and *etailing* ['electronic retailing']. Another is the retaining of the period found in electronic addresses within certain compounds, as a kind of infix, seen in *net.legend, net.abuse, net.police,* and *net.citizen*, or sites beginning with *alt.* (with the punctuation mark often spoken aloud as 'dot'). As already noted (p. 20), *dot* is itself increasing in frequency, as in *dot address, dot file, dotcom organizations*. Reduced sentences and phrases may appear as words, as in the *whois* instruction (for looking up names in a remote database) and *whowhere* (a means of finding a person's e-address by entering a name and location).

Other means of word-creation are also used, at least in the playful jargon used by hackers. It is not clear just how widespread or influential individual coinages are, but in aggregate they are certainly a noticeable feature of many Netspeak conversations. Lexical suffixes are often extended. For example, the noun-forming suffix -*ity* (as in standard English *brief* → *brevity*) might be used in *dubiosity* (from *dubious*), *obviosity* (from *obvious*), and other such -*ous* instances. Other popular ludic Netspeak extensions include -*itude* (*winnitude, hackitude, geekitude*), -*full* (*folderfull, windowfull, screenfull, bufferfull*), and -*ification* (*hackification, geekification*). In a development which will cause delight to all Anglo-Saxonists, the -*en* plural of *oxen* is found with some words ending in -*x*, such as *boxen, vaxen* ['VAX computers'], *matrixen*, and *bixen* ['users of BIX', an information exchange system] – a usage which could well increase, given that so many computing names end in -*X*. Word-class conversion is important, too, usually from noun to verb: *to mouse, to clipboard, to geek out* ['talk technically'], *to 404* ['be unable to find a page'].

The various types of abbreviation found in Netspeak have been one of its most remarked features. Acronyms are so common that they regularly receive critical comment, as observed by Steve G. Steinberg, quoted in *Wired Style*:[20] 'When it comes to technology, the greater the number of acronyms, the higher the bullshit factor'. A tiny sample would include *BBS* ['bulletin board system'], *BCC* ['blind carbon copy'], *DNS* ['domain name system'], *FAQ* ['frequently asked question'], *HTML* ['hypertext markup language'], *ISP* ['Internet Service Provider'], *URL* ['uniform resource locator'], *MUDs* and *MOOs* (see chapter 6), and the names of many firms and sites, such as *AOL, IBM, IRC*. Letter-plus-number combinations are also found: *W3C* ['World Wide Web Consortium'], *3Com* [a data-networking organization – the *Coms* standing for Computer, Communications, Compatibility], *P3P* ['Platform for Privacy Preferences'], *Go2Net*. The chatgroups and virtual worlds also have their abbreviations, some of which turn up on e-mail and in personal Web pages.[21] Some of the commonest ones are listed in Table 3.2. Newer technology, such as the WAP-phones ['Wireless Application Protocol'] with their tiny screens, have

---

[20] Hale and Scanlon (1999: 188).   [21] A list is available at <http://www.netlingo.com>.

Table 3.2. *Some abbreviations used in Netspeak conversations (both upper- and lower-case forms are used).*[a]

afaik	as far as I know	hhok	ha ha only kidding
afk	away from keyword	hth	hope this helps
asap	as soon as possible	ianal	I'm not a lawyer, but...
a/s/l	age/sex/location	ic	I see; [in MUDs] in
atw	at the weekend		character
awhfy	are we having fun yet?	icwum	I see what you mean
bbfn	bye bye for now	idk	I don't know
bbl	be back later	iirc	if I remember correctly
bcnu	be seeing you	imho	in my humble opinion
b4	before	imi	I mean it
bfd	big fucking deal	imnsho	in my not so humble
bg	big grin		opinion
brb	be right back	imo	in my opinion
btw	by the way	iou	I owe you
cfc	call for comments	iow	in other words
cfv	call for votes	irl	in real life
cm	call me	jam	just a minute
cu	see you	j4f	just for fun
cul	see you later	jk	just kidding
cul8r	see you later	kc	keep cool
cya	see you	khuf	know how you feel
dk	don't know	l8r	later
dur?	do you remember?	lol	laughing out loud
eod	end of discussion	m8	mate
f?	friends?	mtfbwu	may the force be with you
fotcl	falling off the chair	na	no access
	laughing	nc	no comment
f2f	face-to-face	np	no problem
fwiw	for what it's worth	nwo	no way out
fya	for your amusement	obtw	oh by the way
fyi	for your information	o4u	only for you
g	grin	oic	oh I see
gal	get a life	otoh	on the other hand
gd&r	grinning ducking and	pmji	pardon my jumping in
	running	ptmm	please tell me more
gmta	great minds think alike	rip	rest in peace
gr8	great	rotf	rolling on the floor
gsoh	good sense of humour	rotfl	rolling on the floor laughing

(Continued)

Table 3.2. (*cont.*)

rtfm	read the fucking manual	tuvm	thank you very much
rtm	read the manual	tx	thanks
ruok	are you OK?	tyvm	thank you very much
sc	stay cool	wadr	with all due respect
smtoe	sets my teeth on edge	wb	welcome back
so	significant other	w4u	waiting for you
sohf	sense of humour failure	wrt	with respect to
sol	sooner or later	wtfigo	what the fuck is going on?
t$^+$	think positive	wtg	way to go
ta4n	that's all for now	wu	what's up?
tafn	that's all for now	wuwh	wish you were here
thx	thanks	X!	typical woman
tia	thanks in advance	Y!	typical man
tmot	trust me on this	yiu	yes I understand
tnx	thanks	2bctnd	to be continued
ttfn	ta-ta for now	2d4	to die for
tttt	to tell the truth	2g4u	too good for you
t2ul	talk to you later	2l8	too late
ttyl	talk to you later	4e	forever
ttytt	to tell you the truth	4yeo	for your eyes only

[a]Not all are found in every situation. Some refer to specific chatgroup interactions (e.g. *afk*) and procedures (e.g. *cfv*), or are more likely in text-messaging (p. 229).

motivated a whole new genre of abbreviated forms. The acronyms are no longer restricted to words or short phrases, but can be sentence-length: *AYSOS* ['Are you stupid or something?'], *CID* ['Consider it done'], *CIO* ['Check it out'], *GTG* ['Got to go'], *WDYS* ['What did you say?']. Individual words can be reduced to two or three letters: *PLS* ['please'], *THX* or *TX* ['thanks'], *WE* ['whatever']. Some are like rebuses, in that the sound value of the letter or numeral acts as a syllable of a word, or are combinations of rebus and letter initial: *B4N* ['Bye For Now'], *CYL* ['See you later'], *L8R* ['later']. Further examples are given on p. 229.

Distinctive graphology is also an important feature of Netspeak. The range extends from an enhanced system (by comparison with traditional writing) with a wide range of special fonts and styles, as in the most sophisticated Web pages, to a severely reduced system, with virtually no typographic contrastivity (not even such 'basic' features as italics or boldface), as in many e-mails and chatgroup conversations. All orthographic features have been affected. For example, the status of capitalization varies greatly. Most of the Internet is not case-sensitive, which thus motivates the random use of capitals or no capitals at all. There is a strong tendency to use lower-case everywhere. The 'save a keystroke' principle is widely found in e-mails, chatgroups, and virtual worlds, where whole sentences can be produced without capitals (or punctuation):

> john are you going to london next week

The lower-case default mentality means that any use of capitalization is a strongly marked form of communication. Messages wholly in capitals are considered to be 'shouting', and usually avoided (see p. 35); words in capitals add extra emphasis (with asterisks and spacing also available):

> This is a VERY important point.
> This is a * very * important point.
> This is a v e r y important point.

There are, however, certain contexts where capitals need to be recognized. Domain names in Web addresses are lowercase; but pathnames (after the first slash) are case-sensitive. A capital letter may be obligatory in a business name (especially if trade-marked). Indeed, a distinctive feature of Internet graphology is the way two capitals are used – one initial, one medial – a phenomenon variously called *bicapitalization* (*BiCaps*), *intercaps*, *incaps*, and *midcaps*. Some style guides inveigh against this practice, but it is widespread:

> AltaVista, RetrievalWare, ScienceDirect, ThomsonDirect, NorthernLight, PostScript, PowerBook, DreamWorks, GeoCities, EarthLink, PeaceNet, SportsZone, HotWired, CompuServe, AskJeeves.

More complex examples include *QuarkXPress* and *aRMadillo On-line*. Some of the new names cause difficulty, in that long-standing orthographic conventions are contravened: for example, sentences can begin with small letters, as in *eBay is interested* or *iMac is the answer*, a problem that faces anyone who wants to start a sentence with a lower-case username or program command.

Spelling practice is also distinctive. In English, US spelling is more common than British, partly for historical reasons (the origins of the Internet), and partly for reasons of economy, most US spellings being a character shorter than British ones (*color* vs *colour*, *fetus* vs *foetus*, etc.). New spelling conventions have emerged, such as the replacement of plural *-s* by *-z* to refer to pirated versions of software, as in *warez, tunez, gamez, serialz, pornz, downloadz*, and *filez*. Non-standard spelling, heavily penalized in traditional writing (at least, since the eighteenth century), is used without sanction in conversational settings. Spelling errors in an e-mail would not be assumed to be an indication of lack of education (though they may be) but purely a function of typing inaccuracy. Opinions vary (see chapter 4). Chatgroups and virtual worlds also make a great deal of use of non-standard spellings which reflect pronunciation, such as *yep, yup, yay, nope, noooo*, for *yes* and *no*, or such forms as *kay* and *sokay* ['It's OK']. Emotional expressions of horror, shock, and the like make use of varying numbers of vowels and consonants, depending on the ferocity of the emotion: *aaaiiieee, yayyyyyyy*. Some deviant spellings have become so widely used as to be virtually standard in this variety, such as *phreak, phreaker, phreaking* for *freak* (etc.). Some are still restricted to certain groups of users, such as the *-y-* spelling (from *byte*) introduced into certain expressions for bit blocks of different sizes: *tayste* or *tydbit* (2 bits), *nybble* (4 bits), *playte* (16 bits), and *dynner* (32 bits). The dollar sign sometimes replaces *S*, if some sort of dig is being made about costs, as in *Micro$oft*, and a £ sign can replace *L*, as in *AO£*. Teenage users, in particular, have introduced several deviant spellings, such as *kool* [cool] and *fone* [phone], and the replacement of a lower-case *o* by a zero, as in *d00dz* [dudes] and *l0zers* [losers], or percentage sign, as in *c%l*. Among this group of users, the *k* is often used as

an emphatic prefix, producing such forms as *k-kool, k-awe?*
and *k-k-allright*. The extent to which deviant spellings and esoteric neologisms can be used to produce a cool jargon has been
dubbed *leeguage* by some. Ihnatko explains its etymology:[22] 'Originally named in honor of Pamela Anderson Lee's bosom, which,
like this language, is completely unnatural, constructed with tor-
tuous effort, and conforms to some vaguely perceived standard no
one comprehends.' He gives an example: *Hay! Odz r he wen 2 Radio
Hack 4 a nu crys 4 hiz rainbow boxx!*[23]

Punctuation tends to be minimalist in most situations, and completely absent in some e-mails and chat exchanges.[24] It is an important area, for it is the chief means a language has for bringing
writing into direct contact with (the prosody and paralanguage of)
speech, as well as conveying a great deal of information about grammatical construction. For Naomi Baron, punctuation 'reveals how
writers view the balance between spoken and written language'.[25]
A lot depends on personality: some e-mailers are scrupulous about
maintaining a traditional punctuation; others use it when they
have to, to avoid ambiguity; and some do not use it at all, either
as a consequence of typing speed, or through not realizing that
ambiguity can be one of the consequences. On the other hand,
there is an increased use of symbols not normally part of the traditional punctuation system, such as the #.[26] Unusual combinations
of punctuation marks can occur, such as (to express pause) ellipsis
dots (...) in any number, repeated hyphens (---), or the repeated use
of commas (,,,,). Emphasis and attitude can result in exaggerated
or random use of punctuation, such as *!!!!!!!* or *£$£$%!*. Some

---

[22] Ihnatko (1997: 112).   [23] I don't understand it either.
[24] This is not the only instance where punctuation is absent. Certain genres of legal language
do without it (Crystal and Davy, 1969), and it is absent or minimal in a great deal of
advertising copy, television captions, newspaper headlines, and other 'block language'
(Quirk, Greenbaum, Leech, and Svartvik, 1985: 845 ff.).
[25] Baron (2000: 167).
[26] A range of new slang names for punctuation marks has emerged: the # has been called
a *hash, sharp, crunch,* and *cross-hatch*; the tilde (∼, used to mean 'about' or as part of
a Web address) has been called a *squiggley*; an exclamation mark is a *bang, pling, excl,
shriek, smash, cuss, boing, yell, wow, hey,* or *wham,* among others; the asterisk is a *star,
splat, wildcard, dingle, spider, aster, times,* or *twinkle.*

odd combinations of punctuation marks can appear at the end of a sentence: *Is this true of Yahoo!?* (where the exclamation mark is part of the name). All of these may of course also be found in traditional informal writing.[27]

Rather different are the symbols borrowed from programming languages, which appear in hacker-influenced interactions, such as an initial exclamation mark to express negation (*!interesting = not interesting*) or an arrow to express location (*dc ← holyhead =* 'dc lives in holyhead'). And new combinations of punctuation marks can be given fresh values, as in the case of smileys (p. 36). Underbars are usually used to express underlining, as in the name of a text, though other pairs of marks will be seen:

> I've been reading _ Hamlet _
> I've been reading #Hamlet#
> I've been reading =Hamlet=
> I've been reading \Hamlet/

A potential contrastivity seems to be emerging, in the use of some pairs, notably the scope of emphasis indicated by the asterisk. The following two sentences convey rather different effects:

> This is a * very * important point.
> This is a * very * * important * * point.*

The latter is much slower and more emphatic. However, the asterisk is still developing a range of other functions, and is at times used somewhat idiosyncratically. For example, some users mark imaginary actions or facial expressions by asterisks (e.g. * grin *, * groan *), though a more widely used convention is the angle bracket (e.g. <grin>, <groan>). Similarly, people use the caret (^) in a variety of ways, sometimes as an emphasis signal, sometimes as part of a more sophisticated convention, such as the ^H sequence used in one kind of programming notation to mark an erasure of the preceding symbol. Hence, if someone typed

> Hear what my mad^H^H^Hnice computer has done now.

---

[27] For the contrast between formal and informal letters, see Crystal (1995: 402).

this would be equivalent to saying

Hear what my nice computer has done now

but by showing the 'erased' element, the sentence adds an ironic effect. Virtually any piece of programming notation might be encountered in hacker-influenced conversation, and thus end up as a part of Netspeak in general. For example, the angle brackets used in HTML in pairs, to indicate the beginning and end of a command (the latter preceded by a forward slash), can be seen in such pseudo-instructions as:

<moan> I've got an interview tomorrow </moan>
<flame> You've got no sense at all </flame>

The most general features of Netspeak distinctiveness are currently found chiefly in graphology and the lexicon – the levels of language where it is relatively easy to introduce innovation and deviation. As with language change in general, grammatical variation is less frequent or widespread. When it does occur it tends to be restricted to a particular situation or group of users. For example, the phenomenon of *verb reduplication* occurs in some chatgroups, and occasionally elsewhere, but as yet is not a universally encountered feature. A verb (from a fairly small set) is used twice in immediate succession to express a range of functions, such as an expression of pleasure or pain, as a sarcastic or exasperated reaction, or simply as a turn-taking marker, showing that an utterance is ended.

You should see the reaction. Flame, flame.
How about that! Win, win. ['the program has performed
    successfully']
I deleted your message. Lose, lose! ['I'm stupid']
What you do that for? Barf, barf. ['I'm disgusted']

Reduplication is sometimes seen elsewhere – for example, jokey topic groups on Usenet sometimes use a triple final element, as in *alt.sadistic.dentists.drill.drill.drill.* But on the whole the effect has limited Internet presence. Likewise, the use of programming devices that affect or replace conventional grammatical constructions tends to be very restricted in its occurrence. For example, the symbol *P* (a notation from the programming language LISP) is sometimes added at the end of a word to turn it into a question, usually of a 'yes/no' type:

GlobeP = are you going to the Globe?

Cognoscenti might respond with *T* ['true'] or *NIL* ['no']. Again, the effect is indicative of a restricted genre among in-group enthusiasts rather than of a productive strategy being employed by Internet users in general. Features of this kind, along with associated discourse features, are thus best discussed in relation to the individual Internet situation in which they occur.

This chapter has discussed the main linguistic features which people consider to be part of Netspeak. In some cases, the features are genuinely present, encountered on most online visits. In others, they are assumed to be present, though in fact the assumptions made are often wide of the mark. And in yet others, people want them to be present, on the basis of a private belief about the way Internet language should develop. The lexico-graphological distinctiveness described above, along with the general characteristics of the medium outlined in chapter 2, provide a solid basis for the impression I have of Netspeak as a genuine language variety. On the other hand, the differing expectations, interests, and abilities of users, the rapid changes in computer technology and availability, and the rate at which language change seems to be taking place across the Internet (much faster than at any previous time in linguistic history) means that it is difficult to be definitive about the variety's characteristics. Doubtless some of the linguistic features described above will still be contributing to Netspeak's identity in fifty years' time; others may not last another year. Already hacker guides talk routinely about features which were commonplace 'back in the mid-90s'. In discussing the frequency of a Netspeak idiom with a hacker friend, I was told that its popularity was 'last year', and 'nobody uses it now'. These are the influences which require guidebooks, such as *Wired Style*, to have frequent new editions, if they are to reflect the real cyberworld. At the same time, some features seem not to be changing, or are changing only slowly. It is a complex and mixed-message scenario, which can really only be understood by a detailed consideration of the individual Internet situations described in chapter 1, and to these I now turn.

4   *The language of e-mail*

At one level, it is extremely easy to define the linguistic identity of
e-mail as a variety of language; at another level, it is surprisingly
difficult. The easy part lies in the fixed discourse structure of the
message – a structure dictated by the mailer software which has
become increasingly standardized over the past twenty years. Just
in the same way as we can analyse the functionally distinct elements
that constitute a newspaper article (in terms of headline, body copy,
illustration, caption, etc.) or a scientific paper (in terms of title,
authorship, abstract, introduction, methodology, etc.), so we can
see in e-mails a fixed sequence of discourse elements. They will be so
familiar to likely readers of this book that they need only the briefest
of expositions. The difficult part, to which the bulk of this chapter
relates, lies in the range of opinions about the purpose of e-mail, as
a communicative medium, and about the kind of language which
is the most appropriate and effective to achieve that purpose. With
over 800 million people using e-mail by 2000,[1] and 100 million
or so being sent each day, a consensus seems unlikely, especially
when age, sex, and cultural differences are taken into account. At
the same time, it ought at least to be possible to identify what the
parameters of disagreement are, to develop a sense of the range of
linguistic features which any characterization of e-mail would have
to include.[2]

---

[1] From estimates provided by the Internet Society (<http://info.isoc.org>) and Matrix
Information and Directory Services (<http://www.mids.org>) in 2000 there were almost
100 million Internet hosts, though there were signs of a slowing in the host growth rate,
over 30 million registered domain names, and over 800 million e-mail users.

[2] In this chapter, I have used data taken from my own e-messages, supplemented by examples taken from messages sent to a younger generation, kindly supplied by my 23-year-old
son and 26-year-old daughter. The desirability of a corpus of e-mail data is stressed by
Johansson (1991: 307-8), and also Yates (1996: 30).

Structural elements

An individual e-mail consists of a series of functional elements, for which terminology varies somewhat, all of which are similar in purpose to those found in traditional letters and memos. 'Compose' screens typically display a bipartite structure, with a preformatted upper area (the *header* or *heading*) and a lower area for the main text (the *body* or *message*). In some systems, if we choose to attach a file to the e-mail, a third space becomes available, in which an icon representing the attachment is located.

Headers

The underlying format of the header contains four core elements (different systems vary in the extent to which they display all four, and the order in which they display them):[3]

- the e-address (or addresses) to which the message is being sent (following *To:*), typed in full manually or inserted automatically by typing a prompt which calls up a character-string from an address-book (either the full e-address or a more memorable short form, or nickname); this is an obligatory element;
- the e-address from which the message has been sent (following *From:*), inserted automatically; this is also an obligatory element;
- a brief description of the topic of the message (following *Subject:*), inserted manually; this is an optional element, but the software will query its absence (e.g. 'This message has no subject. Are you sure you want to send it?'), and it is considered efficient practice to include it (see below);
- the date and time at which the message is sent (following *Date:*), inserted automatically by the software.

---

[3] For the 'header wars' (over what should be included in the header) in the early days of the Internet, see Naughton (1999: 149).

The fact that these are core elements is supported by the information electronically recorded once a message is sent. These are the chief elements represented in the Outbox and Sent folders, under the headings *To*, *Subject*, and *Sent* (often, along with an indication of the server account employed). When a message is received, they are the chief elements represented in one's Inbox (with *From* replacing *To* and *Received* replacing *Sent*).

In addition, several optional elements are available within the header area:

- a space for addresses which are to receive a copy of the message (following *Cc:*, which stands etymologically for *carbon copy*, but which is often glossed as *courtesy copy*), inserted manually or automatically; here too, short and full forms of an address are available, the latter usually being placed within angle brackets; the message's prime recipient is informed that these copies have been sent;
- a space for addresses which also receive a copy of the message (following *Bcc:*, for *blind carbon copy*), but without the prime recipient's knowledge;
- a space in which a symbol (such as a paper-clip) appears if an attachment has been added to the message; this also appears along with the summary in the Outbox and Sent folders, and appears on the recipient's screen;
- a space in which a symbol (such as an exclamation mark) appears if a priority is to be given to the message when it is received (it does not have anything to do with the speed at which the message will be electronically transmitted); low, normal, and high priorities are usually recognized.

There is very limited scope for usage variation, within headers, because so much of the information is dictated by the software. The conventions of e-address structure (the registered two-part designation on either side of the @ symbol) are fixed, and if not followed exactly, the message will either not be accepted by the sender's software or will be returned ('bounced back') by the server to which the sender is connected (it may also disappear into cyberspace and never be seen again).[4] The same considerations affect copies of messages – though e-mail manuals additionally raise the pragmatic question of the decision-making behind copied messages.[5] The sending of time-wasting, unnecessary copies is criticized, and caution is expressed over the use of blind copies – for instance, if people other than the intended recipients learn of their existence, the motives of the writer may be questioned. If there are several main or copy recipients, the question of the order in which their addresses are listed may be relevant: in strongly hierarchical institutions, senior people may expect to see their names at the front of a list. A principle of alphabetical order is often advocated to avoid provoking unintended misinterpretation. So is the avoidance of excessive use of the priority feature: if every message is marked urgent, the convention ceases to be meaningful.

The language of the subject line, however, has received a great deal of attention. Because it is the first thing that the recipient receives, along with the sender's name, it is a critical element in the decision-making over what priority to assign to it or whether to open it at all (in the case of someone who receives many e-mails every day). A great deal of junk-mail, if not automatically filtered out, is known to be junk only because of the subject description. Subjects such as 'Free Your Life Forever', 'Win $31,000,000 dollars and a PT Cruiser!', and 'Confidentiality Assured!' can be confidently categorized as junk (though I am not thereby denying its interest to some), as can most messages whose subject is in capitals throughout ('DO YOU HAVE THE YEN TO BE A MILLIONAIRE?',

---

[4] In general text, e-mail addresses are often placed within angle brackets to show that any adjacent punctuation is not part of the address. Typographical difficulty can arise if an e-address needs to be broken at the end of a line, as an unhyphenated break will leave it unclear whether a space is intended as part of the address, and a hyphenated break will leave it unclear whether the hyphen is part of the address or not. Usage guides suggest that the only unambiguous place to break is before or after the @ symbol (without hyphen). Similarly, an address at the end of a sentence may need to be separated from the sentence-ending punctuation. In this book, all e-addresses are placed within angle brackets.

[5] Examples of such manuals are Angell and Heslop (1994), Lamb and Peek (1995), Flynn and Flynn (1998).

'DON'T GO TO SLEEP WITHOUT READING THIS') or which have certain words emphasized ('Technology for YOU', 'For Serious Marketers ONLY!'). For messages which do not fall within this category, other considerations apply. Because there is a limit on the number of characters to be displayed in the recipient's Inbox summary, lengthy subject descriptions will be truncated, often intriguingly, such as 'New edition of the Cambridge Encyclopedia and ...', and may be so unclear as to be informationally empty. Clear, brief, relevant, and concrete subject descriptions (cf. Grice's maxims, p. 48) are recommended in the various guides, with the most important bit of information put at the beginning of the line. Deliberately misleading subject lines (as sometimes encountered in e-mail from advertisers) are considered a breach of netiquette. It is also important for correspondents to make continued use of a subject description, once it is chosen, to enable groups of related messages (a *thread*) to be placed together, especially if messages are forwarded. Even an apparently simple switch such as 'My review' (in the sender's subject line) to 'Your review' (in the subject line of the receiver's response) can be the source of difficulty – not immediately, but in due course, if the whole correspondence relating to this topic needs to be gathered together, for the first message will (typically) be sorted under M and the second under Y.[6] Electronic filters require exact matches. Similarly, subject lines need to be very specific, otherwise they will not be easy to retrieve at a later date: among the messages in my folder are some with the subject 'Your message', 'Reply to letter', and 'Re: visit', none of which are going to be helpful should occasion to search out a specific thread of messages arise. 'Writing a subject line with *real oomph*' is the heading in one usage manual,[7] and as long as a reasonably broad notion of oomphiness is permitted, I have no problem with that.

---

[6] This procedure only makes sense, of course, if senders ensure that the content of their messages match the subject. It is unclear just how many e-mail users retain an earlier subject heading in a reply, but enter a message which has nothing to do with the stated subject. This is especially easy when people respond by using 'Reply to Sender' (selected in 71% of cases, in Li Lan (2000)), replacing the earlier message body completely but leaving the header alone.

[7] Flynn and Flynn (1998: 15).

Although the header is formally distinct from the message area below, it is not always functionally separate. It is possible to disregard the identity function of the subject line, and use it as an introductory element in the message itself. An e-mail from my daughter, enclosing a promised message, consisted of the following subject:

> here it is . . .

The body of the message then began:

> . . . all in one piece.

Another example had, as subject, 'friday nights gonna be alright', which was followed by the opening sentence, 'on the 10th that is'. This dependence of the body copy on the subject line is also sometimes seen in advertising mail, where the subject may be expressed as a question ('Do you want to . . . ?') to which the opening sentence of the body gives the answer ('Yes, you do!'). A further variation is a message which contains a greeting in the subject line: an example was 'Dear Mr Pinter', which the body copy then continued conventionally.

Greetings and farewells

Turning now to the body of the e-mail, this too can be viewed in terms of obligatory and optional elements. The obligatory item is, patently, a message of some sort. What is interesting is the extent to which it is preceded by a *greeting* (or *salutation, opening*) and followed by a *farewell* (or *signature, closing*). Several types of e-mail have no greeting at all. They include first messages from people who do not know the recipient, and are therefore typical in the case of public announcements and junk-mail. Some messages include an automatically derived 'Dear X' or 'Hi, X' in their openings, often with bizarre results. Automatic junk-greetings in my case have included 'Hi, Professor D', 'Hello, Crystal', and 'Dear Mr Wales'. Automatic acknowledgements, indicating that a message has been received by a system, or that the recipient is away from the office, do not usually greet, though the range of auto responses received by my son include:

> Dear BEN CRYSTAL
> Dear b.crystal@restofaddress.com
> Dear bcrystal

Within institutions, e-mails can be mainly used for the sending out of information and instructions to all members of staff, in the manner of a traditional memo, so that a personalized greeting is unnecessary. A general enquiry posted to a group of recipients (in the manner of an asynchronous chatgroup, p. 11), where the aim is to obtain information for the benefit of all, is also unlikely to be opened with a greeting (unless it is of the 'Dear all', 'Dear List Member' type) and just as unlikely to generate personalized responses.

Between people who know each other, greetingless messages are usually promptly sent responses, where the responder sees the message as the second part of a two-part interaction (an *adjacency-pair*), for which an introductory greeting is inappropriate. For example:

> Arriving message: David, will 7.30 be OK for the talk? Colin
> Response message: Fine

where the following would be unlikely:[8]

> Response message: *Colin, Fine.

or, even less so:

> Response message: *Dear Colin,
>   Fine.

The longer the delay in responding, the more likely the response will contain a greeting, if only an apology for the time-lag.

By contrast, two-thirds of a sample of 500 e-mails in my Deleted folder from people who know me contained an introductory

---

[8] Here and below, this use of the asterisk indicates an expression considered to fall outside the rules governing usage in a variety.

greeting.[9] They express a wide range of effects, from most formal to most informal, and indicate several kinds of social relationship and intimacy. They could be classified in many ways, but an important variable is the use of an initial endearment (+*Dear* messages were twice as common as –*Dear* messages).

–*Dear*

General word:[10] *Hi, Hello again, Hi there!, Bonjour*

General word plus ID: *Hi from Pete, Goodday from Oz*

Intimate name alone: *David, david, Dave, DC, Dad*

Combination of general word and intimate name: *Hi David, Hey D, Hello David, Hello DC, Good morning David, Howdy David, Hi dad*

Formal name: *Professor Crystal, Professor*

[but never (yet): General word and formal name: * *Hi, Professor Crystal,* * *Hello Professor*]

+*Dear*

With intimate name: *Dear David, Dear Dave*

With whole name: *Dear David Crystal, Annwyl David Crystal* [Welsh: 'Dear']

With title and surname: *Dear Professor Crystal, Dear Dr Crystal, Dear Mr Crystal, Estimado profesor Crystal*

By far the most frequent individual greeting formula was *Dear David*, followed by *David*, then *Hi David*, confirming the general view about the medium as a means of informal interaction between people who know each other. On the other hand, such a range of

---

[9] This is similar to Gains (1998), where 34 out of 54 (63%) interpersonal e-mails had a greeting. On the other hand, contextual differences are important: in an institutional setting, where messages were being sent out to all members of staff, 57 out of 62 (92%) had no greeting. Li Lan (2000) points out that the distinction between native and non-native speakers can also be important: in his sample from Hong Kong, using non-native speakers, far more interpersonal e-mails had a greeting than in Gains' native-speaker sample (73 out of 77, or 95%); and in Li Lan's institutional setting only 41 out of 76 (54%) had no greeting. The samples in these studies are small, but even small samples are enough to demonstrate the existence of great variation.

[10] This category was much more varied in the e-mails addressed to my children: *Hey, Heyyy, Hiya, Hello folks* (an unusual plural, given the singular recipient), *Hi darlin*, etc. Exclamation marks also proliferated, and several greetings were in capital letters.

greetings defies easy generalization. Other factors than social relationship enter in: only a mixture of subject-matter, time-pressure,
and mood can explain why my editor at Cambridge University
Press switches throughout the year from *David* to *Dear David* (in
a ratio of 1:2) in his messages, and doubtless I am just as variable
in my labelling of others.[11]

Another factor is the location of the name, once it is used. The
majority of my messages place the greeting at the head of the
message body, usually spaced away from the maintext as in a traditional letter. This is always the case in +*Dear* openings. With
informal −*Dear* openings, however, the location varies. It is most
often spaced and separate (in a ratio of 3:1, in my corpus). When
it is on the same line, it is usually the first word, but is sometimes
placed later, especially in replies (*Thanks, David*; *OK David*; *Thanks
for your message, David*), which to my intuition is more informal
than an initial placement. It is unusual for an inserted name to appear much later in the opening paragraph, or in later paragraphs –
though occasionally one finds instances of 'rapport renewal', such
as (from a third paragraph):

> Sorry to put you to this bother, David, but . . .

This is no different from what is done in traditional informal letter-
writing.

Farewells display fewer possibilities for variation, but the same
points of principle arise. Two elements are available: a pre-closing
formula (of the *Best wishes* type) and the identification (ID) of
the sender. Most interpersonal messages (80%, in my case) end
with both elements present, and the influence of traditional letter-
writing is evident in the overwhelming tendency to place each
element on a separate line, usually spaced away from the message body. The remaining 20% give a name, and dispense with the

[11] In Gains (1998), only 9 out of 54 used *Dear* interpersonally, and only 1 out of 62 institutionally. By contrast, Li Lan (2000) found 31 out of 77 using *Dear* interpersonally and 35
out of 76 institutionally – again suggestive of the existence of a pull towards traditional
usage in non-native speaker settings.

formula. I have only one instance in my files of a closing formula which was not followed by a name – the sender perhaps thinking that it was not needed, given its presence in the header (alternatively, it might have been the result of forgetfulness, or have been mysteriously lost in transmission).[12] The usual range of formulae, known from traditional letter-writing, is employed, with the same range of functions (affection, gratitude, expectation, communicative intent, and so on): *Lots of love, Thanks for everything, See you soon, Let me know if this isn't clear,* etc. The informality of the medium is reflected in the relative absence of the *Yours sincerely* type (turning up in only 5% of my messages, though it seems to be increasing). There seems to be no difference between old and young in their predilection for formulae, though preferences vary dramatically, as we would expect. (I cannot see myself ever using the *ta ta babe* used by one of my children to her friend.)

IDs can be manually or automatically inserted. The manual ones are of three kinds: first name, initial letter(s), and first name followed by surname (or vice versa in languages where the ordering convention differs). Titles, qualifications, and other 'letters after the name' may be present, depending on the formality of the message; and there may also be a status or origin identifier on a separate line (e.g. *Course Organizer, Personnel Department*). In informal interaction, it is common to see the use of initialisms – either the initial letter of just the first name, or of both the first name and surname – even between people who do not know each other well. One reason for this is the bridging option it provides between the message body and a customized signature. In a situation such as the following, (1) may be considered too impersonal, and (2) redundant, whereas (3) combines an element of personal acknowledgement with the full information.

---

[12] I have no instances of the avoidance of a farewell, in my interpersonal e-mail; on the other hand, e-mails from junk-mail organizations rarely end with a farewell. Gains (1998) had 5 instances out of 54 in his interpersonal sample and 5 out of 62 in his institutional sample. Here too there seem to be cultural differences. In Hong Kong, Li Lan (2000) found 13 out of 77 interpersonal e-mails without a closing and 19 out of 76 institutional ones (25%).

(1)
... so I hope to hear from you soon.

Dr James Smith
333 Some Street, Somewhere, POSTCODE, UK
Tel: ...

(2)
... so I hope to hear from you soon.

James Smith

Dr James Smith
333 Some Street, Somewhere, POSTCODE, UK
Tel: ...

(3)
... so I hope to hear from you soon.

JS

Dr James Smith
333 Some Street, Somewhere, POSTCODE, UK
Tel: ...

Automatic signatures are inserted by the mailer software, using text created by the sender and stored in a file. They can be quite complex pieces of writing, though the usage manuals consider lengthy signature files wasteful of time and space. Some consist simply of a person's full name (perhaps with title and qualifications), address, and communication details (phone, fax, e-mail, website). Some add a character note, often framed typographically (commonly within asterisks), such as a slogan, logo, favourite quotation, piece of personal promotion, or even a 'picture' (constructed out of keyboard symbols).[13] For some reason I receive few e-mails from people who go in for slogans and quotations, but when they do occur they all follow the name and are typographically distinguished in some way:

> James Smith * AVENUES TO SUCCESS * [i.e. the title of a
> conference]

---

[13] Sometimes referred to as 'ASCII art'. On Internet impression formation, see Wallace (1999: ch. 2).

By contrast, most of my son's contacts do add such messages. E-mail guides are circumspect in their advice, noting that the novelty, freshness, or impact of a character note quickly fades, and that ill-chosen items can return to haunt the senders once their interests or status have moved on. 'Cool dude' might have suited John Doe as an office junior, but he may not like to be reminded of his former e-identity now he is a company vice-president. Messages can last a long time, in e-mail archives. And, as Wallace puts it: 'Most of us enter cyberspace ... giving little thought to the online persona – how we come across to the people with whom we interact online.'[14]

The farewell element has two important functions in e-mails, as distinct from traditional letters. First, it acts as a boundary marker, indicating that further scrolling down is unnecessary. There may indeed be additional automatically generated material on the screen, such as an advertisement for a mailserver company, a notice saying that the message has been checked for viruses, or a statement of confidentiality such as the following:[15]

> This e-mail is confidential and should not be used by anyone who is not the original intended recipient. If you have received this e-mail in error please inform the sender and delete it from your mailbox or any other storage mechanism.

The farewell has come to indicate that no further personalized text is following – and it is this expectation which makes the use of postscripted text unwise. Many e-mail readers do not look beyond the signature. Secondly, the farewell has an extended identity function. Obviously it identifies the sender to the immediate recipient (typically providing information which is not present in the header, especially useful if the e-address is opaque), but it also makes this fuller identification available to others who may eventually see the message, in the case of forwarded or attached mail.

---

[14] Wallace (1999: 14).
[15] Some writers, especially in the business world, place suggestions about further contact before the farewell, as the last element in the body of the message.

The overriding impression I have, even from such a small sample of material, is of the remarkable amount of variation which is found within the medium. E-mail guidebooks present a much more standardized picture, and in their recommendations reduce the range of options quite considerably. One of them is unequivocal in its support for first-name only: 'Start the message with the person's first name if you're communicating with a person you know on that basis.'[16] It is equally opposed to what it calls 'outdated or gender-specific forms, such as *Dear Sirs* or *Gentlemen*, from traditional business correspondence'. Similar points are made in relation to farewells. Forms such as *Yours sincerely* are proscribed; single-word formulae such as *Thanks* or *Best* (or abbreviated forms, as with *THX* or *TTFN*, p. 85) are commended. At the same time, this guide is aware that cultural differences exist: 'Be aware that greetings tend to be more formal and traditional in some parts of the world, such as Japan and Europe' (the authors are writing from a US perspective, hence the unitarian view of Europe). No recognition is given to the possibility that cultural differences of other kinds exist, which should also be allowed for – such as the differences of taste between people of different ages, personalities, professions, and social backgrounds. I actually find the spontaneous mateyness of many Americans congenial, readily accept first-name usage, and use it to others myself whenever there are no contra-indications that I might be causing upset; but I also know that many people have a personality or background which does not allow them this freedom of address, and who feel uncomfortable when their familiar and established address procedures are contravened. They immediately feel excluded from the medium. After reading one particularly prescriptive usage manual – prescriptive in its recommendations for informality, that is (p. 73) – a retired teacher commented, 'So e-mail's not for me, then'. Of course it is. It is the manual that needs revision.

---

[16] Angell and Heslop (1994). These quotations are from pp. 21–2 (for greetings) and p. 31 (for farewells).

As with other domains, allowing a range of linguistic options increases the communicative power of a medium, and usage manuals need to recognize this. In any case, people are voting with their feet: as with traditional spoken or written usage, they will be more influenced in their e-mail practice by the behaviour of their correspondents than by the recommendations of style guides. As e-mail becomes a routine part of social life, at all levels, it will inevitably be influenced by the linguistic mores of its users. Already many people use it as a more immediate and practical way of sending formal letters and greetings cards (especially when there is a postal strike). In recent months I have received official invitations, letters of agreement, and many other formal communications through this medium, and replied to them in the same way. Some publishers (such as the *Times Higher Education Supplement*) now ask for reviews to be sent primarily as e-mails. It is likely that the technological benefits of the medium (in terms of speed, forwarding, automatic typesetting, etc.) will eventually be a more important driving force than the fact that it permits a greater degree of informal communication than existed before. My prediction is therefore that e-mail in a few years' time will display a much wider stylistic range than it does at present, as the medium is adapted to suit a broader range of communicative purposes, and the legal issues surrounding the status of certain types of message come to be resolved. The contemporary bias towards informality therefore needs to be kept in perspective.

The body of the message

The content of the many e-mail style books is largely devoted to giving advice about how to write effective message body copy. One set of prescriptions is given in Table 4.1. Little of this is new. Virtually identical material can be found in books devoted to older methods, such as letter-writing, typing, and business communication. Although the orientation is electronic, the content is largely

Table 4.1. *Five rules of using e-mail (Flynn and Flynn, 1998: 14)*

Rules	Gloss
Write as though Mom were reading	'Write to the widest audience imaginable.' 'If your message is too personal, confidential or important to write generically, reconsider e-mail as your vehicle.'
Think big picture	'Always provide a brief executive summary at the beginning of the document'.
Keep an eye on spelling, grammar and punctuation	'You can be sure your readers will notice.'
Don't use e-mail to let off steam	'Compose yourself before composing your message'. 'Never use obscene, abusive or otherwise offensive language.' Don't flame (p. 55).
Don't send to the world	'Respect others' electronic space, as you would have them respect yours.' Don't spam (p. 53).

traditional, giving advice on eliminating wordiness and cliche, and guidance on grammar (addressing the usual shibboleths, such as whether it is right to use passives, or to end a sentence with a preposition, p. 64). At times, such books resemble a standard grammar, with tables listing the irregular verbs, frequently misspelled words, and commonly confused words (such as *complement* and *compliment*). Over half of any e-mail guide will be devoted to such matters. The influence of the prescriptive tradition is clear: for example, Flynn and Flynn[17] have a section called 'Bending a few rules to strike an appropriate tone'. They choose: 'contractions [e.g. *aren't, isn't*] aren't bad', 'feel free to end a sentence with a preposition', '*I, we* and *you* belong in business writing', and 'start your sentence with a coordinating conjunction'. Although this is a reaction *against*

---

[17] Flynn and Flynn (1998: 37).

traditional prescriptive pedagogy, the effect is nonetheless to re-inforce a highly selective view of what language is all about, by focusing on a tiny set of rules to the exclusion of the more general properties of language which characterize the maintext of e-mail messages. These properties result from the two chief factors which define the e-mail situation: the limitations imposed by the screen and the associated software; and the dynamic nature of the dialogue between sender and receiver.

A widely held view (dating from the earliest days of e-mailing) is that the body of a message should be entirely visible within a single screenview, without any need for scrolling. Often, this is not a whole screen, because the upper part is needed for a list-ing of incoming messages. Insofar as people use e-mails for brief and rapid conversational exchanges, fitting a message into a sin-gle screen is easily achievable,[18] and in my corpus most people do: 70% of my e-mails fit within the 16-line depth my screen makes available for the first sight of incoming messages. When the mes-sages get longer, and especially when documents of considerable length are sent (as in much business e-communication), the style guides strongly recommend that special attention is paid to the information which appears on the opening screen – providing a strong first paragraph or a summary. An analogy is often drawn with the 'inverted pyramid' style familiar from newspaper writing – the important information should appear in the opening para-graph, with less important information in the next paragraph, and so on.[19] The analogy is apt. Just as a newspaper editor will often trim an article to fit a space working 'bottom up', by cutting the final paragraph first, then the penultimate, and so on, so an e-mail writer should assume that information located at the end of the message might never be seen, if the reader decided not to scroll down any further. The pressure to provide an executive summary

---

[18] Less easy if inroads are made into the lower area, as can happen if a long list of Cc addresses is present, header information is reproduced (as when a message is forwarded), or space is devoted to some automatically generated copy (such as a confidentiality warning).

[19] Crystal and Davy (1969: ch. 7).

is especially strong in manuals of business communication, but the principle has wider relevance.

The clarity of the message on the screen is a dominant theme of e-mail manuals. Clarity in this context involves both legibility and intelligibility. Legibility chiefly refers to ways of avoiding a screenful of unbroken text. Writers are recommended to use a line-of-white between paragraphs, for example, or to highlight points in a list using a bullet or numbering facility.[20] (The increased use of bullet points is an important stylistic feature of e-mails, having previously been rare in letters and typewritten documents.) They are advised to use short, simple sentences, long ones being felt to be more difficult to read on screen. But all questions of legibility have to be considered from two points of view – the reader's as well as the writer's. This is one of the unique features of e-mail communication: there is no guarantee that the message as reproduced on the writer's screen will appear in the same configuration when it reaches the reader's. A common problem is for the line-length settings to differ, so that a message which sat neatly in 100-character lines at the sender's terminal is reproduced with a highly erratic sequence of long and short line-lengths on the receiving screen, or fails to wrap around at all (requiring an awkward repeated right-scrolling manoeuvre), or is processed so that the end part of each line is simply left out. Many manuals, accordingly, advise writers to keep their line length to 80 characters, to minimize the risk of this happening – or even 70, if message-forwarding is likely, as the tab character which is inserted in front of each line of a forwarded message uses up several characters of space. In addition, any special formatting (such as the use of bold or italic typefaces) may be lost in transmission. And attachments may be unreadable at the other end. No other type of written communication presents us with such potential asymmetry.

The pressure to maintain a message's intelligibility might be thought to be no different from that encountered in any other

---

[20] In the paragraph survey described below, only 4 out of 50 personalized messages failed to use white space between paragraphs; white space was always present in the institutional-ized messages.

communicative domain. But the speed and spontaneity with which e-mails can be written and sent makes it more likely that the processes of reflection normally used with written language (see chapter 2) will not take place. Evidently many people do not read through their message before sending it – often with the unintended consequence that the first reply they receive is a request for clarification. The style manuals differ over the question of just how much editing should take place: on the one hand, they are anxious to maintain their belief in the medium's informality; on the other hand, they are driven by their awareness that, the more idiosyncratic behaviour departs from the norms of standard English, the greater the likelihood of unintelligibility. Most of these manuals, written with a business readership in mind, end up paying lip-service to an informality-induced deviance and coming down hard on the side of the orthodox rules of the standard language. Misspellings, for example, are a natural feature of the body message in an e-mail (not in headers, where senders are usually scrupulous, knowing the consequences of error). They occur, regardless of the educational background of the writer, in any situation where there is fast typing and a lack of editorial revision.[21] For the most part, these errors cause little or no disruption to the communicative process. No-one is likely to be misled by such e-lines as the following:

> I'll procede with the practical arrangements.
> Hav eyou got the tikcets yet?

Nor is the reader going to make a social judgement about the writer's educational ability, on the basis of such data – a contrast with what *would* happen if someone wrote a traditional letter containing such errors. On the other hand, some misspellings can make a reader pause, or make an utterance ambiguous or unintelligible:

> Cab we reach you by 8?

---

[21] Even this must not be overestimated. Casting my eye over the last 50 messages I received, from people aged early 20s to mid-60s, with several intimate or from my own peer-group, only 2 had spelling errors, and these were isolated ones. My correspondents evidently revise greatly. (After reading which, my son adds: 'Of course we do. We're writing to a linguist! We might be used as data, otherwise!')

The latter examples are rare, in my experience. Of the hundreds of
e-mail typing errors I have seen, hardly any really interfere with the
meaning. Nonetheless, some manuals are hotly against misspellings
of any kind:[22]

> For every grammar mistake in an e-mail message there are an
> average of three spelling mistakes. If you think that you're saving
> time by not correcting spelling errors, think again. The time saved
> not checking your spelling is multiplied by the time that it takes
> for a reader to decipher the misspelled words. Misspelled words jar
> your reader's concentration by diverting attention away from the
> idea you are expressing. Not only are misspellings annoying and
> confusing, they also cause the reader to question your credibility.
> Misspellings make you look sloppy or, worse yet, incompetent.

And the same anxiety is expressed over punctuation errors – which
in e-mails normally refers to omissions: 'Underuse of punctuation
in e-mail can impede communications.'[23] The attitude doubtless
has some force in the context of business communication, where
prescriptive attitudes are likely to be strongly present, consciously
or unconsciously. But as a principle of general guidance for all
e-mail users, it is unreal. Most spelling errors do not distract from
the content of a message. Lightly punctuated messages, given the
relatively short sentence lengths (see below), pose few problems of
ambiguity. Nor, on receiving personalized e-mails, is the credibility
of a misspeller or mispunctuator ever seriously questioned, because
receivers are fully aware of the situational constraints under which
the message was written. They are aware of it because, several times
a day, they know they write under the same constraints themselves.

More important, in relation to intelligibility, is the question of
a message's coherence, arising out of the inherently dialogic character of e-messaging. Although some e-mails are sent without any
expectation of a response, the vast majority do expect a reply –
and get one. Accordingly, the communicative unit, as in everyday
conversation, is the *exchange*. The chief linguistic evidence for exchanges is the frequency with which response messages begin with

[22] Angell and Heslop (1994: 83).   [23] Angell and Heslop (1994: 99).

an acknowledgement that there has been a previous message: direct feedback expressions, just as in everyday conversation, or elliptical and anaphoric (referring-back) devices, as the square-bracketed queries illustrate in the following selection of opening sentences:

> Yes, I think you're right [about what?]
> No, I won't be there [where?]
> Fine by me [what is?]
> Indeed – couldn't have put it better myself [put what?]
> He'll meet you at the station [who he?]

An explicit acknowledgement of the existence of a previous message is common: excluding replies which have been automatically generated (usually because the recipient is away), 70% of my messages begin with an acknowledgement:

> Thanks for your message
> Many thanks for your thoughts
> Sorry for the delay in replying

Formality varies greatly (*Thank you, Thanks, THX, Ta*...). In my corpus, the majority of the messages *without* any acknowledgement were very short – often one line or one word in length. This is understandable: it would be anomalous to add an acknowledgement which would be longer than the meat of the response. The following seems highly unlikely.

> ?*Thanks for your message. Yes.

Acknowledgement is also sometimes omitted when the full text of the previous message is reproduced further down the screen, as when use has been made of the 'Reply to Author' option. The opposite situation also occurs, with a reply message consisting solely of an acknowledgement, such as *Thanks*. I have only four examples, so it is difficult to say anything useful about them. Usage manuals differ in their views about this practice: some warm to the fact that a courtesy has been expressed; others castigate it as a time-wasting device.

The length of the text comprising the body of an e-mail is relatively short. A sample of 50 personalized e-mails sent to me averaged 10.9 lines of body copy per message (excluding greetings, farewells, and attachments). There is considerable individual variation: the last 50 of my own e-mails to others averaged 6.56 body lines per message. (I am evidently a briefer respondent than many of my interlocutors.) The vast majority fitted easily into a single screen view. E-mails from institutions (ads, newsletters, business reports, press releases, etc.) were much longer – 20 such e-mails showed an average of 30.65 lines per message (though this figure is more difficult to calculate, due to the insertion of all kinds of extraneous matter into the body copy, such as hypertext links). In terms of paragraphs, my incoming personalized e-mails averaged 3.28 paragraphs per message; my outgoing ones averaged 2.0. Institutionalized e-mails were much longer (as we might expect) – an average of 8.35 paragraphs per item.

Paragraph structure is short. Table 4.2 shows that 80% of my personalized incoming messages were 4 lines or less.[24] Here there is no difference from what is found in institutionalized messages – nor, indeed, in my own outgoing messages, with 78% of my paragraphs being 4 lines or less. (I was surprised to encounter a 22-line paragraph, in one of my e-mails. I now find this difficult to read, and wish I had restructured it before sending.) One difference between personalized and institutionalized messages is that the former use three times as many single-line paragraphs; this seems to reflect the need for length to enable institutions to make their various expository (informational, marketing, etc.) points. Institutional one-line paragraphs tend to be the occasional slogan-like observation to which the writer is giving paragraph prominence (e.g. *There'll never be a better time to buy*). In personalized e-mails, the one-liners tend to be a brief acknowledgement (*See you there, Thanks*), real or

---

[24] It seems to make no difference whether the format displays longer or shorter lines in larger or smaller type: there seems to be a general tendency to keep the overall paragraph length short. On the other hand, it follows from this that paragraphs will contain different amounts of content: four long lines in small type must carry more information than four short lines in small type.

Table 4.2. *Paragraph length (in lines) in a personal sample of e-messages*

No of lines in a paragraph	Personalized incoming messages ($N^a = 50$)	Institutional incoming messages ($N = 20$)	My outgoing messages ($N = 50$)
1	37 (22.6%)	11 (6.6%)	33 (33%)
2	33 (20.1%)	51 (30.5%)	20 (20%)
3	35 (21.3%)	38 (22.7%)	15 (15%)
4	26 (15.8%)	19 (11.4%)	10 (10%)
5	9	18 (10.8%)	6
6	11	10	7
7	6	12	2
8	2	2	2
9	3	3	1
10	1	1	
11	1	1	2
12		1	
15			1
22			1
Totals	164	167	100

$^a N$ = number of messages

rhetorical isolated queries (*What time do you want me to arrive?, Wasn't the concert fine?*), or a response to an individual point (*The Smith book sounds intriguing, The session starts at 12*).

The dialogic character of the body element in an e-mail is made totally explicit when the 'Reply to Author' option is activated, and respondents add reactions which refer directly to the whole of a received message. The process is facilitated by the software, which makes a clear typographic distinction between original message and reaction. After early experiments using indention, standard practice is now to insert a right-pointing angle bracket (sometimes a colon or vertical black line) at the beginning of each line of the original message (including the paragraph-separating lines-of-white), so that (1) becomes (2):

(1)
I hope to be there by six, though everything depends on the
trains. Will you be coming by train yourself, or are you driving this
time? I know Fred is bringing his car.

(2)
>I hope to be there by six, though everything depends on the
>trains. Will you be coming by train yourself, or are you driving
>this time? I know Fred is bringing his car.

The reaction may then be added, in any of three locations: above the
whole of the received message, below it, or within it – repeatedly,
if necessary.

	Above	*Within*	*Below*
	reply	>received message	>extract from
	>received message	reply	received message
		>extract from	reply
		received message	
		reply	
		>extract from	
		received message	

The procedure is a little like adding notes at the beginning or end
of a letter, or in the margins, and returning it to the sender – but
with the difference that in e-mail both parties end up with a perfect
copy of everything.

All three methods have their advantages and disadvantages.
Putting the reply first gets to the point straight away, but the receiver
often has to scroll down to be reminded of what the person is reacting to – often necessary, if time has passed since sending the original
message. Putting the reply at the end avoids this problem, but forces
the receiver to scroll through a message which may be totally familiar – as it would be if it had been sent only a few minutes before. The
former option is preferred in many professional settings, where it
has become standard practice to reply to a steadily growing chain of
e-messages by adding the latest response at the beginning, because
when a tailback of messages becomes extensive, it is then very awkward to find a message located at the end and to print it out. In those

companies which retain a paper record of their messages, printing out the most recent ones (as opposed to the entire message history) is very much easier if they are at the beginning of a chain, as there is no way of knowing which pages to select for the printer if they are at the end, since e-mail pages are not formatted on-screen in terms of printer pages. 'Print pages 1–2' is an easy instruction; 'Print pages 11–12' requires research. ('Print all', of course, is also an easy option – but at the expense of increasingly bulging filefuls of duplicated pages.)

Some usage manuals disapprove of the within-message reaction. 'Add your reply above or below – *never within* – the original message.'[25] In fact, within-message commenting is very common, when several points are being made which require individual attention. A within-message reply to (1) above might read:

> >I hope to be there by six, though everything depends on the
> >trains.
> I know – remember last time?
> >Will you be coming by train yourself, or are you driving this
> >time?
> Car
> >I know Fred is bringing his car.

It would not be intelligible to give this sequence of responses at the end of the message:

> >I hope to be there by six, though everything depends on the
> >trains.
> >Will you be coming by train yourself, or are you driving this
> >time? I know Fred is bringing his car.
> I know – remember last time?
> Car

or at the beginning:

I know – remember last time?
Car
>I hope to be there by six, though everything depends on the
>trains. Will you be coming by train yourself, or are you driving
>this time? I know Fred is bringing his car.

To make either intelligible would require major rewriting, with more explicit cross-reference to or paraphrasing of what the sender had said. In business communication, where documents can be very long and reactions to individual points erratically located, guidebook advice to avoid within-message reactions is well taken. A point might easily be missed, and it would be difficult to work out the nature of the overall reply from a sequence of individual, widely separated reactions. In professional correspondence, accordingly, there is a widespread preference for (3) as opposed to (4):

(3)
With reference to your points A, B, and C I think P, Q, and R respectively.

(4)
>Point A
Point P
>Point B
Point Q
>Point C
Point R

But in most interpersonal e-mail, (3) is simply not an option, because of the rewriting (and rethinking) which would be involved.

Message intercalation of the type illustrated by (4) is a unique feature of e-mail language, and a property which could only succeed in an electronic medium. And there is a further refinement. It is possible for recipients to respond to an original message not by adding reactions to selected parts of the original text, as illustrated above, but by editing the original text so that only those parts which require reaction are left. The procedure is, effectively, one of quotation. Thus, for example, I sent the following paragraph (5) to someone, who replied as (6), cutting one of my sentences and pasting it into the new message:

> (5)
> There are still several loose ends for the Tuesday. We've had a lot of people wanting to contribute, and our original proposals for timing seem to be out. Do you think it would work having two sessions in the afternoon? It would mean cutting down on the tea-break, and maybe even timing dinner a half-hour later than usual. That in turn would push the evening session on a bit, but I don't see any problem there, as everyone is staying the night.
>
> (6)
> >Do you think it would work having two sessions in the
> >afternoon?
> Good idea

The longer a sender's paragraphs, the more likely the recipient is to respond in this way. The result has been described as *framing*, because of the way in which the quoted text is demarcated typo-graphically, either through an angle-bracket or a vertical line.[26] Framing is a consequence of the ease with which people can cut and paste from an original message. It is also a feature of chatgroup interactions (p. 141), where an extended discussion may make use of extensive quotation from several participants, providing the context for a reaction.

Framing has both strengths and weaknesses. It is a convenience, in that a series of points can be responded to rapidly and succinctly, either in the order in which they were made or in some fresh order – much as we can strategically recapitulate a series of points made by an interlocutor in a face-to-face discussion. Time and memory are saved, as it is no longer necessary to trawl back through an

---

[26] This is an extension of the notion of perceptual framing found in psychology and semi-otics: see Bateson (1972), Mabry (1997), Wallace (1999: 127). It should not be confused with the use of the term *frame* (in several senses) in grammar (*sentence frame*), conver-sation analysis (*discourse frame*), and elsewhere.

e-mail thread to find the original remarks. And dealing with several points at once (a common strategy in asynchronous chatgroups, p. 163) saves repeated e-mailing. Reactions to reactions are also possible, with each new reaction retaining its own framing device, so that the page takes on a nested appearance (as shown by the increasing angle brackets):

>B's extract from A's message
>>A's extract from B's message
>>>B's extract from A's extract ...

On the other hand, everybody knows the difficulties which arise when quotations are being used extensively: meaning can change dramatically when words are quoted out of context, whether innocently or deliberately. Deliberate out-of-context quotation may seem a strange concept to people expecting the e-mail or chatgroup worlds to be inhabited by polite, well-mannered, Gricean (p. 48) individuals. But analysis of the reasons for flaming in e-interaction shows that misquotation, in order to score a point, is commonly implicated.[27] It may even involve pre-editing of the paste: Tom finds an extract in Dick's message which doesn't quite suit the point he wants to make, so he alters it in some way, and then quotes it as if it were Dick speaking. In the hurly-burly of a chatgroup, nobody (apart perhaps from Dick) is going to take the trouble to check back; and retracing a thread of e-mails to find the relevant point (assuming the relevant items have not been deleted) can be just as laborious. It should also be noted that the option of misquotation is available to both sides: Dick can deliberately edit himself, too.

A framed message is certainly a most unusual object, not like anything else in language use. The stylistic consequences of cutting and pasting text from an earlier message – either our own or someone else's – are also unusual; here, too, there is nothing remotely like it in other domains of writing. Where else would we find so many physically adjacent but semantically unrelated paragraphs of text? In traditional writing, such texts would be penalized for lack

---

[27] Mabry (1997).

of organization and logical progression; but in an e-mail, where the points are taking up different issues in a previous message, such overriding considerations are waived. The bottom line is that, with e-mail, a new document is created with every transaction. The permanence of e-writing is only a superficial impression. Although a single piece of text may be preserved throughout a thread of messages, via forwarding or replying to author, each screen incarnation gives it a different status and may present it in a different form – either through electronic interference from the software or editorial interference from the new user. Linguistics has yet to devise ways of capturing such dynamic characteristics in its stylistic descriptions.

The issues go well beyond the linguistic. Traditional letter-writing, through such features as its choice of notepaper, letterhead typography, style of paragraphing, and signature format, presented a facet of the writer's personality and standing. People can spend ages worrying over these matters – when ordering new notepaper, for example. In some circumstances – such as the writing of references, job applications, or referee reports – the choices made inevitably affect the receiver's perception of the character of the sender, and influence the outcome in all kinds of unconscious ways. The 'meaning' of a message is much more than the semantic content of its constituent words. But when this kind of material is submitted by e-mail – as it increasingly is – all this extra meaning is lost. Publishers, for example, commonly paste extracts from readers' e-reports on a book proposal into a single document for submission to an editorial board. Instantiating this point, my Cambridge in-house editor remarked:

> Inevitably a small part of the 'meaning' as intended by the author of the report is then lost, and some of the authorial control of the text has shifted to me as editor. I now have the power to undertake subtle but acceptable editorial interventions and juxtapositions which would have been barred from me in the era when the physical page was part of the message intended by the author.... Until a year ago [he writes in December 2000] authors of reports remained uncomfortably aware of all this, and there was a

nervousness about losing control of format; but then suddenly that bridgehead collapsed, and now anyone will send you more or less anything by e-mail, accepting that an editorial re-formatting will inevitably come into play.

The willing surrender of control over one's written or spoken output is not in itself novel: journalists, for example, have long been used to having their copy altered by senior editors before it appears in print; and one never knows just how much of a radio or television interview will end up being used, or in what way editorial 'cutting and pasting' will affect what one has said. But e-mail permits the extension of such practices to a very wide range of communicative behaviours previously immune to such 'interference', and the consequences have yet to be explored.

Features such as screen structure, message openings and closing, message length, dialogic strategies, and framing are central to the identification of e-mail as a linguistic variety. This is not to deny the presence of other, more local points of stylistic significance, in relation to graphology, grammar, and lexicon, but these are not so critical. There has been a tendency to highlight the informal features of messages – such as the use of contractions, loose sentence construction, subject ellipsis (*Will let you know*), colloquial abbreviations (*bye, cos, v slow, s/thing*), and 'cool' acronyms (*LOL, CU*, p. 85) – but these are plainly not indicative of the variety as a whole, as many messages do not use them. Doubtless, given the question/answer basis of many exchanges, an analysis of sentence types will reveal a distinctive bias; for example, the intensity of questioning seems to be greater than in traditional letters, or even in conversation (where rapid-fire questioning of the type illustrated below would be considered a harangue):

> Am I asking too much? Does this seem workable to you? Can you get to it, do you think? Do you * want * to get to it?!

Rhetorical questions also seem to be commoner in e-mails than in other varieties of written English, apart from certain types of literary expression. Advertising e-mails are full of them, reflecting a style that is more likely to be heard in commercial broadcasting than in graphic advertising:

> How would you like to win...?
> Why wait?
> What could be more addictive than both Pokémon and pinball... except for a blend of both? Catch 'em early by pre-ordering for just £22.99.
> Have you ever wanted to see... if it's sunny in San Francisco? if there's new snow at Vail? what traffic is like on Interstate 10 in Phoenix? Well, you can!

The status of a question – whether the sender expects or does not expect a response – is often ambiguous. Self-answering is more common than I recall seeing elsewhere:

> Will Mary turn up? I doubt it, after last time. Who knows? Not Jim, anyway.

But these impressions need to be supported by some detailed survey-work before they can be proposed as distinctive features of the variety.

A similar caution needs to be expressed over e-mail graphology. The variety is plainly distinctive at a graphic level (p. 7), in view of the widespread characterless large bland typeface which provides the default for many mailers: 90% of all my incoming mail uses it. But the fact that an HTML option is also widely available as a sending format means that it is not an obligatory feature of the e-mail situation. Much of the graphological deviance noted in messages is also not universal, being typical of informal Internet exchanges especially among younger (or at least, young at heart) users. I have already referred to misspellings (p. 111), but examples such as the following hardly fall into that category:

> Hellllllooooooooo!

There is also a reduced use of capitalization, which may involve either grammar (e.g. sentence-initial) or lexicon (e.g. proper names), or both, as in these examples:

> log onto the address below and you will see a mock up of our site
> the above is an advert I noticed for New Deal
> an excerpt from a tommy cooper forward i got

The usual range of punctuation expressiveness may be seriously extended:

> Yes!!!!!!!!
> WHAT?????
> You've got a $^\wedge$&*! cheek

Smileys (p. 36) are available for use, though they are by no means as frequent as the explanatory literature suggests. Common enough in the exchanges between teenagers, they are almost totally absent in my own incoming mail (apart from two instances from one of my children). Angell and Heslop comment: smileys 'are the equivalent of e-mail slang and should not be used in formal business e-mail messages'.[28] But they do not seem to be much used in non-business circles either. Ingenious keyboard typography may also be used to make material stand out, using asterisks, hyphens, bullets, pipes, and other symbols to create panels, boxes, and borders. Colour is also present, being routinely used to highlight hypertext links (www or @ addresses). The range of typographical options is bound to grow, as technology progresses. MIME (multipurpose internet mail extension) already exists as a standard for sending audio, graphics, and video files as e-mails. But at present, there are few graphic or graphological features that are universally present. Stylistic conformity there may be among particular groups of e-mail users (e.g. undergraduates, teenagers), but in the variety as a whole the potential for significant group differentiation exists.[29]

---

[28] Angell and Heslop (1994: 111).

[29] The point about a growth in conformity has been addressed by McCormick and McCormick (1992); see also Wallace (1999: 62–4). Danielson (1996) draws a contrast between the homogeneous look of incoming e-mail and the much greater sortability of incoming snail mail (on the basis of envelope type, colour, size, address typography, and so on). Stylistically, there is no reason why such variability should not appear in e-mailing too. The potential is there.

The uniqueness of e-mail

Writers repeatedly draw analogies between e-mail and other forms of communication, in order to locate it in communicative 'space'. It is:

> a cross between a conversation and a letter, email is as fast as a telegram and as cheap as a whisper[30]
> a telegraph, a memo, and a palaver rolled into one[31]
> faster than a speeding letter, cheaper than a phone call[32]
> a strange blend of writing and talking[33]

Homer Simpson has it explained to him in this way:[34]

> Homer: What's an e-mail?
> Lenny: It's a computer thing, like, er, an electric letter.
> Carl: Or a quiet phone call.

From the above analysis, it is clear that e-mails do indeed have elements of the memo about them, notably in their fixed header structure. The informal letter analogy is also appropriate, with the medium's reliance on greetings and farewells, and the use of several informal written features in the message body. The telephone conversation analogy is also proper, given the way a dialogue style can build up over time; and the cheapness of the medium has often been remarked. And some e-mails are highly telegrammatic in style. But e-mail, in the final analysis, is like none of these. The consensus seems to be that it is, formally and functionally, unique.

Functionally, e-mail does not duplicate what other mediums can do. It is better than the telephone in eliminating what has been called 'telephone tag' (in which people repeatedly leave messages

---

[30] Hale and Scanlon (1999: 3). [31] Hale and Scanlon (1999: 78).
[32] Angell and Heslop (1994: 1); see also Hatch (1992). The similarity of electronic discourse to the language of public interviews has also been noted (Collot and Belmore, 1993).
[33] Naughton (1999: 143), who goes on to characterize it as resembling 'stream-of-consciousness narratives, the product of people typing as fast as they can think'.
[34] 'The computer war menace shoes', Episode 12A6 of *The Simpsons* (Fox TV).

with each other to 'call me back'); on the other hand, if an immediate response is essential, and face-to-face communication is impossible, you cannot beat the telephone. E-mail is better than the letter in obtaining a quick response to an enquiry; but not for every kind of message. There is a widespread feeling that letters are better than e-mails for expressing negative content, such as breaking off a relationship or reporting a family death, and that telephone or face-to-face conversation is also better in such cases, where the full range of vocal nuance is needed to do justice to the meaning. On the other hand, it has been noted that people have a greater tendency to self-disclose on the computer, compared with telephone and face-to-face conversation – a factor which, some think, partly accounts for the growth in e-romances.[35] E-mail has also emerged as a means of communication where nothing was easily available before – such as between professionals whose erratic life-style meant that they were never predictably at the end of a telephone line, between parents and their children at university, or between partners separated by distance, for whom the cheapness of the medium is a godsend.

E-mail has come to be used for some of the purposes traditionally carried out by the letter (e.g. the sending of CVs or job applications, certain types of form-filling), but it has not yet supplanted conventional mail for others (e.g. contractual matters), because of issues to do with privacy, security, and legal tradition. While we may make copies of a will, or of our house deeds, the 'real' documents have a special status which it will be difficult, perhaps impossible, for e-mail to replicate. Certainly, at present, the incompatibilities between software systems (mentioned above) disallow any privileged status for a document where layout is critical, such as a legal document or a commercial advertisement. The limitations of e-mail, as a communicative medium, are in fact still being discovered. There is no way of controlling an e-mail, once it has been sent; nor is

---

[35] See the discussion in Wallace (1999: 151). Baron (2000: 235) suggests that the private nature of e-mail dialogue accounts for its 'laissez-faire' character, so that it can be used for virtually any subject-matter. Her illustrations include condolences, which for me oversteps a boundary.

there any way of knowing who will eventually see it or edit it. The e-mail guides are thus very emphatic in their advocacy of caution: 'Don't write anything to or about another that you would not feel comfortable saying face-to-face.'[36] 'Watch what you say', says another, 'Big Brother is watching you' – noting that employers and law-enforcement agencies may search your mailboxes.[37] The exploration of the legal implications is in its infancy. Many issues are known, some extremely serious. There have been complaints about e-bullying (e.g. in e-mail staff reprimands), sexism, sexual harassment, the use of libellous language, and rudeness (often arising out of a misplaced attempt to be funny or ironic). There can also be ambiguities of an international kind: e-mails which refer to a local time (or date), without making it clear which time-zone is involved; e-mails which write the date in one way, forgetting that the convention is different elsewhere (e.g. 7/3/00 is 7 March in the UK, 3 July in the USA); e-mails which talk about '3 o'clock' without making it clear whether morning or afternoon is intended; e-mails which assume that local abbreviations (e.g. *ABC*) will be universally familiar (whereas it means one thing in the USA and another in Australia); e-mails which assume that a local geographical reference will be known (e.g. *East Coast*); and so on. Many e-mail users are still getting to grips with these matters (see further, chapter 8).

The evolution of e-mail style is in its infancy,[38] and perhaps the only thing we can say for certain is that it will soon no longer be as it currently is. Generalizations about the medium have hitherto been heavily influenced by its technical origins and early years of use. There is an understandable tendency to think of e-mailing solely in terms of informality. It feels temporary, indeed, and this promotes a sense of the carefree. Messages can be easily deleted, which suggests that their content is basically unimportant. Because of its spontaneity, speed, privacy, and leisure value, e-mail offers

---

[36] Flynn and Flynn (1998: 3).
[37] Angell and Heslop (1994: 6). In 2000, in the UK, a number of sackings for e-mail violations brought considerable publicity to the issue of employer powers vs. employee rights, highlighting the existence of widely different regulations between companies and countries.
[38] See further: Thompson and Ahn (1992), Baron (1998a; 1998b; 2000: chs. 8–9).

the option of greater levels of informality than are found elsewhere in traditional writing. But as the medium matures, it is becoming apparent that it is not exclusively an informal medium, and received opinion is going to have to change. Hale and Scanlon observe: 'A well-written electronic missive gets to the point quickly, with evocative words, short grafs, and plenty of white space. Spelling and punctuation are loose and playful. (No-one reads email with red pen in hand.)'[39] The evidence is growing that an awful lot of people actually do keep such a pen in mind, in educational, business, and other workplace settings, where e-mails are routinely seen as providing a more convenient professionalism (one that can speed up decision-making and build strong daily working relationships) rather than just an opportunity for a chat. Certainly, the spirit of the e-mail style manuals is very much towards being careful, stressing the communicative limitations of the medium (such as those discussed in chapter 2). In due course, this emphasis seems likely to gain ground. The result will be a medium which will portray a wide range of stylistic expressiveness, from formal to informal, just as other mediums have come to do, and where the pressure on users will be to display stylistic consistency, in the same way that this is required in other forms of writing.[40] E-mail will then take its place in the school curriculum, not as a medium to be feared for its linguistic irresponsibility (because it allows radical graphological deviance) but as one which offers a further domain within which children can develop their ability to consolidate their stylistic intuitions and make responsible linguistic choices. E-mail has extended the language's stylistic range in interesting and motivating ways. In my view, it is an opportunity, not a threat, for language education.

[39] Hale and Scanlon (1999: 3).
[40] Baron (2000: 242) also concludes that two styles of e-mail will emerge in due course, one edited, the other unedited. Punctuation preferences, likewise, are likely to evolve two standards, one following grammatical prescriptions, the other following the rhetorical patterns of speech.

5   *The language of chatgroups*

The Internet allows people to engage in a multi-party conversation online, either synchronously, in real time, or asynchronously, in postponed time (chapter 1). The situations in which such interactions take place have been referred to in various ways, partly reflecting the period in Internet history when they were introduced, and partly reflecting the orientation and subject-matter of the group involved, such as *chatgroups, newsgroups, usergroups, chatrooms, mailing lists, discussion lists, e-conferences,* and *bulletin boards.* In this book, I have used *chatgroups* as a generic term for world-wide multi-participant electronic discourse, whether real-time or not.[1] There is a technical overlap with e-mailing: a mailing list is essentially an e-mail address which redirects a message to a set of other addresses. It is also possible for pairs of chatgroup members to arrange to communicate privately by e-mail or using some other messaging facility. However, from a linguistic point of view it is important to distinguish the chatgroup from the e-mail situation (chapter 4), in that the latter is typically between a pair of named individuals (or institutions), with message-exchanges often limited to a single transaction, and relating to a specific, pre-planned question. Chatgroups, by contrast, typically involve several people,[2]

---

[1] Many people restrict the term *chat* to real-time contexts only. It should also be noted that some systems are very sensitive to the correct use of their own terminology: for example, Usenet users operate in *newsgroups* (or *groups*), WELL users in *conferences*; Usenet managers are called *news administrators*; Internet Relay Chat managers are *operators*.

[2] Asynchronous groups have far more members, because there is no limit to the number of people who can access the group, and there is no complication caused by members belonging to different time-zones. Synchronous groups can get clogged if too many people try to talk to each other at once, and many organizations try to limit population growth. This issue is also a problem in virtual worlds: see p. 186. For a directory of e-groups in the scholarly and professional spheres, see Diane Kovacs' compilation at <http://www.n2h2.com/KOVACS>.

with message-exchanges often anonymous, continuing indefinitely, and dealing with a wide and unpredictable range of issues. Although there are several points of linguistic similarity between the two situations, the linguistic features and strategies taken up by chatgroup participants are very different from those typically employed by e-mail users.

In a synchronous setting, a user enters a chat 'room' and joins an ongoing conversation in real time.[3] Named contributions are sent to a central computer address and are inserted into a permanently refreshing screen along with the contributions from other participants. The online members of the group see their contributions appear on screen soon after they make them (all being well: see below), and hope for a prompt response. In an asynchronous setting, the interactions also go to a central address, but they are then stored in some format, and made available to members of the group only upon demand, so that people can catch up with the discussion, or add to it, at any time – even after an appreciable period has passed. It is not important for members to see their contributions arrive, and prompt reactions are welcomed but not assumed. Of the two situations, it is the synchronous interactions which cause most radical linguistic innovation, as we shall see, affecting several basic conventions of traditional spoken and written communication. It is therefore better to begin this chapter with the asynchronous type, where many of the interactions are much more like those familiar in e-mail and in traditional written genres such as the letter or essay.

Asynchronous groups

Discussion groups proliferated so remarkably in the 1990s that it is difficult to make statements of any generality. The WELL (= Whole Earth 'Lectronic Link), founded in 1985, had over

[3] How this is done (the various procedures and types of participation – by subscription, permission, open access, etc.) is not the concern of this book, except insofar as the list-owner or moderator exercises linguistic influence: see below.

260 groups (referred to as *conferences*) by mid-2000.[4] The groups on Usenet (referred to as *newsgroups*) are so multifarious that they are organized in a hierarchy, with over 50 major domains dealing with such topic areas as recreation, science, business, computing, and news. The recreation domain, for example, in mid-2000 consisted of over 300 groups devoted to such areas as comics (represented by 9 groups), games (51 groups), pets (10 groups), and sport (19 groups), as well as more specific domains such as guns, heraldry, juggling, and woodworking. Most of these headings contained further groups, dealing with still more specific aspects of the topic.[5] LISTSERV®, first developed in 1986, is a software system for managing electronic mailing lists (the lack of a final -*e* in the name reflects the 8-character name-processing limitation of computers at the time). It was handling over 180,000 lists by October 2000, over 40,000 of them in the public domain.[6] At that date of enquiry, there were no less than 162 devoted to the topic of 'language' and 44 to 'linguistics'. Looking at one of these areas in further detail: LIN-GUIST, a specialized linguistics list founded in 1990, had developed 70 conferences by late 2000.[7]

Introductions, helplines, and pages of FAQs (frequently asked questions) all stress the variety of style and tone, coverage and treatment, which exists among these groups. 'It is almost impossible to generalize over all Usenet sites in any non-trivial way', observes the writer of an introduction to that system,[8] and a WELL writer warns newcomers to the conferences it uses to illustrate the system not to assume that other groups will be the same: 'each conference has a distinct style'.[9] In the light of this diversity, and in the absence of in-depth comparative surveys,[10] an introductory account can do little more than illustrate the type of activity that takes place,

---

[4] Further information at <http://www.well.com>. Quotations below are from this site.
[5] Further information at <http://www.faqs.org/facs/usenet>.
[6] Further information at <http://www.lsoft.com>.
[7] Further information at <http://www.linguistlist.org>.
[8] <http://www.faqs.org/facs/usenet/what-is/part1>, under 'Diversity'.
[9] <http://www.well.com/aboutwell.html>.
[10] But see Yates (1996), who compared a selection of features from a corpus of conference data with spoken and written corpora.

point to the variety of approaches which already exist, and identify some of the linguistic issues to which operations of this kind give rise.

The aims of a group are indeed as diverse as it is possible to conceive. Many are formed because of an interest in a particular subject-matter, whether amateur or specialist. Others are there just to talk or play games. The constituency of a group may be academic, professional, governmental, commercial, or social. As the WELL writer comments, 'regulars check in frequently to offer expertise, debate ideas, play word games and indulge in banter and gossip'. The informal descriptions capture this diversity. LISTSERV has been described as a 'virtual coffee house';[11] Usenet as a 'fair, a cocktail party, a town meeting, the notes of a secret cabal, the chatter in the hallway at a conference, a friday night fish fry, post-coital gossip, the conversations overheard in an airplane waiting lounge that launched a company, and a bunch of other things'.[12] Some systems permit the presence of extraneous content, such as commercial advertisements; others do not. The more specialized the topic, the more likely the content will be focused – and several groups use moderators to ensure that the conversation does not diverge from the subject too much (go *off-topic*).[13] However, the amount of identity and responsibility given to contributors varies greatly. Some allow anonymity of membership (see below), others insist on real names being used. All emphasize the freedom of expression that is present in the situation, while at the same time warning users against the incautious use of that freedom. The WELL aphorism, 'You Own Your Own Words' (YOYOW), stresses this element of personal responsibility, and draws attention to the need for 'mutual respect and co-operation' (cf. Grice's maxims, p. 48).

[11] <www.lsoft.com/manuals/1.8d/user/user.html>. However, it has both public (or open) and private (or closed) lists, the latter with some degree of controlled access.
[12] <http://www.faqs.org/facs/usenet/what-is/part2>.
[13] Though what counts as off-topic is not always clear. A reference to the weather might be considered off-topic by some, but good group rapport-forming by others.

The systems all operate in roughly the same way.[14] An organization provides a set of group options – such as the hierarchically organized set of newsgroups on Usenet – which individuals who have the appropriate software choose to join. Members then send (*post*) their contributions (*articles, messages, posts*) to the group, and the system makes these available to all addresses it holds, some of which may be other networks of addresses. Messages may be saved in files for future reading or searching (*archives, notebooks, logs, conferences*), and catalogued with varying depth of detail in terms of date, topic, author, etc. The management of each group, or of a particular task within each group, is in the hands of an individual person or small team, identified by such role-labels as *list-owner, editor, host, postmaster, maintainer,* or *moderator*. Different systems are known by their use of one or other of these labels, and often more than one; for example, the person who owns a list and knows its content may be labelled differently from the person who maintains the list computationally. In this book, I use *moderator* as a convenient generic term for anyone who has managerial influence on the operation of a group. Moderators exercise varying amounts of power – for example, deciding whether a message is relevant or offensive. Several groups have moderators whose power consists only in whether to allow a message to appear or not (WELL hosts fall into this category). Other groups allow their moderators to have editing as well as filtering powers, enabling them to shorten an overlong message, or to cut out obscenities, spam (p. 53), flaming (p. 55), unauthorized advertising, and other unwanted material. Issues of censorship and taste inevitably arise, in such contexts, and

---

[14] However, the 'life' of a group is not the same. Although many groups have an indefinite lifespan envisioned, others are created for specific and restricted periods of time. A school or college may decide to create a conference chatgroup for a single year, or term, or for part of a term, or for a particular project (as in the group studied by Davis and Brewer, 1997). Also, the students may only be able to access the group when in school, which restricts operations to certain times of day. An academic group may decide to hold an electronic conference over a precise period, allowing time for participants to have read certain papers and to respond to them. For example, a linguistics online conference (the first to be organized by the LINGUIST list) was held from 14 October to 4 November 1996 on the subject of binding theory.

'metadiscussions' about the role of the moderator are common-place. In all cases, moderators belong to individual groups within a system. There is no 'super-moderator' for a chatgroup system as a whole, and no 'big brother' watching – benevolently or malevo-lently – over the whole Internet chatgroup system, notwithstanding popular suspicions to the contrary.

Many servers can circulate a message very quickly, within a minute or so; it would be unusual for a delay to exceed half an hour, though as always this depends on such factors as the com-puter system used and the part of the world to which the message is sent (cf. p. 31). Because messages can arrive at any time, and users may not want to read them as they come in, some systems (e.g. LISTSERV) provide a digest of all messages received during a particular period of time, which can be accessed in one go at a later stage. An index of the messages received in a period may also be available, which users can scan before deciding which ones to read. Additional files may be stored for access by group mem-bers, such as minutes of meetings, magazine articles, agendas, and academic papers. However, it is important to bear in mind that some mail systems do not accept very large messages or message digests (e.g. larger than 64kB or 100kB). Technologically imposed length constraints are an important factor influencing the linguis-tic character of chatgroup messages, therefore, over and above the pragmatic pressure on individuals to keep their contributions rela-tively short. Chatgroups are unlikely to be a domain where lengthy monologues or balanced dialogues – speeches, lectures, commer-cial presentations, formal debates, and suchlike – are found. Or, putting this another way, it would be pointless for anyone to try to use in this way a medium which is designed to provoke and accept short messages and multiple reactions. The point may be obvious, but it is nevertheless a distinctive linguistic feature of the chatgroup situation.

The asynchronous nature of the interaction is the heart of the matter. Individual contributions to a group are saved and dis-tributed as they come in, which may be at any time and separated by any period of time. In one group I observed, several contributions were coming in every day; in another, over a hundred messages were present, but spread out over a year; in a third, a group had received no contributions for several years (and thus, I imagine, was defunct). Each contributor leaves a linguistic 'footprint', in that what is said has a permanent pragmatic effect. In face-to-face communication, pragmatic effects are typically immediate and direct. In an asynchronous list, the effect of a contribution is preserved over an indefinable period of time – in much the same way that contact with a broadcast interview can be indefinitely renewed, as long as there is interest in it. It is a standard technique to embarrass politicians, for example, by retransmitting their words years after they were spoken. But it is not just politicians. Which of us, in everyday conversation, have not had occasion to bless the fact that our utterances are not being taken down to be later used in evidence? Yet this is precisely the situation which obtains in asynchronous chatgroups, where we ourselves put everything down, using our own keyboards. Our individual e-conversations may come to an end, but the text remains. We should not therefore be surprised if, at some point – even years later – someone uses what we have said in a way we did not intend, or quotes us out of context. The group managers repeatedly warn their members about the long-term effect of their contributions. As the WELL site says:

> Remember that words you enter in a burst of inspired passion or indignant anger will be there for you (and everyone) to read long after your intense feelings are gone. This isn't meant to discourage spontaneity and the expression of feelings on The WELL, but merely to remind you of the long-term existence and effects of what you write.

This pushes the situation much more in the direction of the written language, as encountered in articles, books, and other 'permanent' literature. There is an autonomy about the text, once it is posted, much like that encountered in a book. Indeed, in looking at the topic-list within a particular group, with its main headings and sub-headings, there is a distinct resemblance to conventional book divisions. Boyd Davis and Jeutonne Brewer found that, after the

student conference they studied was over, it came to be read differently: 'topics become chapters, even in print-out'.[15]

Indeed, the reactions of the participants in the Davis and Brewer
study are interesting for another reason, as this further quotation
suggests:

> Students forgot how to read across to find their entries. When one
> group was presented with the print-out of the full conference, they
> were momentarily puzzled until they could spread it out across
> space and re-created the sense of connection they had when they
> were part of the conference. Reading the artifact after the fact
> demands a topical orientation which is not always sequential and
> can be thematic across time and space.

The non-linear nature of the interaction is highlighted here, and
this as we shall see has all kinds of linguistic consequences. Just as
we can 'dip into' a book, so we can dip into a group. When joining
a group, we can call up a recent or distant topic, then begin with
the most recent postings, or go back to ones made days, months, or
even years ago. There is no given chronological beginning-point.
Topics are classified thematically or by author within directories.
Within a topic, there is a stronger sense of chronological linearity,
as messages are organized in the order in which the server received
them. However, this is a presentational linearity only, of no communicative consequence: there is no guarantee that a sender E,
responding to message A, has read any of the messages B, C, D
which may have been sent to the group in the interim. Indeed, E
does not know whether A will read E's response – or whether anyone ever will. A may have logged off by the time E responds. And
it is always possible that a cluster of other messages may come in
(perhaps taking a topic in a different direction), so that when A
next logs on, E's message may be so far back in the queue that it
will not be noticed. Because there is no obligation on E to respond,
and no expectation on A's part that E *will* respond, A may not go
looking for it. People's time is limited: Davis and Brewer found,
on the basis of internal evidence in their corpus (the way senders

[15] Davis and Brewer (1997: 162).

explicitly refer to previous messages), that members of their conference read on average only between five and seven other postings
before sending their own.[16]

With arbitrary entrance-points, and an ongoing accumulation
of topics, the adequate indexing of the messages in an asynchronous
chatgroup is critical. Attention needs to be paid to both coverage
(the range of subject-matter indexed) and treatment (how the indexed information is presented). A traditional alphabetical index
of the group content will be only partly informative – it will be
useful for contributors' names, for example – but topical content
needs a thematic approach, so that subsets of semantically related
messages (*threads*) can be identified. Readers (as the student conference example illustrates) need to be provided with a thematic
'map' of the message-structure of a group, when they access it.
In the students' case, their data was processed using the conference management program, VAXNotes (VAX = 'Virtual Address
eXtension' minicomputer), with each message assigned an ID, date,
topic title, and file-number; for instance, item 3.16 would be the
16th reaction to topic 3. The required approach has been called
topographic – 'a writing with places, spatially realized topics'.[17] And
the controlling semantic notion is the title assigned to the message
topic. Titles, as Davis and Brewer put it, enable us to 'read the "map"
of the conference as if we lived in the territory'; they give us a guide
to the 'conference topography'.[18] They are in many ways analogous
to the 'subjects' of e-mail, and operate under similar constraints
(p. 98). If they are too vague they are useless. If they are altered, it
becomes difficult to trace message themes.

Title threads grow in number as the theme of the conference
broadens. If I decide to set up a group called 'Influence of hamsters

[16] Davis and Brewer (1997: 131). It is by no means clear whether this is due to practical
reasons (e.g. time availability) or psycholinguistic reasons (e.g. the amount of 'semantic
distance' required before someone loses the thread of a discourse). I am reminded of the
magic number seven, plus or minus two (Miller, 1969).
[17] Bolter (1991: 25).
[18] Davis and Brewer (1997: 54–5). Especially when the time-frames are extensive, there is an
urgent need for some sort of co-ordination mechanism to flag new relevant documents,
to stop one user's updates interfering with others: see Adams, Toomey, and Churchill
(1999).

in binding theory', then those who see such a group and decide
to join in are likely to be members of a fairly closed constituency,
interested in that highly specific topic and not expecting to encounter unrelated topics along the way. Relatively few threads are
likely to be encountered (though one never knows). On the other
hand, if I set up a group called 'Language in the modern world' I
can expect to encounter a huge range of topics, which will generate
a large number of different title threads in the course of time. A
college group called 'Ideas for projects' or 'Reactions to course 300'
is likely to generate even more differentiated reactions. The titles do
far more than identify a particular topic; just as often they express
the intention, attitude, or viewpoint of the writer. So, alongside
specific content titles, which might be anything from 'Aardvarks'
to 'Zarathustra revisited', we find the following (taken from a variety of groups, but the first five from Davis and Brewer):[19]

> gut reaction
> rambling
> Calla's reply
> response to Candace
> Calla's response to Peter
> my project, keep it going
> am I still on this list?
> that's true
> yeah good question
> hasty apology
> quik question
> I agree, Jeff

The analogy with newspaper style is compelling – especially those
which use such headlines as 'We agree, Tony', 'A good question',
'Our response to the colonels', and 'Gotcha'. Headlines which are
idiosyncratic and ludic attract the reader, and make it more likely

---

[19] Davis and Brewer (1997: Appendix D2). The authors also note the occurrence of particular
fads (especially involving language play) in titles – for example, a two-word formulaic
game which some of their students played for a while: *Spud speaks, Sandra responds,
Crawford adds* ... (pp. 66 ff.).

that their accompanying articles will be read. The same point applies to chatgroup messages. With so much competition for readership, the message which has the intriguing title is the one more likely to be picked up and responded to. This is another important difference from the e-mail situation. Both e-mail writers and chatgroup writers look for responses, but whereas the e-mail writer is surprised if no response arrives ('Didn't you get my e-mail?') the chatgroup writer is not unduly disturbed if a message fails to elicit an individual reaction. Chatgroup messages are contributions to an ongoing discussion. The aim is to influence the discussion, to correct a misapprehension, to express agreement, to remind people that you exist, to 'sound off', to 'have your say'. If anyone is minded to reply specifically, it is a bonus. A lack of reply is not taken personally. Even in those cases where a writer asks a specific question of a group ('Does anyone know where I can get...?'), the absence of a reaction probably means only that nobody who read the message knew. There is no sense of personal responsibility here – unlike that which obtains in an e-mail situation, where we will respond with a 'No' to such a question, if we do not know, apologise for our lack of knowledge, and even apologise for the delay in sending the 'No' if we have not replied promptly.

The pressure to maintain a practicable route-map of a discussion means that, even in groups where titles in some groups are prone to idiosyncrasy and ludic treatment, certain formulae do recur in titles, focusing on the content of the discussion. Examples include:

Reply/response/reaction to X [where X is the writer or the topic]
Re: X
To X
Agree with X
Disagree with X
Further to 6.16

This last example, citing a previous message number, arises because this sender was conscious of the screen distance which intervened between his message and the one he was responding to. Here there was a concern to keep the message thread going. Not everyone co-operates, of course. Some senders seem to be so little concerned with the status of their contribution that they may not bother to title their message at all – which therefore appears in such a form as <No title>. But the majority of contributors are more single-minded about their interaction. They want others to read their message. Therefore a clear and unambiguous title is crucial, and one which will ensure that their message is related to the other relevant messages in a thread. This is an important difference from the role of the subject in e-mails. When an e-mail comes in, it will very likely be read, or at least opened, simply because it is there – often with no particular attention being paid to the subject line.[20] The identity of the sender is typically far more relevant than the content; indeed, in most cases the person is known to the receiver, and a personalized, unidirectional message is anticipated. The common observation is 'Ah, so-and-so has replied' or 'There's a message from so-and-so', and not 'Ah, here's an interesting topic' or 'That topic has come up again.' You can avoid using the e-mail subject-line at all, and many people do, or (feeling obliged to put something in, because the software has prompted them) insert something vacuous, such as 'various' or 'message'. This would be totally self-negating in a mailing list, where people on the list will only be motivated to read a message if they feel the topic is of interest to them. And in such situations as classroom conferences, the same pressures obtain. In these cases, the only means senders have of influencing others to read their messages is through their titles.

The existence of personal and interactive elements in titles means that they take on some of the character of a greeting. We would not expect a message titled 'Response to Jeff' to begin 'Dear Jeff' or 'Hi Jeff'. The link has already been made. In any case, the message is not solely to Jeff; it is to the group as a whole. Jeff is simply the hook on which to hang a particular response. Indeed, once a personal name gets into a title, it becomes a theme in its own right: a whole sequence of messages may come to be titled 'Re response to Jeff'. Jeff

---

[20] There are certain exceptions – such as a virus alert in which people are warned to look out for a message with a particular subject line. Also, many e-mail users become adept at filtering out messages which contain distinctive typography (p. 97).

may in due course become a generic term: a message titled 'more on Jeff' does not have anything to do with Jeff as a person, but with the content of the message he sent. The one-to-many nature of the interaction thus makes a formal greeting unlikely.[21] Newcomers to the group, or people renewing contact after an absence, may begin their message with a 'Hello everyone' type of remark, especially if the group is small and closed in membership (as in a school class conference).[22] 'Ordinary' people writing to a personality (e.g. in a group which has been set up to discuss a particular work, with the involvement of the artist or author) often begin with the personality's name. And when personalities respond, they tend to greet their interlocutors by name, dealing with a series of messages all at once (in much the manner of a framed e-mail, p. 118). Teachers in classroom conferences also count as personalities, in this respect. But most writers go straight into the body of their message without any greeting.

A common technique is to introduce a message with an explicit reference to a previous posting, usually in the form of a quotation from it or a paraphrase of it, as in these opening sentences:

(1) We're all democrats at heart? I don't think so.
(2) I never thought I'd hear someone talking about people power, not in 2000.
(3) >I was living in a different universe. [The writer has pasted this sentence from a previous message.] Isn't that the truth!
(4) Animated more, I'd say. [The writer is referring to a previous question: 'Are we animals?']

Lengthy quotation is unusual – indeed, unnecessary, because the previous messages are readily available in full. Little attention is paid to the accuracy of quotation, and quotation marks are unusual. It is the spirit rather than the letter of a message which is seen to be significant, and earlier phrasing can be adapted to suit the new

---

[21] In this situation. An important difference between asynchronous and synchronous groups is that contributors to the latter do acknowledge the group in greetings and farewells. Indeed, it is considered bad form if they do not (pp. 154–5).

[22] 'Hello' sequences, often ludic, were a feature of the classroom sample studied by Gillen and Goddard (2000).

writer, as in the last example above. Even when contributions do not start in this way, the body of the message contains a significant re-use of salient individual lexical items. The term *democrat*, used in (1), resurfaced in several succeeding messages from different participants, until the conversation moved on. Extensive lexical repetition (in words and phrases) was found to be a major feature of the Davis and Brewer student conference, for example, suggesting that a useful way of identifying thematic threads (or topic shifts) in this kind of data will be to trace the use of individual lexical items and their sense relations (synonyms, antonyms, hyponyms, etc.).[23]

From a pragmatic (as opposed to a semantic) point of view, what is interesting about a quotation is that it performs two roles. First, it conveys the illusion of adjacency, and thus makes the interaction more like the real conversational world. Second, it is another way of acknowledging group membership. In some respects, the explicit harking back to previous content performs some of the function of a greeting. Indeed, the strategy is common enough in face-to-face conversation, where we may hear people beginning a conversation by quoting something from their previous communicative encounters. An arrival at Holyhead railway station was met by someone whose opening remark was 'Who's never going to travel on Sundays ever again, then?' – the point being that it was a Sunday, and the person being met had evidently vowed, in those words, never to undergo that experience again. Then there was the following exchange, based on the participants' shared knowledge:

> Colleague [introducing me]: This is David Crystal
> New contact: Ah, Language Death.

The reference was to my narrative not causative role in this topic, I am pleased to say, my book on that subject having recently appeared. In such a circumstance, the quotation acted exactly as a greeting, and I replied with a perfectly ordinary 'Pleased to meet

---

[23] For sense relations in semantics, see Crystal (1997a: 104ff.). Textual links in an introductory statement were a 'prototypical' feature of the corpus studied by Herring (1996b: 88).

you'. In a Stoppardian setting, I can imagine several lines of play dialogue being taken up in this way.

Quotation is not the only way in which chatgroup messages are linked, of course. All kinds of anaphoric cross-reference are also found in opening sentences (p. 113):

> Another good tool is ...
> The last time I tried it ...
> She does a good job ...
> Perhaps I should be clearer ...

And sentence connectivity is present, especially among members who are monitoring the messages so frequently that the interaction verges on the synchronous (see below):

> Or you could just ...
> Except you can't ...
> And it is easier to ...

General feedback or back-channelling reactions are also found as opening sentences – 'Yeah', 'Thanks', 'Wow!', 'Great idea' – as well as discourse features such as 'Well' and 'Umm'. What is surprising, of course, is that sometimes these close-binding links may appear in messages separated by long periods of time. The impression is always of a rapidly moving conversation – until we look at the headers, to find that G wrote his message in April and H wrote her reaction in December.

An interesting pragmatic asymmetry operates in some chatgroups. They may not greet, but they do close. In some classroom situations, virtually all the messages conclude with a farewell of some kind – usually a simple name, but often preceded by a closing formula, such as 'Cheers' or 'Take care', or an expression of affiliation ('All power to the Jeffs of this world'). Although the name of the sender is clear from the header or directory listing, there is also a strong tendency to add a personal signature, sometimes with all the trimmings encountered in e-mails (p. 99). This is less likely in a small group, or in one with closed membership (signatures were not a feature of the Davis and Brewer corpus, for example). Hardly any of the members of those WELL conferences that are publicly available[24] end with a formal closure, though there is the occasional greeting and mid-body naming. On the other hand, in a sample of 200 personal contributions taken from several groups on the LINGUIST list (that is, excluding circulars, conference announcements, calls for papers, etc.) over 90% ended with some sort of farewell, ranging from a casual 'Thanks a lot' to a formal affiliation signature.[25] A great deal of variation in practice evidently exists.

The body of a chatgroup message does, however, display a few typical features. Susan Herring identified a number of functional macrosegments in her data, and concluded that 'participants are aiming at an ideal message schema comprised of three functional moves: an introduction, a contentful message body, and a close'.[26] Within the body, she found three further elements to be typical: a link to an earlier message, an expression of views, and an appeal to other participants. So, a typical message might be:

> Introduction: *Good to see that people are worried about this issue.*
> Body: Link: *Smith thinks that X is the case.*
> Expression of view: *I disagree.*
> Appeal: *Am I alone in this view?*
> Close: *I look forward to hearing more on this.*

This, along with any epistolary conventions of greeting and signature, made a 'balanced communicative unit'.[27]

Also typical of chatgroup messages is their length, which tends to be short. While I have seen contributions, especially to the more in-depth discussions of professional groups, running to over 100 lines – or even reproducing whole articles – the vast majority are very short indeed. A sample of 113 contributions – all the contributions made to three WELL groups (each of which had at least 30 members) – produced an average of 3.5 lines per

---

[24] As of October 2000, there were two of these: Inkwell.vue and Point.vue.

[25] A similar asymmetry between greetings and signatures was found by Herring (1996b: 87): in her discussion groups, only 13% of the messages were preceded by a salutation, whereas 80% were followed by a signature.

[26] Herring (1996b: 90–1).

[27] The reference is to Halliday (1978: 187), who recognizes three functional components within a language's semantic system: *textual* (i.e. links to other text), *ideational* (i.e. language as reflective content), and *interpersonal* (i.e. language as action). In Herring's terms, the introduction to a message is a textual link, the expression of views is ideational, and the closing is interpersonal.

message;[28] 20% of all messages were just 1 or 2 lines. The average number of paragraphs per message was 1.45; 70% were just a single paragraph; the maximum number of paragraphs was 5, and that happened in only 5 messages. Notwithstanding the gaps in real time which separate the messages, the dialogue positively races along, with succinct, punchy contributions. In classroom conferences, the length is naturally greater, as students are making their points in front of their teacher and peers, and the class teacher often responds at length. Even so, in a sample of 50 messages from a group discussion of a novel in a US college, available on the Web, the average message length was only 8.1 lines, and half of the contributions were 6 lines or less. One student who wrote an emotional response of 30 lines (the longest contribution in the sample) ended his posting with an apology for its length.[29]

Short responses are one of the features which give a chatgroup interaction a dynamic, conversational feel. However, the fact that they tend to be fairly consistent in length is actually a difference from face-to-face conversation, which is by no means so balanced in its turn-taking.[30] Everyday conversation is a perpetual competition for 'who gets the floor', which becomes greater as more people become involved. Depending on the interest of a topic, the personality of a speaker, and other such factors, so the turn-taking in a conversation takes on a wholly asymmetrical and unpredictable character. A short comment from A might elicit a lengthy narrative from B; or a question from B directed at A might be interrupted by C. In a common scenario, several people overlap in their speech or talk at once. These factors simply do not arise in asynchronous chatgroups, where interruptions and overlaps are impossible, and nobody can grant anyone else the floor.[31]

---

[28] A line was full-screen width, in this count.

[29] In Davis and Brewer's (1997) conference, lack of familiarity with the technology promoted shortness of message length. The initial space available on the bottom half of the students' screens was limited to some 5–7 lines – the top half showed the message being replied to – and most users stuck to that, until they gained in confidence and began to use the downward scrolling feature.

[30] See Crystal and Davy (1969: ch. 4; 1976).

[31] A degree of floor-granting takes place in those synchronous chatgroups where a moderator intervenes and organizes a queue of speakers. See p. 184.

Another conversation-like feature is the unpredictability of the subject-matter. Although a particular topic motivates a message, there is nothing to stop the writer from introducing a new topic, angle, or allusion into it. Davis and Brewer use an ornithological metaphor to capture the 'flocking' behaviour of their students, as a cluster of writers 'migrate' to a new topic.[32] However, there is nothing in asynchronous chatgroups quite resembling the randomness of the subject-matter in face-to-face conversation.[33] Perhaps it is the sharpness of focus which comes from joining a group, or perhaps it is something to do with the act of typing or the time available to the typist, but the vast majority of messages I have seen do stay surprisingly on-topic. Relevance (p. 49) seems to be a powerful motivation, which all members share. If a contribution strays too far from the subject-matter of a group, a moderator (if there is one) may intervene, or other members may criticize. In Usenet, for example, there is the convention *ob-* [= obligatory] placed in front of a word to show that an attempt is being made to bring a topic back to the point, after it has gone off in various directions (e.g. *obpassports* was used after a discussion about passports had got sidetracked into one on holidays). Contributors are only human, of course, so they do find themselves going off-topic, from time to time, but they usually realize this and often apologize for doing so. One writer deleted (*scribbled*) his message to a group, then immediately sent another message apologizing for having done so and explaining why – his first message had been off-topic, as it had been intended for some other group, and he was sorry for the distraction. Anyone who writes persistently off-topic is likely to be excluded. Moderators are mercifully absent from everyday conversation, and topic-shift is not normally corrected by participants or apologized for. Anyone may say 'That reminds me...' and change the conversation's direction, without feeling self-conscious about it or running the risk of being told to leave the room. Although chatgroup discussion is much less tightly structured by comparison with virtually all other varieties of written language, it rarely

---

[32] Davis and Brewer (1997: 137).
[33] Again, synchronous chatgroups are a different matter: see p. 162.

becomes as unfocused, rambling, and inconsequential as everyday conversation.

A further feature of face-to-face conversation which is found in chatgroups is that the members accommodate to each other.[34] Although they come from many different backgrounds, and write in many different styles, their contributions progressively develop a shared linguistic character – the equivalent of a local dialect or accent. Everyone comes to use certain types of grammatical construction, slang, jargon, or abbreviations. Often the accommodation is short-lived. A particular locution may be taken up as a fad by several members, and be used intensively for a while before it dies away – though it may become part of the group's communal memory, being resurrected from time to time. A typographical error can prompt a train of deviant spellings. A certain competitiveness can exist, especially among smaller groups, with members trying to 'one up' each other, perhaps by taking one writer's pun and coining others on analogy, as in face-to-face examples of 'ping-pong punning'.[35] Davis and Brewer found regular stylistic shifts in their student group: a new device (e.g. a student using a particular feature, such as direct address) would influence others for about five contributions before there was a change.

A sample of messages from any chatgroup is likely to display a similar use of certain linguistic features. The medium privileges the personal and idiosyncratic contribution, and this has immediate linguistic consequences. Davis and Brewer noted several features: the 'overwhelming use of the pronoun *I*'; the frequency with which *it* was used to introduce a personal comment (e.g. *it seems to me*); and the reliance on private verbs (e.g. *think, feel, know*).[36] Herring also identified the importance of these features in her data, under the heading of 'expressing views', and also notes *it seems to me,*

---

[34] For the notion of accommodation, see Giles, Coupland, and Coupland (1991).
[35] See Crystal (1998: ch.1). For an analysis of humour in a Usenet context, see Baym (1995).
[36] Davis and Brewer (1997: 85ff.). Private verbs are those where the activities cannot be publicly observed; they contrast with the public verbs, such as *say* and *tell*: see Quirk, Greenbaum, Leech, and Svartvik (1985: 1181).

among others.[37] A very important feature is the use of rhetorical questions or tag questions both to express a personal attitude and to give extra emphasis to what one has just said. A typical strategy is to make a statement and then query it oneself, as in these examples:

> . . . we just can't afford it. Am I right?
> . . . a machine for every student. Does X live in this world?
> . . . would give everyone a qualification. What has that got to do with it?
> . . . would mean that we would all have jobs. Can we believe this?
> . . . this is just a waste of time, don't you think?

Only occasionally do other members take such questions literally, and respond directly to them.

The language of asynchronous messaging is a curious mixture of informal letter and essay, of spoken monologue and dialogue. Authors search for comparisons:

> Conference discourse in our corpus was neither oral conversation nor, usually, planned and edited exposition. Instead, with its heavy contextualization and its extemporaneous keyboard composition, it was more like a multiparty conversation among strangers who are becoming acquaintances.[38]

At the same time, it lacks some of the most fundamental properties of conversation, such as turn-taking, floor-taking, and adjacency pairing (p. 33). Reading through a conference log, we may get the impression that such behaviours exist, but these are purely an artefact of the corpus. As Davis and Brewer put it:[39]

> There is no real turn taking in electronic conference discourse. Instead, there is an asynchronous exchange of messages about a particular topic. . . . the contact is not with the other students, but with the texts that the students have left behind.

There is moreover an element of tension between the motivation to be spontaneously informal and the nature (and technological

---

[37] Herring (1996b: 89).   [38] Davis and Brewer (1997: 161).
[39] Davis and Brewer (1997: 28).

limitations) of the medium. Experienced chatgroup members, familiar with a group's software, owning sophisticated personal hardware, and with time available to be regular participants, can forget that many aspiring chatgroup participants meet none of these criteria. They may be working with machines that have very limited editing facilities, for example, so that their messages take on a draft-like character, with errors difficult to correct. But everyone has to learn to live with the fact of data persistence, with their messages becoming part of a corpus that cruelly retains all the infelicities which characterize unplanned and unrevised text. Errors or inadequacies of expression last, in principle, for ever. Even if a sender posts a later message correcting a misunderstanding, there is no guarantee that future readers will see it.

This is just one of the cautionary points that relate to this medium. College instructors who ask for feedback from their chatgroup students quickly encounter other problems. Several criticisms of the asynchronous situation are made. The idea of getting messages from a lot of people sounds exciting, at first, but the experience of being flooded with messages on a particular class discussion point can be overwhelming. Thirty or forty might come in at once, and it is not as if each of these messages is going to be interestingly different from the others. There is likely to be a great deal of repetitiveness and banality. Forty people all saying that they 'did' or 'did not' like a chapter in a novel soon ceases to be inspiring. Every teacher knows the boredom that can set in when marking large numbers of essays. In an electronic classroom, the boredom element is distributed to all. As one student put it: 'I don't want to know what *everyone* else in my class thinks *every* week.' The problem, however, is not the classroom, but the medium. The asynchronous chatgroup is a medium that promotes redundancy. Because members do not know what others have said until their messages appear on screen, duplicated subject-matter is inevitable.[40]

On the other hand, the benefits which come from the medium are considerable. In the classroom case, both students and teachers cite

---

[40] This affects synchronous chatgroups too: cf. the 'losing' convention, p. 184.

the opportunity it provides for equal participation. Students who might be reserved in a real-world class, or who find no opportunity to make a contribution there (perhaps because of class sizes or the presence of hyperverbal classmates), now have an equal chance to make their voice heard – and several of those voices *will* have novel and stimulating things to say. Such groups are especially valued by those students with limited or irregular hours – perhaps because they have to work for their living in order to attend college – and for whom communicative flexitime is a godsend. The situation also helps them get to know the other members of their class, especially if the class does not meet often (infrequent real-life encounters increase the motivation for engaging in a chatgroup). But above all, the classroom conference facilitates the exchange of ideas among a population operating at the same educational level – as opposed to interactions with teachers or other experts. And it is this peer-group factor which characterizes asynchronous chatgroups in general. People join a group because they know they are talking to their peers. They are assumed to be equals (whether they are, in real life, or not) and will be judged as such, on the basis of the quality of their messages. Language, accordingly, becomes the primary means of establishing and maintaining group membership and identity.

It seems likely, then, that – once proper descriptive work has been carried out – asynchronous chatgroups will emerge as a distinct variety of language (p. 6). Some writers, conscious that we are dealing with a relatively recent technology, have been uncertain about this. Davis and Brewer, for example, describe their classroom conference as 'a new register in written electronic discourse, more complex than one would at first assume', and at the end of their study cautiously suggest that it is 'apparently an emergent register'.[41] Their caution is chiefly due to the fact that their users – students engaged in a specific task – were involved for only a relatively short period of time, and thus had little opportunity to evolve the kind of communal linguistic conventions that a register would require. Yet the amount of shared linguistic distinctiveness which did emerge

---

[41] Davis and Brewer (1997: 34, 157).

among their students is impressive, and the fact that several of these features are found in other asynchronous group settings is a persuasive argument for the status of this mode of electronic communication as a linguistic variety.

Synchronous groups

In a synchronous group, electronic interactions are taking place in real time. But there are several ways of making this happen. Some systems are designed to facilitate communication between just two users; others among several users. *Unix (or UNIX) Talk* is an early example of the first type.[42] A conversational exchange of text can take place between two people, A and B: when a connection is made, using a normal phone connection between e-addresses, each person's monitor screen is split into an upper half and a lower half. Everything A types is displayed in the upper half of A's screen and the bottom half of B's screen, and vice versa. The words are displayed as they are typed, character by character. Both people can be typing at the same time, with input coming in simultaneously with output. The communication is private, like e-mail; there is no moderator. Related Unix developments include a *Write* facility which allows A to send an *instant message* to someone who is already logged in: B is notified on screen that someone is trying to make contact. There is also a *Ytalk* facility, which enables *Talk* messages to be sent to more than one person.

Internet Relay Chat (*IRC*) is the chief example of the second type.[43] This allows several users to be simultaneously in touch with each other. They connect to one of the IRC servers on a particular network, and join one of the *channels* (or *chat rooms*) held there, each one devoted to a particular topic and prefixed by a hash symbol. Some are identified by country name (e.g. #gb), some by common interests (e.g. #sport, #poetry), some by age group

---

[42] For UNIX, see <http://www.bell-labs.com/history/unix>.
[43] For IRC, see <http://www.irchelp.org>, Rheingold (1993). IRC data is the basis of a study by Werry (1996).

(e.g. #41plus) or the use of a technology (e.g. #mac, #www). A large network, such as EFnet, Undernet, IRCnet, or DALnet, has thousands of channels, and regularly connects tens of thousands of people, each of whom is identified by a session nickname (*nick*). Many medium-size and local networks also exist. Any user can create a new channel and become its *operator* (*op*); operators have total control over their channel, deciding who joins or is excluded (*banned*). Like Talk, it is a text-only medium. Unlike Talk, it uses the whole screen, though most communicative activity takes place at the top. Also unlike Talk, it allows either private communications, between just two people (who may or may not be on the same channel) or public communications (where everyone on your channel can see what you type). It may or may not be moderated.

Both types of synchronous chat depart from the principles underlying face-to-face conversation (see chapter 2). As with asynchronous groups, the notion of turn-taking and its associated concepts (such as interruption) is once again undermined. Even in the one-to-one situation of Unix Talk, it is not always the case that A waits for B to finish typing a message before A sends a reply. Often the two parties are typing simultaneously or in an overlapping mode:

> A sends message 1
> B starts to reply to message 1
> A sends an afterthought to message 1 while B's reply is still coming in
> A reacts to B's reply
> B reacts to A's afterthought
> B makes another point
> etc.

If A's message becomes at all lengthy, B may react to the first part of it, not waiting for A's later points to be made. A may then choose to postpone making those points, and take up what B has said, or choose to ignore B's intervention and carry on with them. A may then look back at B's intervention and react to it, along with any other interventions B may also have made in the interim, in one go. And so the conversation proceeds, in a mixture of sequence, simultaneity, and overlap. This is not something A would have been able to do in face-to-face conversation, where interruptions either succeed or they are crushed, and overlapping speech is minimal. The scenario of two people talking in parallel and at length while retaining full mutual understanding is inconceivable. It should also be remembered that A's messages are in the upper half of the screen and B's below (or vice versa):

> A sends message 1
> A sends an afterthought to message 1 while B's reply is still coming in
> A reacts to B's reply
>
> B starts to reply to message 1
> B reacts to A's afterthought
> B makes another point

It therefore becomes extremely difficult to follow the sequence of events involved in the interaction. Even in a case where each party obediently waits for the other to finish before replying, the split-screen display does not make this clear:

> A sends message 1
> A sends message 2
> A sends message 3
>
> B sends message 1
> B sends message 2
> B sends message 3

There is no way of knowing, from a log of this interaction, whether the messages alternated neatly, or whether two of B's three messages were sent after A's second message, or whether some other sequencing took place.

With multiparty interaction, the situation immediately becomes potentially much more confusing. You enter a chatgroup at a random point, not knowing how many other people are involved, who they are, or what they have been talking about. You might find yourself in the middle of a conversation like this (the nickname of each member appears at the beginning of the line and is shown in angle brackets):

> <Allvine> why on earth not?
> <Roughneck> cos nobody wants to buy any
> <Looopy> I'd buy some anytime
> <Allvine> yeah but we aint all as rich as you
> <Tootle2> you wouldnt
> <Annjewel> Beatles CDs are real cheap at our local store...

You can find out a little about who the participants are (by typing a /whois command),[44] but the only way to find out what is going on is to sit back and watch for a while. 'Make sure you follow the conversation before interrupting someone' says the Chatnet manners file,[45] and other networks offer similar advice. When you do decide to join in, you need to adopt a different conversational strategy and set of expectations about interaction. As with asynchronous groups, even basic conventions, such as greeting and leave-taking, are adapted. There is no symmetry to the exchange, for example. When signing on, the IRC software tells the other users that you have arrived (showing that the message is software-generated by the use of the triple asterisk):

> ***DC has joined channel #linglang

You may greet everyone if you wish, by saying 'Hello everyone' or the like, but few if any of the other members will reply. If everyone did, after all, it would flood the screen. There is an automatic greeting facility, whereby the system immediately says 'Hi all', or suchlike; however, many consider auto-greet to be poor chatgroup etiquette, because it removes the personal element which is a part of the medium. Some IRC help manners pages are quite firm on the point: 'Scripts that automatically greet people are considered rude and not welcomed.'[46] Similarly, when you are about to leave,

---

[44] /whois elicits a small piece of information originally provided by the group member, e.g. a self-description, an e-mail address, a favourite like or dislike, or a favourite quote.
[45] <http://www.chatnet.org/etiquette.htm>.
[46] From the Galaxynet NETiquette page: <http://www.galaxynet.org>.

you may precede your departure with a reason – good etiquette, to avoid any suggestion that you are leaving in a huff – but again, few if any others will acknowledge.[47]

Following your arrival, you may decide to send a comment relating to what Allvine, for example, has just said. However, you do not know if Allvine will react to it, or even see it (he – if it is a he, for the gender of a nick is often unclear, as we shall see – may not be watching the screen at that moment). Others may choose to react to it instead – and more than one person may react at the same time, making the same point independently. Further new arrivals to the group, in the meantime, will react to a point without having seen the earlier points that a member has made, which may already have anticipated their reaction. There is a permanent shifting of the goalposts. Nor can any real-world time-scale be taken for granted: the order in which messages arrive is governed by factors completely outside the control of the participants, such as the speed of their computers and the processing capacities of the service providers. None of this makes for a 'conversation' in the conventional sense of the term.

The point about timing is of especial relevance for synchronous chatgroups. In chapter 2 (p. 31) I discussed the notion of *lag* – the time it takes for a sender's typing to appear on the screens of others. Lag is not a serious issue in asynchronous groups, as computer-mediated delays will not usually be noticed, given the elongated time-frames involved; but in synchronous groups it is critical. If an intervention is delayed too long it becomes irrelevant, as the conversation has moved on. And all lags add a degree of disruption to what is already a fairly complex interaction. Chatgroup lags range from slight delays of a few seconds to the total disappearance of group members. A particularly disturbing situation is the 'Netsplit' which happens in IRC, where one of the servers

---

[47] The variety of group practices must be respected, nonetheless: the IRC group studied by Gillen and Goddard (2000) did make use of greeting and farewell sequences, including ludic variants. In their group, though, the names of the participants who are on-line at any time are shown in a panel on the screen, which perhaps establishes a greater sense of personal presence in the interaction, and thus raises expectations that such sequences will be used.

(e.g. in Australia) loses its connection with the others (e.g. in the UK, Canada, USA, Japan). In this illustration, any Australian participants in the chatgroup would suddenly sign off, without warning, leaving unanswered communications in cyberlimbo. From the point of view of the other members, there is no way of knowing whether someone has left deliberately or not. The situation only clarifies when the link is restored and the other participants emerge online again.

The widespread experience of lag, and the knowledge of its causes, must be one of the factors which influence the overall length of chatgroup messages. People are under pressure to keep their messages short, over and above the natural tendency to save time and effort while sending. IRC makes this very plain in its help manners file:

> Do not 'dump' to a channel or user (send large amounts of unwanted information). This is likely to get you kicked off the channel or killed off from IRC. Dumping causes network 'burps', connections going down because servers cannot handle the large amount of traffic anymore.

The principle applies not just to large amounts of text, but to all chat messages. 'Do not repeat in a channel', says the Galaxynet NETiquette page. And indeed, there are several signs of a marked trend towards succinctness: paragraph-like divisions are extremely rare; contributions tend to be single sentences or sentence-fragments; and word-length is reduced through the use of abbreviations and initialisms. Typical contributions are:

> i feel much better now
> think I'll sit this one out
> where R U
> how it going?
> hi Rococu
> who wanna msg me [= message]
> yeah right
> someone has taken my nick!!!!!

A sample of 100 direct-speech contributions taken from published log data showed an average of 4.23 words per contribution, with

80% of the utterances being 5 words or less.[48] The words themselves are short: nearly 80% of 300-word samples of direct-speech
taken from logs (excluding proper names) were monosyllabic; indeed, only 4% were words longer than 2 syllables. This places synchronous chatgroup utterances a little behind everyday conversation, which is even more monosyllabic, and ahead of journalism,
which is much less so.[49] Certainly, such short utterances help to
promote rapid distribution and enable the conversations to take
on more of a real-time dynamic.

   The fact that messages are typically short, rapidly distributed (lag
permitting), and coming from a variety of sources (any number
of people may be online at once) results in the most distinctive
characteristic of synchronous chatgroup language: its participant
overlap. This example from a study by Susan Herring illustrates
the textual character of overlap in a short interaction between five
participants:[50]

1.	\<ashna\> hi jatt
2.	*** Signoff: puja
3.	\<Dave-G\> kally i was only joking around
4.	\<Jatt\> ashna: hello?
5.	\<kally\> dave-g it was funny
6.	\<ashna\> how are u jatt
7.	\<LUCKMAN\> ssa all
8.	\<Dave-G\> kally you da woman!
9.	\<Jatt\> ashna: do we know eachother?. I'm ok how are you

---

[48] Typical extracts are reproduced in Werry (1996), Bechar-Israeli (1996), and Paolillo
(1999). 'Direct speech' here excludes activity descriptions (e.g. 'P has left channel Z'),
reports of nickname changes ('X is now known as Y'), and other formulaic statements.
In such cases, the sentence length is somewhat longer – 6.08 words per statement (for a
sample of 100). Werry (1996: 53) also found an average of 6 words in his data. Direct-
speech contributions in virtual worlds are longer still (see p. 187), but this is because of
a greater proportion of longer utterances; about a half of the contributions there are still
5 words or less.

[49] The conversational data in Crystal and Davy (1969: ch. 4) showed 84% monosyllabic
and 11% disyllabic. The two journalistic extracts (1969: ch. 7) showed (for the *Daily
Express*) 63% and 25% respectively, with words up to 5 syllables in length, and (for *The
Times*) 62% and 18% respectively, with words up to 7 syllables in length. The main point
of contrast is in trisyllabic words, where *The Times* has four times as many trisyllables as
IRC.

[50] Herring (1999: 5)

10. *** LUCKMAN has left channel #PUNJAB
11. *** LUCKMAN has joined channel #punjab
12. <kally> dave-g good stuff:)
13. <Jatt> kally: so hows school life, life in geneal, love life, family life?
14. <ashna> jatt no we don't know each other, i fine
15. <Jatt> ashna: where r ya from?

Messages from one exchange routinely interrupt another. If we disentangle them, we can see that there are basically two exchanges: Ashna and Jatt are carrying on one conversation:

1. <ashna> hi jatt
4. <Jatt> ashna: hello?
6. <ashna> how are u jatt
9. <Jatt> ashna: do we know eachother?. I'm ok how are you
14. <ashna> jatt no we don't know each other, i fine
15. <Jatt> ashna: where r ya from?

Dave-G and Kally are carrying on another:

3. <Dave-G> kally i was only joking around
5. <kally> dave-g it was funny
8. <Dave-G> kally you da woman!
12. <kally> dave-g good stuff:)

Jatt then starts another conversation with kally:

13. <Jatt> kally: so hows school life, life in geneal, love life, family life?

In addition, Puja and Luckman leave the session (the asterisks show messages produced by the IRC software):

2. *** Signoff: puja
7. <LUCKMAN> ssa all
10. *** LUCKMAN has left channel #PUNJAB
11. *** LUCKMAN has joined channel #punjab

Each exchange is interrupted by messages from the other, destroying any conventional understanding of adjacency pairing (p. 33).

Moreover, this is a fairly simple example, compared with those where a given message may result in multiple replies from participants, or where replies come in after a considerable gap (separations of stimulus and response by as many as fifty messages have been noted). A further confusion arises if a message from one member of the group is repeated. Herring reports, in another of her studies, that over a third of all participants ($N = 117$) who posted messages received no response, which led to some of them sending their message more than once (cf. spamming, p. 53). She concludes: 'Violations of sequential coherence are the rule rather than the exception in CMC [computer-mediated communication].'[51] The effect somewhat resembles a cocktail party in which everyone is talking at once – except that it is worse, because every guest can 'hear' every conversation equally, and every guest needs to keep talking in order to prove to others that they are still involved in the interchange. In a real-life party, if someone is not talking, you can at least see that (s)he is still paying attention. In a chatgroup, silence is ambiguous: it may reflect a deliberate withholding, a temporary inattention, or a physical absence (without signing off). That is one reason why some of its conversations seem so pointless: the contributors are talking to maintain their screen presence, even though they may not in fact have anything to say.

The use of nicknames (*nicks*) is a highly distinctive feature of synchronous chatgroup language. Some use of nicks is also found in asynchronous groups, sometimes replacing, sometimes supplementing the use of a real name; they may also be a feature of e-mail addresses. But nick practice is primarily associated with synchronous groups and the interactions of virtual worlds, where people rarely use their real name. The choice of a nick is a ritual act, demanded by the culture to which the individual aspires to belong, and – as with all naming practices – a matter of great complexity and sensitivity. However, unlike traditional nicknaming, chatgroup practice is influenced by extraneous factors, notably the

---

[51] Herring (1999: 9).

principles introduced by the network.[52] The core principle is that nicknames are not owned, in any permanent sense. When you join a chatgroup, you may choose any nick you wish (within the limitations imposed by the system – see below), but if someone else in the group has already chosen that nick the software will not allow you to use it. Nick clashes are not permitted. The task, then, is to create a nick that is so distinctive that other people will not also hit upon it, and thus enable you to stay with the same nick every time you log-in to a particular group. As with all self-selected names (such as car licence plates and CB handles), owners get attached to them. The nick is their electronic identity: it says something about who they are, and acts as an invitation to others to talk to them. People who feel they belong to a particular group will wish to retain that identity, if only to ensure that they are recognized as being the same person each time they log on.[53] They get upset if they find they cannot use it, for some reason – such as the German character described by Haya Bechar-Israeli, *Bonehead*, who found his name had been taken over by real-world neo-Nazis, and who was thus forced to find an alternative (*cLoNehEAd*).[54] Unless the group is very small, therefore, ordinary names (e.g. *Fred*, *Sheila*) are thus unlikely to appear as nicks, because they stand a greater chance of being duplicated. On the other hand, weird and wonderful nicks are very much the norm, and their study is going to provide onomastics with a fascinating domain in due course.

The devising of a nick is not as easy a task as might at first be thought. Users are restricted to a single string of characters (in the case of IRC, up to nine, with no spaces allowed). Any upper- and lower-case letters can be used, along with numerals, hyphens, and a few other keyboard symbols not already functional within the

---

[52] It is also different in that chatgroup nicks are chosen by the users themselves, and not given to them by others. In real life, also, a person may have several nicknames at once, depending on the social circumstances, whereas only one at a time is allowed on a chatgroup channel.

[53] There have even been software programs written to help people preserve their nicks, e.g. NickServ, a Germany-based nickname registration service. This ran from 1990 to 1994, when problems of maintenance and equitable application forced it to close.

[54] Bechar-Israeli (1996).

software program. The nicks may be words or phrases, sense or nonsense. Because the number of possible real name-like words is limited, people regularly play with the typography or morphology, producing linguistic creations of sometimes virtuoso quality. Bechar-Israeli classified the nicks in one corpus of 260 names in terms of the semantic preferences expressed.[55] Almost half related to characteristics of the self (a person's character, appearance, profession, hobbies, location, age, etc.), with other categories, in preference order, as follows:

Self: <shydude>, <sleepless>, <pilot>, <Dutchguy>, <irish>, <cloudkid>, <oldbear>, <bfiancee> <EKIMslave>
Names to do with technology and the medium: <pentium>, <pcman>
Names to do with flora, fauna, and objects: <froggy>, <tulip>, <BMW>, <cheese>
Names to do with famous characters, real or fictitious: <Godot>, <BeaMeup>, <Elvis>, <Stalin>
Names to do with sex and provocation: <sexpot>, <buttspasm>, <HITLER>, <HAMAS>

Names were also 'empty' (<me>, <so_what>), sonic (<tamtam>, <tototoo>), ludic (<gorf> [= frog]), and typographically playful (<myTboy>, <cLoNehEAd>). It is possible to change one's nick at any time, and some groups do actually play around with their nicks, informing the other members that '<flurb> is now known as <slonk>', and initiating a series of temporary changes at great speed. Everyone in the interaction may change their name in a certain way – for example, adding a numeral to their nick, or adopting the name of an animal – before changing back.

Nicks have a discourse value, also, in that they provide a crucial means of maintaining semantic threads in what is otherwise a potentially incoherent situation. When interactions become complex, members name each other – usually before, sometimes during or

---

[55] Given the idiosyncratic nature of many names, classification is a real problem. Many items are highly ambiguous or uninterpretable.

after the body of their message – as a discourse signal to the intended recipient. This is not necessary when just two or three members are holding the floor on a single topic, or where people are directly addressing a topic rather than an individual, or where a topic is so distinct from the surrounding 'noise' that any contributions to it are unambiguous. But relatively few synchronous chats are so well organized, and the use of nicks in direct address thus becomes an invaluable means of linking sets of messages to each other. They are analogous to the role of gaze and body movement in face-to-face conversation involving several people: in talking to A, B, C, and D, I can single out B as the recipient of a question simply by making eye-contact, and while I am doing that other people can talk to each other without confusion. Naming is unnecessary in such circumstances. It would be most unusual to hear:

> Mary: John, are you going to rehearsal tonight?
> John: Mary, yes I am.
> Mary: John, what time?
> John: Mary, about six.

Initial naming of this kind takes place in spoken interaction only when the parties cannot see each other, such as a telephone conference call, or in radio programmes where an interviewer is dealing with several people at once:

> Frank Smith, what are your views on this?

Even there, it is not so common as in the chatgroup situation.[56]

Unlike asynchronous conversations, topics decay very quickly. It is in fact not at all easy for group members to keep track of a conversation over an extended period of time. Not only do other people's remarks get in the way, some of those remarks actually act as distractions, pulling the conversation in unpredictable directions. The pull may even take the entire interaction well away from the supposed topic of the channel. In one of Herring's studies,

---

[56] Initial clarificatory naming was conventional practice in Werry's (1996) IRC samples.

nearly half of all turns were off-topic.[57] It may only take a slight semantic shift to start a drift towards another topic – such as might be triggered by a playful remark. A comment about *Tony Blair*, for example, elicits a rhyme on *hair*, which leads to a participant wishing he (the participant) had more hair ... and gradually the topic moves in a new direction. In unmoderated channels, it may never get back to where it was. Nor is 'where it was' a clear concept, as there are often several topics being discussed in parallel – not only between different pairs of discussants (as illustrated above), but by the same discussant. P writes on topic X to Q while Q writes on topic Y to P. Sophisticated performances can be found among experienced chatgroup members, with someone keeping several conversations going simultaneously (sometimes even on different channels, using different screen windows).[58] But for most people, following a multidimensional conversation is extremely difficult, with the need to maintain close attention to a rapidly scrolling screen.

Several formal features of synchronous chatgroups make this variety of Netspeak highly distinctive. The nick-initiated lineation, with names in angle brackets, is one such feature. Another is the identification of message-types generated by the software. In IRC, for example, as we have seen, system messages are introduced by the triple-asterisk convention. These formulaic messages give information about such matters as which participants are present, who is joining or leaving a channel, or whether someone is changing identity:

> ***DC has joined channel #suchandsuch
> ***Signoff: DC
> ***DC is now known as CD

---

[57] Herring (1999: 10).
[58] Presumably this often happens, not because people have several equally competing interests, but because they find a single channel insufficiently stimulating. Cynical observers might conclude that such 'multi-taskers' are trying to escape the boredom which must be present on many channels, with most of the participants having nothing to say. It is difficult to avoid the impression that, in some groups, an issue that might give people cause to worry (p. 1) is more to do with poverty of content than of language.

Actions or comments on the part of participants are in this system introduced by a single asterisk:[59] when someone types /*me* followed by an action, the software substitutes the person's nick, and expresses the action as a commentary-like narrative, usually using the 3rd person singular present tense. For example, if I (nick: <DC>) type

> /me is totally confused

it will appear on the communal screen as

> *DC is totally confused

There are several other sources of visual distinctiveness, most of which can be found in other Internet situations. Smileys (p. 36) – or, at least, one or two basic types – are fairly common. Rebus-like abbreviations and colloquial elisions give sentences an unfamiliar look (e.g. *are > r, you > u, and > n*), as does the transcription of emotional noises (e.g. *hehehe, owowowowow*), filled pauses (e.g. *um, er, erm*), and comic-book style interjections (e.g. *ugh, euugh, yikes, yipes*). Christopher Werry found similar features in his French sample: *qqn* ['quelqu'un'], *c* ['c'est'], *t* ['tu'].[60] Also distinctive are the character sequences found in nicks, which combine symbols in unusual ways (e.g. *DC77DC, aLoHA!, TwoHands*). Internal sentence punctuation and final periods are usually missing, but question-marks and exclamation-marks tend to be present. The apostrophe is commonly absent from contracted forms, in a manner reminiscent of George Bernard Shaw. Emotive punctuation is often seen in an exaggerated form (p. 89), such as *hey!!!!!!!* An entire message may consist of just a question-mark, expressive of puzzlement, surprise, or other emotions. Perverse spellings (e.g. *out of > outta, see you > cee ya, seems > seemz*, French *ouais* ['oui' = 'yes']: p. 88) and typographical errors are frequent. Capitalization is regularly ignored, even for *I*, but is scrupulously recognized in nicks. Typical sentences are:

---

[59] This use of the asterisk should not be confused with its linguistic function as a marker of ungrammaticality: p. 100.
[60] Werry (1996: 55).

i dont know why
you da right person
how ya doin
wanna know why
i got enuf
it wuz lotsa lafs

Grammar is chiefly characterized by highly colloquial constructions and non-standard usage, often following patterns known in other dialects or genres. The following examples show the omission of a copular verb (a form of *be* as main verb), an auxiliary verb, non-standard concord between subject and verb, and the substitution of one case form for another:

i fine
me is 31
you feeling better now?

Nonce-formations are common – running words together into a compound (*what a unifreakinversitynerd*), or linking several words by hyphens (*dead-slow-and-stop computer*). Word play is ubiquitous. New jargon emerges – *bamf!*, for example, which some use to mark their final utterance when leaving a live group (the word is from the *X-Men* comic book, where one of the characters makes this noise before teleporting).

Although the use of non-standard formations, jargon, and slang varies from group to group, all synchronous chatgroups rely heavily upon such processes, presumably as a mechanism of affirming group identity. It is notable just how many distinct conventions have grown up in such a short time. Different systems have their individual command-dialects. The use of screen colours varies greatly, with some channels banning coloured text or an excessive use of colour. Certain abbreviations or terms are associated with a particular system or channel. Feedback preferences vary – whether a group says <grins> or abbreviates it to <g>, for example. A particular kind of misspelling may have privileged status in one group, due to its having attracted everyone's attention at some time. A newcomer quickly realizes that everyone in the group spells, say, *computer* as *comptuer*, or as *commuter*, and does the same. Each group has its own history, and a group memory exists (often semi-institutionalized in the FAQs for that group) and is respected. In a multilingual group, the way others code-switch will be an important index of identity.[61] Maintaining the identity of the group is the important thing, especially as there is no other sort of identity to rely upon, given that personal anonymity is the norm.

The anonymity of the medium is one of its most interesting features, in fact, though a discussion of this phenomenon leads us away from linguistics and into social psychology.[62] Yet it is important to note that, when participants are anonymous, the language of the interaction, as presented on screen, is all other group members have to go on. Subconsciously, at least, participants will be paying special attention to everyone's choice of words, nuances of phrasing, and other points of content and presentation. Although the ideal involvement is one of trust, commentators and participants alike are well aware – from years of hoaxes, viruses, name forgeries, and other misbehaviour – that the Internet is a potentially deceptive, dangerous, and fraudulent medium. Who knows what the intentions are of the latest visitor to a chatroom or the new role-player in a fantasy game? They may or may not be genuine new members. Members are very largely dependent on newcomers' choice of language to determine their *bona fides*, and this fact alone is beginning to prompt a great deal of interest and research. For example, because it is very difficult to become quickly adept in a new variety of language, interlopers are likely to stand out. If an adult chose to visit a teenage chatroom, it would be very difficult for the visitor to adopt or maintain the assumed teenage identity, given the many linguistic differences (especially of slang) between the generations. Similarly, a male in a female chatroom (or vice versa) – an extremely common occurrence – would also encounter difficulties in adopting the right persona, given the many points of difference which sociolinguists have noted between male and

---

[61] Paolillo (1999) notes the use of local languages as a marker of in-group identity in regional or immigrant groups, e.g. the use of Hindi on the #india channel. Werry (1996: 56) found a use of *re* borrowed from English by his French IRC community, in the sense 'hello again'.
[62] It is a major theme of Wallace (1999), for example.

female speech.[63] Some studies have already identified salient contrasts in certain Internet situations. One study of an academic newslist showed that males, *inter alia*, sent longer messages, made stronger assertions, engaged in more self-promotion, made more challenges, asked fewer questions, and made fewer apologies. Another study, of material from newsgroups and special interest groups, showed that women used more smileys (p. 36) than men.[64] Not enough research has been done to determine how far differences of this kind will translate into reliable intuitive impressions about gender, age, or other personal characteristics. But there is undoubtedly much of social–psychological–linguistic interest here.

Why chat?

The distinction between asynchronous and synchronous situations is not absolute. Some authors have noted the 'asynchronous quality [of] synchronous computer conferences'.[65] If someone is offline, in a synchronous chatgroup, messages can be left in that person's buffer to be read later. Or again, it is possible to save the text of a real-time business meeting so that it can be replayed later to another group (perhaps in a different timezone) who will comment upon it. These comments are then saved and returned to the first group for further comment; and so the discussion continues.[66] Moreover, several of the issues we have noted as important for

---

[63] For example, Lakoff (1975), Tannen (1990), Coates (1993), and, in the context of chatgroups, Herring (1996b). Some authors think the adoption of a female persona is a common occurrence in MUDs, where the stratagem evidently guarantees extra attention from male players (Bruckman, 1993; Wallace, 1999: ch. 11). Cherny (1999: 65) thinks that the incidence of gender-swapping is low in MUDs, where many players know each other off-line.

[64] Witmer and Katzman (1997), though as only 13.2% of the sample included graphic accents, the results need further support. Unexpectedly, this study found that challenges and flaming were more common in women than in men.

[65] See the references in Cherny (1999: 151).

[66] This procedure is the basis of *PAVE*, the 'PAL Virtual Environment': see Adams, Toomey, and Churchill (1999). People communicate by typing text into a box which appears on the screen as a cartoon balloon. Because long utterances result in large balloons, which can block out the rest of the screen, users develop the habit of breaking their long remarks into smaller segments, using carriage returns – a nice example of how a development in technology influences language structure.

Netspeak apply to both kinds of chatgroup situation: the etiquette files of each domain routinely caution against flaming, harassment, abusive language, spamming, and advertising; they issue the same sort of warnings about privacy and security. And both types of situation raise the same puzzling question: how is it possible for chatgroups to work at all? How can conversations be successful, given the extraordinary disruptions in time-scale and turn-taking which both asynchronous and synchronous types permit? Participants ought to be leaving chatgroups in droves, incapable of handling the confusion and incoherence, and complaining about the waste of time. But they are not. Indeed, the opposite attitude is typical: most people seem perfectly happy to be there.

Two reasons probably account for this. The first raises the question of what people want from chatgroups. If the answer was 'information exchange', pure and simple, then I suspect there would indeed be a problem. Information is the sort of thing that the Web routinely provides (chapter 7). Chatgroups provide something else – a person-to-person interaction that is predominantly social in character. The semantic content and discourse coherence of a chatgroup is likely to be stronger within the asynchronous setting, but even there significant social elements operate. And it would seem that, even in the most contentless and incoherent interactions of the synchronous setting, the social advantages outweigh the semantic disadvantages. The atmosphere, even when a topic is in sharp focus, is predominantly recreational (as the common metaphor of 'surfing' suggests). Language play is routine. Participants frequently provide each other with expressions of rapport. Subjectivity rules: personal opinions and attitudes, often of an extreme kind, dominate, making it virtually impossible to maintain a calm level of discourse for very long. If you are looking for facts, the chatgroup is not the place to find them. But if you are looking for opinions to react to, or want to get one of your own off your chest, it is the ideal place. Trivial remarks, often of a strongly phatic character, permeate interactions.[67] 'Gossip-groups' would

---

[67] For 'phatic communion', see Malinowski (1923: 315).

be a more accurate description for most of what goes on in a chat-group situation. And gossip, as in the real world, is of immense social value.[68]

The second reason follows from this. It would seem that, when the social advantages are so great, people make enormous seman-tic allowances. Several authors make the point that the presence of linguistic confusion and incoherence could be inherently attrac-tive, because the social and personal gains – of participating in an anonymous, dynamic, transient, experimental, unpredictable world – are so great. The situation 'is both dysfunctionally and advantageously incoherent', according to Herring.[69] Participating in the most radical synchronous chatgroups must be like playing in an enormous, never-ending, crazy game, or attending a perpet-ual linguistic party, where you bring your language, not a bottle. The shared linguistic behaviour, precisely because it is so unusual, fosters a new form of community. The point is made by Davis and Brewer:[70]

> The repetitive, rambling, discursive, recursive features of electronic conference writing may actually, then, serve the purpose of creating community among its writers, even though that community is short-lived.

The type of community has been described as 'hyperpersonal' rather than 'interpersonal',[71] and there is some merit in this. Com-munication does seem to transcend the individual exchange, being more focused on the group, or its textual record.

People interpret the chatgroup experience in many ways. Patricia Wallace, for example, has provided a thorough discussion of the im-plications in social psychological terms.[72] From a linguistic point of view, I find chatgroup language fascinating, for two reasons. First, it

---

[68] For the social functions of gossip, see Goodman and Ben Ze'ev (1994). For an evolutionary perspective, see Dunbar (1996).

[69] Herring (1999: 2). In her view, it is 'the availability of a persistent textual record of the conversation [which] renders the interaction cognitively manageable'.

[70] Davis and Brewer (1999: 34).   [71] See Walther (1996).

[72] Wallace (1999). The fact that romantic attachments can arise out of chatgroup interac-tions (being followed up by e-mails, Website photos, and so on) is strong evidence of the social power inherent in the medium.

provides a domain in which we can see written language in its most primitive state. Almost all the written language we read (informal letters aside) has been interfered with in some way before it reaches us – by editors, subeditors, revisers, censors, expurgators, copy-enhancers, and others. Chatgroups are the nearest we are likely to get to seeing writing in its spontaneous, unedited, naked state. Secondly, I see chatgroups as providing evidence of the remarkable linguistic versatility that exists within ordinary people – especially ordinary *young* people (it would seem from the surveys of Internet use). If you had said to me, a few years ago, that it was possible to have a successful conversation while disregarding the standard conventions of turn-taking, logical sequence, time ordering, and the like, I would have been totally dismissive. But the evidence is clear: millions are doing just that. How exactly they are doing it I am still not entirely clear – though I hope this chapter has suggested some guidelines. Plainly, they have learned to use their innate ability to accommodate to new linguistic situations to great effect. They have developed a strong sense of speech community, in attracting people of like mind or interest ready to speak in the same way, and ready to criticize or exclude newcomers who do not accept their group's linguistic norms. They have adapted their Gricean parameters (p. 48), giving them new default values. And they are aware of what they are doing, as is evidenced by their 'metadiscussions' about what counts as acceptable linguistic (and social) behaviour, and their 'metahumour', playing with the group's own linguistic conventions. It is a performance which shows great adaptability and not a little creativity. As David Porter observes:[73]

> As participants adjust to the prevailing conditions of anonymity and to the potentially disconcerting experience of being reduced to a detached voice floating in an amorphous electronic void, they become adept as well at reconstituting the faceless words around them into bodies, histories, lives... Acts of creative reading... can and do stand in for physical presence in these online encounters.

With virtual worlds, the linguistic creativity becomes even greater.

[73] Porter (1996a: xii).

6   *The language of virtual worlds*

E-mails, chatgroups, and the Web have one thing in common: they are all electronic interactions where the subject-matter comprises – apart from the occasional aberration – real things in the real world. This chapter examines a very different scenario: electronic interaction where the subject-matter is totally imaginary. All communication between participants takes place with reference to the characters, events, and environments of a virtual world. These virtual worlds go by various names, but their most common generic designation is with the acronym: MUDs.[1]

The term MUD has had two glosses, over the years. It originally stood for 'Multi-User Dungeon', in the popular mind reflecting the name of the leading role-play fantasy game devised in the 1970s, and still widely played, 'Dungeons and Dragons'™. Since then, hundreds of such D&D games have been published, extending the concept from fantasy worlds to horror, science fiction, history, and other domains. All have the same orientation. They are played by groups of two or more people. One player, usually known as the 'Game Master', defines an imaginary environment in which the players will move and interact, the kinds of obstacles they will encounter, and the kind of powers they have. Each player creates a character and defines its attributes – size, shape, race, clothing, weapons, and so on. Adventures deal with age-old themes, such as a hunt for treasure, a battle between good and evil, or the rescuing of a person in distress. Games of several hours are normal; games lasting for years are known. The MUD games have close

---

[1] MUDs are also written *Muds*, especially in compound names, and several have now lost their acronymic character. Many people use *muds* as a generic term, without even an initial capital. For an introduction to MUD history, terminology, and practice, see Rheingold (1993), Keegan (1997), Cowan (1997), Cherny (1999: 4), Hahn (1999).

similarities, although the extent to which D&D games were a formative influence on early MUD-thought is contentious.[2]

These days, MUD is more commonly glossed as 'Multi-User Dimension', to get away from the 'monster and combat' (or 'hack 'n slash') associations of the earlier label. Although the virtual equivalents of the older games by no means exclude fantasy play literally of a 'dungeon and dragon' kind, most computer-mediated virtual worlds are very different in subject-matter, and some have little or no fantasy element at all. Some MUDs are games, in which points are scored and there are winners and losers; but many foster collaborative role-playing activities of an educational, professional, commercial, or social kind. A group of people may get together for social chat, as they do in a synchronous chatgroup (chapter 5); the difference is that, if they form a MUD, they talk in a world that they have created for themselves, and adopt personae which fit into this world. The notion has been applied within the educational domain, for example, where groups have constructed MUDs in order to engage in a discussion of academic research or college teaching practice, or to facilitate staff–student interaction. An entire teaching situation might be created within a MUD – whether for seven-year-olds or seventeen-year-olds. The virtual world might be a campus, classroom, or business centre; it might be fictitious or an accurate re-creation of a part of the real world. But whether the purpose is combat or conversation, destruction or debate, research or recreation, MUDs have all had one thing in common: they are interactive databases which create vivid environments in which users interact in real time. And they have all been text-based.

The first MUD was devised in 1979–80, designed by British computer scientists Roy Trubshaw and Richard Bartle at the University of Essex, UK. As the MUD idea caught on, variants developed, and with it a proliferation of acronyms. They include:

- LPMUDs, based on the LPC programming language (the LP is from Swedish computer scientist Lars Pensjö, who developed

---

[2] See the discussion of MUD history at, for example,
<http://www.apocalypse.org/pub/u/lpb/muddex/mudline.html>.

the first version in 1989); they attract programmers interested in making modifications to the virtual environment – adding new features and commands, and generally exploring ways of extending the concept. Originally 'hack 'n slash' in character, LPMUDs now include all types of subject-matter.

- DikuMUDs (the name is from the computer science department at Copenhagen University (Datalogisk Institute Københavns Universitet), where this variant was devised in 1990); written in the C programming language, they permit a greater depth of activity and character development within a single game. They are sophisticated adventure MUDs, and an analogy is sometimes drawn with the 'Advanced Dungeons and Dragons' variant of the real-world game.

- TinyMUDs, so-called because the program used to develop them (first devised by US computer scientist Jim Aspnes in 1989) was smaller than those used in previous MUDs, located within a database system and not relying on an independent programming language. They are all 'talker' MUDs, aimed at providing a social environment within which chat is the chief activity (though nonetheless in an imaginary world).

This is just the beginning. Each genre of MUD has evolved its subgenres, most named acronymically, and generally beginning with an M. Some names are based on the real-world meaning of 'mud', and although written in capitals are not acronyms at all: for example, derivatives of TinyMUDS are MUCKs (or TinyMUCKs) and MUSHes (or TinyMUSHes), where the names are simply ludic variants of the connotations of 'mud'. However, it need not take long for a pseudo-acronym to attract interpretations, and MUSH in due course came to be interpreted as 'Multi-User Shared Hallucination'. Illustrative of the range within the MUCK domain are the somewhat opaque DragonMUCKs, FurryMUCKs, and FuroticaMUCKs, as well as the slightly more self-explanatory Lion King MUCK and X-Files MUCK.[3] With MUSEs, MAGEs, and

---

[3] For more detailed MUCK explanations, see
<http://www.oingo.com/topic/12/12689.html>. An explanatory MUSH site is
<http://gargoyle.strange.com/mush/what.shtml>.

MUGs, there seems to be no end to the lexical inventiveness. Using the wildcard convention, the whole MUD domain is sometimes referred to as MU*.

MOOs do not quite fit within the last abbreviation. MOO stands for 'MUD Object Orientated', referring to the programmed objects (roads, furniture, weapons, etc.) which can be created and manipulated within the imaginary world. First devised by US computer scientist Stephen White in 1990, there are now many MOO genres also, such as LambdaMOO (the most frequented social world), MediaMOO, and the population studied by Lynn Cherny, ElseMOO.[4] Those who retain an affection for MUD as a superordinate term usually refer to themselves as MUDders or MUDsters; those who identify with MOOs as a separate genre refer to themselves as MOOers or MOOsters. Many neologisms exist: MOOmen, MOOwomen, MOOcode, MOOtalk, MOOsex, etc. Someone who is seriously unhappy with the way an interaction is going may have a character commit MOOicide. And just as one can 'mud' ('I was mudding all night') so one can 'moo'. According to the surveys to date, most MUD players are young, aged 19–25, often students (using free college access), though the range reaches into the 40s, and could extend as more people learn about the medium.[5] The majority are male – or claim to be.

Because not all MUDs are games, in the usual sense, there is some uncertainty of usage over how to refer to those who actively participate: the term *players* is widespread, but *users* is preferred by some who want to get away from the gaming connotations, especially in MOOs, which are not games in the sense that people score points, win, and lose. In all cases, though, a distinction needs to be made between players and the *characters* they create. A

---

[4] It is an interesting question whether text-based virtual environments will survive, in their present form, once more sophisticated communicative technology becomes available (see ch. 8). If they do not, then the information in this chapter will in due course become of largely historical interest – though not totally so, for some of the linguistic features identified could be retained by future varieties. Apart from this, the current MUD situation also illustrates very well the sort of linguistic thinking that takes place when people adopt a new medium and adapt it to their individual interests.

[5] Cherny (1999) is a rare example, to date, of an in-depth linguistic study of an Internet variety. As such, its influence on my observations in this chapter will be pervasive.

character is an on-screen persona, with its own name and associated description; several alternative characters (*morphs*) may belong to a single player. In graphical systems, where visual representations are displayed as well as text, characters are often called *avatars*. The player can have a presence on-screen too – a distinction which becomes important when someone stops role-playing but continues interacting 'out-of-character' (OOC).[6] The off-screen human controller of a player is usually called, simply, the 'typist'. Occasionally, even this being can be referred to on-screen (e.g. we might see a sentence such as 'Langman's typist is getting impatient'), but this behaviour is not much appreciated. Characters can be anything at all – human, humanoid, robotic, alien, mythological, mechanical, animal, vegetable, mineral ... though MUDs do sometimes have preferences (e.g. some ban alien characters, some insist on humans). A minimal set of attributes establishes a character's name, gender, and race (human, elf, animal, etc.). MUD-veterans may maintain their character names across different MUDs (there is no limit, other than that imposed by time and sanity, to the number of MUDs one may join).[7]

MUDs are usually in the hands of system administrators, similar in function to the moderators of chapter 5. Their names vary (*wizards, programmers, tinkers, gods, arches, imp[lementer]s*) – I shall use *wizard* as the generic term in this chapter – but they are all players with a lot of experience of the site, usually with programming ability. These are the ones who design quests, introduce objects, and generally moderate the way a game is played. Players who gain experience and skill in a MUD are given more power, and may in due course graduate to be wizards. They have considerable technical powers, and may adopt a disciplinary role against players who do not conform to the rules of the MUD, looking out for instances of spamming, flaming, and spoofing (pp. 52ff.), and

---

[6] Conventions are supposed to distinguish in-character and out-of-character remarks (e.g. the latter within double parentheses), but not everyone follows this.

[7] It is difficult to be really fluent in the commands and dialect preferences of several MUDs. Most of the people in Cherny's (1999) survey were regulars on just two or three, while maintaining characters on a few others. Membership of both an adventure MUD and a social MUD is evidently a popular combination.

observing the manners of visitors to the site (*guests*). MUDs are just as conscious of the need for courtesy as are chatgroups; but in a virtual world, where anything can happen, there are more opportunities for bad behaviour. For example, it is bad manners to eavesdrop (by entering a room silently) or to teleport a character to some other location without the player's consent. Several stories of sexual harassment exist.[8] As with chatgroups, anything which increases lag (such as spamming, or the use of unnecessarily complex commands) is considered inappropriate. Persistent offenders may find themselves temporarily prevented from using their character (*newted*) or find that their character is limited in its capabilities or even completely excluded from the MUD (*toaded*). A *gag* command is also available, enabling player P to 'shut up' player Q, making Q's messages invisible just on P's screen; while Q would not be aware of P's action, an accumulation of gag decisions by several players would soon convey the group's antipathy, inculcating in Q a dawning sense of communicative isolation.

As with chatgroups, it is important to appreciate the size of MUD groups. Most are relatively small, but the largest sites (notably LambdaMOO) have thousands of registered characters, and players often in the hundreds, though the number of people simultaneously playing is much less, and there is some indication that numbers may be diminishing. Cherny's ElseMOO had around thirty users connected at any one time, with another hundred or so who connected sporadically.[9] Nonetheless, thirty interlocutors is by no means a small number, and all the linguistic complications involved in managing such situations, discussed in the previous chapter, will be encountered again here. Lag, in particular, is a serious problem in the larger groups; LambdaMOO even introduced a 'lagometer' on screen at one point. Cherny makes the apposite comment: 'Complaining about lag time is the MUD version of complaining about the weather: it affects everyone, and everyone has something to say about it'.[10] The problem of group size worries

[8] See, for example, Dibbell (1997), and other papers in Dery (1997).
[9] Cherny (1999: 15).   [10] Cherny (1999: 262).

everyone, too; some sites now restrict the introduction of new characters because of spiralling population growth, and do not welcome publicity (which is why I do not give site references in this book). At the same time, MUDs can become defunct, once their players get fed up or move elsewhere. And if groups adopt too exclusive an attitude towards their membership, they reduce their long-term prospects of survival.

Although chat is ubiquitous in virtual worlds – even in adventure games – it would be wrong to think of MUDs as a variety of synchronous chatgroups (chapter 5). The reality which exists in a chatgroup situation, such as in Internet Relay Chat, is a function solely of the online participants. Take away the people, and there is nothing left. The reality which constitutes a MUD, by contrast, is independent of the players. Take away the typists, and the virtual world they have created remains, permitting new players to enter and interact at any time, as long as the server is operational. A MUD world is a database of connected functional spaces (*rooms*), described according to the theme of the MUD: they may be in a castle, city, space station, planet, road, field – or, of course, simply simulating the rooms in an ordinary house. The rooms which exist are textually described within the database. When you log-in, the description of where you are would appear on screen, in such a style as the following:[11]

> You are in a square in the middle of the city of Langscape, on planet Zorb. A large fountain is in the centre of the square. To the north there are sounds of a street battle. To the south you can see a series of shops selling the latest weapons. [etc.]

The compass directions relate to the computer screen: 'north' is to the top of the screen. You navigate through the MUD world by text commands which can be general (e.g. 'move west') or specific (e.g. 'go to control centre'). As you proceed, the screen describes where

[11] For other examples, see Iro (1996), Cherny (1999), and several logs at <http://www.apocalypse.org/pub/u/lpb/muddex>. Because of the concern over privacy, I have constructed most of the examples in this chapter myself, using an imaginary MUD, but all examples are closely modelled on the real virtual examples illustrated in the literature.

you are, and what rooms you pass through. When you reach your destination, and enter the room, you are told what objects are in it, and who is present. In this typical sequence, the player controlling the character 'Langman' types the instruction in the first line:

>go to control centre
You walk to the north ladder.
You climb the ladder and enter the outer office.
You cross the office and enter the control room.
You see:
A box of tapes
A tape recorder
A bunch of bananas
A half-eaten copy of the Journal of Linguistics
Doc is here.
Prof is here.

The players in the roles of Doc and Prof would see the following message come up on their screen:

Langman arrives in the control centre from the office.

Langman may 'speak' to the other characters in the room, and can 'hear' what they say. He can have a private conversation with another character in the same room using a *whisper* command. He cannot hear what is going on in other rooms, but he can talk to someone there through a *page* command. Some MUDs also allow a *mutter* command, which all but one specified player sees. (Not everyone likes the exclusionary commands, and some MUDs warn against them.) It is also possible to find out who everyone is by typing an appropriate command; this calls up from the database the self-descriptions provided by the other players. If someone wants to find out who Langman is, therefore, they could type the following instruction and obtain the relevant response:

>look langman
A 7-foot robot who has been programmed to speak all the world's languages. He always wears a yellow hat and coat. He travels the world looking for monolingual people so that he can teach them a second language.

He is charged up and ready for action.
He carries:
A mobile phone
A case containing dictionaries
A set of calling cards

At any given point, you can type a command which will call up an inventory of the possessions a character has. This is important in a game context, where players negotiate all kinds of difficult situations and gain weapons, treasure, skulls, food, or whatever on the way (as well as points for their score). Depending on the type of MUD, players can add new rooms, objects, scenery, and even types of command, so that sites come to display great variation. Typical commands are @*who*, to find another player logged in; @*where* to find a player's location; *look* or *examine* (followed by the name of a room, person, or object) to elicit the relevant description; *get*, *hand*, and *drop* to manipulate objects; *go*, @*join*, or *teleport* to control character movement. There are conventions for speeding up the typing, by abbreviating the commands.

Probably no other domain within the Internet offers such possibilities for creative, idiosyncratic, imaginative expression, and the likelihood that this situation will produce a distinctive linguistic variety is the main reason for handling MUDs separately in this book. Even if they prove to be a passing phase in the history of Internet applications, they provide a fascinating example of the way in which the medium can foster a fresh strand of linguistic creativity. Although some MUDs are virtually identical in their purpose to synchronous chatgroups, the simple fact that they are set in an imaginary world is enough to motivate differences in the kind of language used. The skill involved must not be underestimated: it takes time to become a competent MUD player, and some MUDders hone their skills over months or years (the 'plot' of a MUD is in principle never-ending, capable of being forwarded by someone in some timezone all day everyday). As the medium becomes increasingly 'expert', accordingly, so the linguistic conventions become more institutionalized and sophisticated. In this chapter, I shall not review those features of MUD discourse which are shared with chatgroups in general, but focus on those which make it different. For example, the communicative problems associated with turn-taking are found here as well as in chatgroups; however, in MUDs, there are additional issues arising out of the range of discourse options that the medium provides. I shall illustrate the procedures in a little more detail than in previous chapters, partly because this Internet situation is less well known, and partly because it is difficult to get access to samples of data.

Two chief modes of communication exist: *saying* and *emoting*.[12] Saying is illustrated by the following extract from a hypothetical conversation between Langman, whom I operate, and the other characters in the control room, operated by other players. To make my character speak I might type:

> >say hello

This would appear on everyone else's screen as:

> Langman says 'hello'.

They might then reply to me.

> Prof says, 'good day'.
> Doc says, 'Where the hell have you been?'

If I wanted to single out one or other of the characters, I could have typed a directed command, such as:

> >say prof hello

which would appear on everyone else's screen as:

> Langman [to Prof], 'hello'.

Of course the player operating Doc might then wonder why I had failed to greet him – the reasons doubtless bound up with an earlier stage of the game.

---

[12] There are others, such as 'thinking' – illustrated by the 'thought-bubble' convention in Cherny (1999: 111).

The *emote* (or *pose*) method of communication allows a player to express a character's actions, feelings, reactions, gestures, facial expressions, and so on. Not all MUDs use them, but they are a dominant feature of those that do. They are typically statements with the verb in the 3rd person singular present tense (though other tenses can be found in certain circumstances).[13] For example, the command to my character

> >emote salute

would result in the following appearing on everyone else's screen:

> Langman salutes.

On my own screen, however, the software changes the message into the appropriate person:

> You salute.

Similarly, I might wish to express the following:

I type	*Others see*	*I see*
>look puzzled	Langman looks puzzled.	You look puzzled.
>pick up the journal	Langman picks up the journal.	You pick up the journal.

Some verbs are especially common in the expression of emotes: in her group, Lynn Cherny noted the frequency of *smile, laugh, wave, greet, grin, bow*, and *nod*.[14] All possible social or cognitive contexts are represented – such as *hug, guess, think, glare, poke*, and *kill*. There are plainly parallels with other language varieties which contain ongoing description, such as broadcast commentary and instructional narratives (as in cookery recipes). But emotes do things that commentaries do not do, as illustrated by this sequence:[15]

> Ray can't remember
> Ray could swear he picked it up ...

---

[13] Cherny (1999: 202) illustrates the use of other tenses in expository narrative: *Tom hated that movie.*
[14] Cherny (1999: 117). [15] Cherny (1999: 123).

This moves the convention more in the direction of stream-of-consciousness narrative. And the feedback function of emotes is also important, conveyed not only through conventional verbs ('X agrees/nods/grins') but by idiosyncratic word-formation:

> Largo hehs. ['says heh']
> Jon acks. ['acknowledges']
> Anthony ohboys.
> Pete actuallies.

The practice of word-class conversion has the best of precedents: 'grace me no grace, nor uncle me no uncle' (*Richard II*, II.iii.86), though the use of adverb > verb and interjection > verb processes is admittedly daring.

The narrative style of emotes gives a somewhat literary flavour to the interaction, which sits oddly alongside the often highly colloquial tone of the direct speech. A sequence such as the following – a piece of word-play, a stereotypical literary description, a conversational interjection, and a somewhat contrived adjectival construction – is not at all unusual:

> lynn says, 'leggo my Lego Tom'
> Bunny eyes Ray warily.
> lynn [to Penfold]: hrmph
> Ray puts the annoying electronic bell in the Christmas tree.

This is an extract from the ElseMOO group studied by Cherny.[16] The 'eye warily' locution is an emote, introduced by ElseMOO players, which caught on, becoming a frequent part of its dialectal idiom ('X eyes Y warily', 'X eyes himself warily'). They would use it essentially as a signal of unease, letting others know that there was some hidden implication or irony in what had just been said. The device falls within the genre of literary allusions, such as is found with Tom Swifties and other self-conscious, humorous linguistic play.[17] Other MUDs have developed their own favourite words and

---

[16] Cherny (1999: 143). A wide range of linguistic routines used in ElseMOO is illustrated on her pp. 96ff.
[17] For Tom Swifties, see Crystal (1995: 409).

expressions, which act as identity-markers for the group, though evidence is anecdotal. The use of gender-neutral pronouns, such as the set invented by Michael Spivak – *e, em, eir, eirs, eirself, eirselves* – are scrupulously employed in some groups, and avoided in others. It is simply not clear, in the absence of several studies of the Cherny type, just how generalized a particular usage is. For example, how many MUDs use reduplication for activities (*Ray nodsnods Shelley, Pete waveswaveswaves*)? We do not know.

Emotes are important as a means of foregrounding the structure of the activity-dimension of an interaction – providing the nonlinguistic context for the direct speech. But they add a further complication to the task of maintaining discourse coherence already noted in chapter 5. As with chatgroups, several conversations can take place at once, timing anomalies are pervasive, and multiple threading (p. 137) is normal. But in MUDs, along with the need to follow the threads of direct speech, there is also the need to relate emotes to their appropriate stimulus. It may not be immediately clear, in the following example, whether Techo's laugh is directed at Prof or Doc. By the end of the sequence, the potential for ambiguity has grown, making it necessary for Doc to spell out who his utterance is aimed at.

> Langman says, 'I've given the tapes to Prof'
> Prof blinks.
> Doc waves at Techo.
> Prof says, 'I didn't get them'
> Prof says, 'where did you put them?'
> Techo laughs.
> Techo says, 'sorry I'm late'
> Langman says, 'in the fridge'
> Prof looks horrified.
> Doc says 'it's the best place'
> Prof grins.
> Doc [to Techo]: don't do it again.

To alleviate turn-taking problems, some MUDs (as with chatgroups) have evolved discourse stratagems – such as a moderator-controlled queue, reminders about the topic, and recognized signals expressing a desire to speak or yield the floor (e.g. handraising, or saying *done* when finished). Players themselves devise co-operative conventions. They tend not to introduce multiple topics within a single message (unlike e-mails). Because they know that the size of a message is entirely determined by the player (interruptions not being possible and feedback not visible until a message is sent: p. 30), they often break their message down into shorter utterances, such as

> Langman finds the situation bizarre.
> Langman has never seen anything like it.
> Langman believes Doc should apologize immediately.
> etc.

or

> Langman says, 'The situation is bizarre.'
> Langman says, 'I've never seen anything like it.'
> Langman says, 'Doc should apologize immediately.'

There is always a risk that another player will insert a message in between these items, of course. Further conventions therefore may be used to signal to others that a longer message is forthcoming, and a player wishes to hold the floor, such as introducing a remark with *well*. If Langman had started

> Langman says, 'Well . . .'

everyone would know that a monologue was in his mind. Another example of a discourse convention is the 'losing' routine Cherny encountered in ElseMOO.[18] This arises when two players both respond to a particular point in the same way. P's response arrives on screen while Q is still typing hers. Q sees that her response is no longer needed, so she does not bother to finish it off, terminating it with 'loses'. She sends the message to the group nonetheless, perhaps automatically, perhaps to let others know that she was

---

[18] Cherny (1999: 98ff.).

also on the ball. An example transferred to the Langscape MUD
would be:

> Langman says, 'what was the name of that book Chomsky wrote
> in 65?'
> Prof says, 'Aspects of the theory of syntax'
> Doc says, 'Aspects of loses'

An analogous behaviour to 'losing' turns up in face-to-face conversation, too, when two people speak at once, and one yields the
floor to the other (*Sorry – you go ahead*).

In the body of a MUD message, a very similar range of linguistic
forms and constructions will be found to those already encountered in chatgroups and other informal Netspeak situations – for
example, players use the usual range of contracted forms (*gonna,
dunno, wanna, usta* ['used to'], *sorta*), abbreviations (*BBL, BRB,
LOL*, etc.: p. 84), and formulaic sound effects (*aieee, mmmm,
arrgh*). But when we step back to look at MUD messages as a
sequence, there are several differences, especially in those MUDs
which make use of emotes. The constant switching between saying and emoting produces one of the most distinctive linguistic
features of MUD style: person shift. There is a perpetual alter-
ation between 1st and 2nd person in direct-address utterances
and 3rd person in the commentary-like emoting, as this example
suggests:

> Langman says, 'I'm sorry'.
> Doc looks at Langman suspiciously.
> Prof says, 'Never mind, there's plenty of time.'
> Doc says, 'Well, five minutes.'
> Prof grins.
> Langman drops the journal.
> Langman looks suitably ashamed of himself.

The use of a 2nd person pronoun in an emote would introduce
ambiguity, and tends to be avoided. If a screen said 'Doc looks at
you suspiciously', players (there may be many in the room) would
not be sure which of them was the intended recipient.

A similar juxtaposition of styles occurs when computer-generated messages are added to the mix of direct-speech utterances and emotes. The latter two, despite their differences, are united by a generally colloquial tone and a readiness to deviate from standard English norms; the computer-generated items are typically in a fairly formal standard English, in terms of spelling, punctuation, capitalization, and construction. The influence of standard English is everywhere present, in fact, notwithstanding the regular efforts to depart from it. Even in direct-speech contexts, MUD players can display a strong sense of standards of communication. Indeed, throughout the virtual worlds situation, as in chatgroups, it is never a matter of 'anything goes'. Taboos are strongly present, and players are sensitive to them. Co-operative linguistic performance is a *sine qua non* of a new player being made welcome. If someone's utterance is wildly inaccurate in typing or spelling, it will be criticized by other players, or even by the player eirself, as in these comments: *I just lost my fingers, I'm a lousey* [*sic*] *typist.*

The overriding impression of MUD language is of a mixture of styles – which is hardly surprising, given the multiplicity of functions they have evolved to meet (from adventure game to exploratory programming to serious discussion to insult forum to gossipy chat[19]) – and their at times explicit concern to evolve unique identities. Preferences vary over the size of the group: some MUDs prefer many players, cultivating the atmosphere of a party; others want the size to be small, finding that parties contain too much noise (spam). Some groups cope with the problem of multiple players by fostering subgroups – a set of players go off into another room, or whisper to each other a lot. Others find such practices anti-social. The style a group uses also depends greatly on the number of participants trying to speak at once. Cherny found that if more than six speakers were talking together within one minute, the number

---

[19] 'ElseMOO is a community run largely by gossip' (Cherny, 1999: 286). However, this is not like face-to-face gossip, for the texts can be reviewed and quoted. The slanging matches sometimes encountered are reminiscent of the verbal duelling noted in face-to-face contexts: Crystal (1997a: 60–3); see also p. 55 above.

of words per minute dropped.[20] The players would use more utterances per minute, but put fewer words into them. Doubtless this is due, as Cherny suggests, to the fact that people have to read other players' messages while they are typing their own, and the more they have to read, think about, and react to, the less time they have themselves to write. Moreover, when a lot of players are sending short messages simultaneously, the screen is scrolling very rapidly. In passing, it seems to me that those players who are trying to study or carry on some kind of job while joining in a MUD must have a tough time – though I am impressed by Cherny's report of a comment, in relation to interactions on TinyMUD, that 'it is possible to do calculus homework and have tinysex at the same time, if you type quickly.'[21]

MUDs also vary greatly with respect to the economy of expression associated with Netspeak interaction. Some groups evolve a succinct pattern of interaction, their utterances taking up only the left-hand side of the screen, with relatively few whole-screen lines: a 100-utterance sample from the 'Gloria' log,[22] excluding the 'X says' formula, produced an average of only 4.75 words per line, with two-thirds of the messages less than 5 words – comparable to the short lengths found in synchronous chatgroups (p. 156). On the other hand, two other samples from the same site showed a much fuller, more discursive set of direct-speech utterances: 'Black Rose' with an average of 8.7 words per utterance, and 'Classic Fiasco' with an average of 7.68 words, both of them displaying several sentence sequences over 20 words in length.[23] Indirect speech (emotes) were also an important feature of these two samples (not so with 'Gloria', where no emotes were used), and these showed a similar

---

[20] Cherny (1999: 165ff.). In her material, it was very unusual to find seven speakers within a single minute of data.

[21] Cherny (1999: 36).

[22] <http://www.apocalypse.org/pub/u/lpb/muddex/gloria-log.txt>.

[23] <http://www.apocalypse.org/pub/u/lpb/muddex/black-rose.txt> and <http://www.apocalypse.org/pub/u/lpb/muddex/classic-fiasco.html>. Cherny (1999: 155) found that most messages in her ElseMOO data were 5–13 words in length. Although my samples were much shorter, their range was not quite the same, with the MUD referred to at fn. 22 having a bias towards shorter messages and the others a more even spread.

range, from the succinct (*Daydreamer smiles*) to the extended (*Zed goes off to @recycle his one room in Classic in token protest. He didn't used to have any objection to the management there.*). The use of more than one sentence in the last example is noteworthy, illustrating just how relaxed the emote construction can become. Indeed, looseness of construction is common, as speakers lose control of their point of view. In the following example, from 'Classic Fiasco', the player switches from 3rd person to 1st person in the same message:

> Mizue points out that the people on two sides of the
> Bruce-bashing are doing things which affect others, too. Maybe
> you aren't _obliged_ to keep your stuff around, but I'd suggest it's at
> least impolite to just zap it to satisfy an opposition to Bruce4 when
> the users of the Mud are also affected.

Probably the longer the message, the more serious the subject-matter, and the more emotionally involved the player, the less care and attention will be paid to maintaining the expressive conventions. These factors of course vary greatly between and within MUDs.

There are some signs of a general concern over economy. For example, function words are frequently omitted – prepositions (*Jon waves Sandy*), copulas (*Mike happy*), auxiliary verbs (*Rick getting there*), and sometimes function-word sequences, giving the utterance a pidgin-like character (*Penfold bad mood*). There is more to deletion than simply achieving a faster typing speed, however. Omissions of this kind are probably better viewed as dialect features which have grown up as the result of the intense pressure to accommodate between group members (p. 147). Economy of typing is not the whole story, as is easily illustrated from the structure of emotes, which often use quite complex expression, and from such examples as *onna* ['on a'] and *atta* ['at a'], which actually use an extra letter keystroke. On the other hand, anything which does speed up typing is going to be appreciated – if only to reduce the risk of repetitive strain injury.[24] An example is the *s/* convention

---

[24] An interesting development is the use by some players of what has been called 'Carpal Tunnel Syndrome Feature Objects' – shorthand verbs which replace very common but lengthy expressions, to cut down on typing.

(cf. p. 90) for correcting some kinds of mistyping, which takes the form: *s/oldstring/newstring*. For example:

> Langman: you should have given me a week's notice
> Langman: s/week/month

This says: 'replace *week* in the previous utterance by *month*' – thereby avoiding the bother of typing the whole sentence out again. Other players can intervene. If Prof felt that even a month was not enough, he might add:

> Prof: s/month/year

This convention is by no means universally used, however, requiring as it does a certain amount of programming awareness.

Variability in usage between MUDs partly reflects synchronic dialect differences among groups that are extremely identity conscious to the point of exclusiveness. Each group will have its favourite jargon, its ritualized utterances, and its idiosyncratic commands. The use or non-use of emotes is one major dialect boundary – what I suppose we could call an *isocybe*.[25] The range and frequency of smileys is another. But the variation also reflects language change. Continual reference is made in the ElseMOO dialogues to 'how things were' – to the linguistic history of the group, to outdated usage, to the origins of its jargon, to ancient jokes and stories, and so on – and linguistic metadiscussion seems to be commonplace in computer-mediated chat situations. It is in fact a perfectly normal manoeuvre, especially when real content is lacking, for a group to look in on itself, and start talking about how it talks. And in listening to these histories, a recurring theme is the extent to which MUDs have split away from other MUDs, adopting new linguistic conventions in the process.[26]

The idiosyncratic linguistic direction of a MUD is often most visible in its predilection for language play. All groups play, but some play more than others and some play with particular linguistic

<hr/>

[25] For isoglosses, and associated *iso-* terminology, see Crystal (1997b: 204–5).
[26] For a range of political, social, personal, and other reasons. See the discussion on MUD community in Cherny (1999: ch. 6) and the papers in Porter (1996a).

features more than others – using unusual ASCII symbols, for example, or comic smiley sequences. Whatever the rules a particular MUD has devised, they are there to be bent and broken. MUDs like ElseMOO, which depend heavily on emotes, will start playing with them – Cherny found several examples of byplay with emotes, and also of what she called 'null-emotes',[27] in which a character deliberately breaks the rules of the discourse:

> Lenny says, 'what's weird?'
> Tom

(In other words, Tom is weird.) This is somewhat like the deviant 'knock-knock' joke:

> Knock-knock.
> Who's there?
> Doctor.
> Doctor Who?
> Oh, you guessed.

As with all fashions in joking behaviour, different MUDs can be extremely critical of what they consider the puerility of other groups' play.

An evolving world

MUDs operate in a curious, Alice-like world, where anything can happen. Two players may find themselves doing logically impossible things. Player P might decide to pick up a piece of chocolate and eat it, and tells everyone she has done so; simultaneously, player Q decides to pick up the same piece of chocolate and eat it, and tells everyone he has done so. People can be killed and become alive again within a turn or two. Objects can change size, shape, and colour. Time-travel and teleporting are normal. With incompatibility a possibility, the associated language begins to be stretched in ways

---

[27] Cherny (1999: 104ff.).

that conventional truth-descriptions cannot manage, giving validity to utterances which would be of questionable or unacceptable status in real-world language.[28] It is a world where, indeed, colourless green ideas can exist, and sleep furiously. The use of role-play further distances MUD interactions from reality. Anonymity allows players to introduce all kinds of exaggerations and deceptions (p. 50).

Perhaps as virtual worlds become less textual and more graphic, they will become more like real life, thereby imposing greater constraints upon the language used. A textual medium can cope unconcernedly with 'colourless green'; a graphic medium cannot. It is therefore important to note that, as with other Netspeak situations, MUDs have begun to evolve a multimedia dimension. Asynchronous interaction and e-mailing already exists in some sites, with messages stored in the database. Mailing lists are often used for such purposes as circulating general information, carrying out petitions, and organizing ballots. The new options are welcomed by some, and opposed by others: asynchronous messaging, for example, is a way of giving more players a greater chance to be involved in the group; however, for those for whom the MUD experience is real-time only, a matter of culture rather than technology, such extensions can be viewed as heretical.

The language of virtual worlds, as of chatgroups in general, is difficult to study, as was informal face-to-face conversation in the early days of linguistic research. Many MUDs do not bother to save their interactions (this is one reason why researching the history of the medium is not easy), and when they do, they can easily be edited. Some of the logs I found, in researching this chapter, had been sanitized in various ways, with presumably sensitive information deleted. Then, once a reliable sample has been obtained, the important question of privacy needs to be considered. Such issues have long been satisfactorily addressed in the large linguistic

---

[28] See Cherny (1999: 220ff.) for a discussion of emoting expressions with reference to tense, aspect, and related considerations.

surveys of recent decades; every major corpus now contains a significant amount of conversational data, and appropriate measures to protect anonymity are these days routine.[29] The study of Netspeak conversations, however, is a long way from this stage, with participants sensitive about the 'ownership' of their utterances, and researchers anguishing over whether such sensitivities should be respected or not. Cherny, who has anguished more than most, points out that the players themselves are uncertain about the status of their situation:[30]

> Fully understanding MUD culture requires understanding the ambivalence of MUDders toward their texts, which remain poised between the transience of speech and the persistence of documents.

The core of the matter seems to be whether such texts are public data or not. On the one hand, it can be argued that, simply by putting your words on a screen which can be accessed by an indefinite number of people you do not know, you have effectively made a public statement, which can be used, with appropriate acknowledgement, in the same way as other public statements (such as newspaper articles) are used. On this view, within the usual conventions of 'fair quotation', I may use extracts from these conversations without first requesting permission. On the other hand, because MUD players see themselves as belonging to virtual communities, interacting with players (or, at least, their characters) who they sometimes do get to know well, and dealing with topics which are at times intimate in nature, there is a widespread feeling that their utterances are private, and should be respected. On this view, I should ask permission of all participants before quoting.

Surveys of linguistic usage have long used both procedures. Because some circumstances are so public, and involve so many people, it is impossible to control a permissions process focused on individuals, and an institutional permission must suffice. I recall, back in the 1960s, a discussion on the Survey of English Usage about

---

[29] The state of the art in corpus linguistics is well illustrated in Aijmer and Altenberg (1991).
[30] Cherny (1999: 293).

who would have to be approached, if it were found necessary to obtain permission from the 'participants' to use a piece of broadcast
cricket commentary. It transpired that, not only would one have to
ask permission of the commentators, but also of the programme
producer, the head of department to which the producer belonged,
every individual cricketer named in the commentary, plus anyone
else incidentally alluded to, including the estate of any deceased
person mentioned! A simple agreement with the BBC, taking into
account the limited purposes of the linguistic description, was the
sensible outcome. On the other hand, privately recorded conversations between three or four people, such as those Derek Davy
and I recorded for *Advanced conversational English*,[31] did require
personal permission, along with appropriate measures to safeguard
anonymity (such as replacing all proper names by phonologically
equivalent forms).

The MUD situation sits uneasily between these two procedures.
This is not because of the uncertain status of the texts as speech or
writing – for exactly the same considerations apply in the written
medium (e.g. in relation to using a transcript of informal letter-
writing). Nor is it anything to do with the intimacy of the subject-
matter: a distinction must be drawn between personal and private
data. Private data may be impersonal, and personal data may be
totally public (as in tombstone inscriptions).[32] Rather it is to do
with the typist/player/character distinction, and whether what we
are dealing with here is fact or fiction, given the anonymity and
virtuality of the whole situation. I remember Anthony Burgess once
being questioned after a lecture, when someone attacked him for
something 'he had said' in one of his novels: Burgess replied, 'I
didn't say that; my character said that.' It is the same here: if I David
Crystal join a MUD as elfonaut 'Davidia', am I responsible for the
utterances of my character, and have I any grounds for objecting
if someone quotes those utterances without my permission? If a
linguist were to approach Davidia later, either on the MUD (as

---

[31] Crystal and Davy (1976).
[32] The point is made by Paccagnella (1997: 7) in his discussion of studies, such as ProjectH,
which have analysed cybertexts without permission (though shielding identities).

Cherny did with her fellow-players) or via e-mail, and ask this character for permission to quote its utterances, and it said no, could the mere typist David Crystal later complain if someone made such a quotation? Ethnographers are very familiar with such issues, which go well beyond language, and Cherny discusses them at length in her final chapter; but the recency of the medium, and the many different attitudes between and within groups, means that the issue is by no means settled. This is why, out of a general respect for the emerging nature of linguistic cyberspace, I have invented my own characters in this chapter, and not used online logs (many of which are now a decade old) for my longer or extended illustrations.

MUD data is not quite as solid a basis for the kind of generalization about linguistic distinctiveness that it has been possible to make in relation to other Netspeak situations. My impression is that a linguistic variety has developed here, involving remarkable ingenuity, but that its defining characteristics are obscured by the existence of a large amount of individual difference. Until more material is made uncontroversially public, it will be difficult to resolve the matter. And as some commentators are already wondering about the possible demise of text-based virtual environments, given the more powerful communicative options being made available by new technology (see chapter 8), maybe the matter never will be resolved, and the subject-matter of this chapter will become an intriguing historical episode in Internet evolution, showing what can happen linguistically as people adapt a new medium to meet their interests and needs. A rather different situation obtains in the next chapter, where we encounter a domain where the public status of the data is not in doubt, where there is hardly a shortage of illustrative material, and where the future of the phenomenon is assured: the World Wide Web.

7   *The language of the Web*

'The vision I have for the Web is about anything being potentially connected with anything.' This observation by the Web's inventor, Tim Berners-Lee, on the first page of his biographical account, *Weaving the Web* (1999), provides a characterization of this element of the Internet which truly strains the notion of 'situation' and the accompanying concept of a 'variety' of Internet language. After all, language, and any language, in its entirety, is part of this 'anything'. The Web in effect holds a mirror up to the graphic dimension of our linguistic nature. A significant amount of human visual linguistic life is already there, as well as a proportion of our vocal life.[1] So can it be given a coherent linguistic identity?

'Graphic' here refers to all aspects of written (as opposed to spoken) language, including typewritten, handwritten (including calligraphic), and printed text. It includes much more than the direct visual impression of a piece of text, as presented in a particular typography and graphic design on the screen; it also includes all those features which enter into a language's orthographic system (chiefly its spelling, punctuation, and use of capital letters) as well as the distinctive features of grammar and vocabulary which identify a typically 'written' as opposed to a 'spoken' medium of communication. Most Web text will inevitably be printed, given the technology generally in use. Typewritten text (in the sense of text produced by a typewriter) is hardly relevant, belonging as it does to a pre-electronic age, though of course it can be simulated, and

---

[1] Anything that can exist as a computer file can be made available as a Web document – text, graphics, sound, video, etc. There is no theoretical limit to the size of the Web, and new sites are being added to it so rapidly that no reliable statistics are available; but growth in the late 1990s was c.40% a year, with the number of pages rapidly approaching a billion. See the review in Lawrence and Giles (1999).

many of the features of typing style have had an influence on the word-processing age. Handwritten text has only a limited presence, being available only through the use of specially designed packages, and is of little practical value to most Internet users. But printing exists in a proliferation of forms – currently more limited than traditional paper printing in its use of typefaces, but immensely more varied in its communicative options through the availability of such dimensions as colour, movement, and animation. And it is here that even a tiny exposure to the Web demonstrates its remarkable linguistic range. Anything that has been written can, in principle, appear on the Web; and a significant proportion of it has already done so, in the form of digital libraries, electronic text archives, and data services.[2]

So, a few minutes Web browsing will bring to light every conceivable facet of our graphic linguistic existence. There will be large quantities of *interrupted linear* text – that is, text which follows the unidimensional flow of speech, but interrupted by conventions which aid intelligibility – chiefly the use of spaces between words and the division of a text into lines and screens.[3] This is the normal way of using written language, and it dominates the Web as it does any other graphic medium. But there will also be large quantities of *non-linear* text – that is, text which can be read in a multidimensional way. In non-linear viewing, the lines of a text are not read in a fixed sequence; the eye moves about the page in a manner dictated only by the user's interest and the designer's skill, with some parts of the page being the focus of attention and other parts not being read at all. A typical example is a page advertising a wide range of products at different prices. On the Web, many pages have areas allocated to particular kinds of information and designed (through the use of colour, flashing, movement, and other devices) to

---

[2] The review in Condron (2000a) includes several major resources, such as the Arts and Humanities Data Service (<http://ahds.ac.uk>), the Oxford Text Archive (<http://ota.ahds.ac.uk>), and the Electronic Text Center (<http://etext.lib.virginia.edu>). Online catalogues, such as those of The British Library and The Library of Congress, are also important gateways to resources.

[3] The dimensions of graphic expression used here are presented in Crystal (1997a: 185ff.), who is following Twyman (1982).

attract the attention and disturb any process of predictable reading through the screen in a conventional way. On a typical sales page, a dozen locations compete for our attention (search, help, shopping basket, home page, etc.). The whole concept of hypertext linking (see below) is perhaps the most fundamental challenge to linear viewing.

But there are yet other kinds of graphic organization. The Web displays many kinds of *lists*, for example – sequences of pieces of information, ordered according to some principle, which have a clear starting point and a finishing point – such as items in a catalogue, restaurant menus, filmographies, and discographies. As the whole basis of the linguistic organization of a search-engine response to an inquiry is to provide a series of hits in the form of a list, it would seem that list organization is intrinsic to the structure of the Web. *Matrices* are also very much in evidence – arrangements of linguistic, numerical, or other information in rows and columns, designed to be scanned vertically and horizontally. They will be found in all kinds of technical publications as well as in more everyday contexts such as sites dealing with sports records or personal sporting achievements. And there are *branching* structures, such as are well-known in family tree diagrams, widely used whenever two or more alternatives need to be clearly identified or when the history of a set of related alternatives needs to be displayed. In an electronic context, of course, the whole of the branching structure may not be visible on a single screen, the different paths through a tree emerging only when users click on relevant 'hot' spots on the screen.

The Web is graphically more eclectic than any domain of written language in the real world. And the same eclecticism can be seen if we look at the purely linguistic dimensions of written expression (p. 7) – the use of spelling, grammar, vocabulary, and other properties of the discourse (the ways that information is organized globally within texts, so that it displays coherence, logical progression, relevance, and so on). Whatever the variety of written language we have encountered in the paper-based world, its linguistic features have their electronic equivalent on the Web. Among the main varieties of written expression are legal, religious, journalistic, literary, and scientific texts. These are all widely present in their many sub-varieties, or genres. Under the heading of religion, for instance, we can find a wide range of liturgical forms, rituals, prayers, sacred texts, preaching, doctrinal statements, and private affirmations of belief. Each of these genres has its distinctive linguistic character, and all of this stylistic variation will be found on the Web. If we visit a Web site,[4] such as the British Library or the Library of Congress, and call up their catalogues, what we find is exactly the same kind of language as we would if we were to visit these locations in London or Washington, even down to the use of different conventions of spelling and punctuation. The range of the Web extends from the huge database to the individual self-published 'home page', and presents contributions from every kind of designer and stylist, from the most professional to the linguistically and graphically least gifted. It thus defies stylistic generalization. All of this is obvious, and yet in its very obviousness there is an important point to be made: in its linguistic character, seen through its linked pages, the Web is an analogue of the written language that is already 'out there' in the paper-based world. For the most part, what we see on Web pages is a familiar linguistic world. If we are looking for Internet distinctiveness, novelty, and idiosyncrasy – or wishing to find fuel for a theory of impending linguistic doom (p. 1) – we are not likely to find it here.

But distinctiveness there is. If the Web holds a mirror up to our linguistic nature, it is a mirror that both distorts and enhances, providing new constraints and opportunities. It constrains, first of all, in that we see language displayed within the physical limitations of a monitor screen, and subjected to a user-controlled movement (*scrolling*) – chiefly vertical, sometimes horizontal – that has no real precedent (though the rolled documents of ancient and mediaeval

---

[4] A *Web site* is an individual computer holding documents capable of being transferred to and presented by browsers, using one of the standard formats (usually HTML or XML). Web sites are identified by a unique address, or URL (*Uniform Resource Locator*), with different pages of data at the site distinguished by means of labels separated by forward slashes.

times must have presented similar difficulties). Scrolling down is bound to interfere with our ability to perceive, attend to, assimilate, and remember text. Scrolling sideways is even worse: a browser that does not offer a word-wrap facility may present line lengths of 150 characters or more, with reading continuity very difficult to maintain between successive lines.[5] Similarly, it is common to experience difficulty when we encounter screens filled with unbroken text in a single typeface, or screens where the information is typographically complex or fragmented, forbidding easy assimilation of the content. And any author who has tried to put text from a previously published book on the Web knows that it does not translate onto the screen without fresh thought being given to layout and design.[6] Research is needed to establish what the chief factors are, as we transfer our psycholinguistic ability from a paper to an electronic medium. For not everything is easily transferrable, and alternative means need to be devised to convey the contrasts that were expressed through the traditional medium of print. For example, the range of typefaces we are likely to find on the Web is only a tiny proportion of the tens of thousands available in the real world. Although there is no limit in principle, and many typographically innovative sites exist, the general practice is at times boringly uniform, with unknown numbers of Web newcomers believing that electronic life is visible only through Times New Roman spectacles. As Roger Pring puts it, arguing for keeping typographic options open:[7]

> Can you imagine a world with only one typeface to serve as the vehicle for all communication. How content would you be to see the same face on your supermarket loyalty card as on a wedding invitation? . . . The way computers work makes it easy to use the same group of faces over and over.

Many users do take the easy option, with the result that innumerable sites present their wares to the reader with the same bland, monochrome look.

---

[5] See the examples in Pring (1999: 20).
[6] The principles are now the focus of several books and conferences: see Pring (1999).
[7] Pring (1999: 176).

The size of the screen has also exercised a major influence on the kind of language used, regardless of the subject-matter. The point is made explicit in manuals which deal with the style of computer-mediated communication. As we have already seen in chapter 3 (p. 74), the *Wired* handbook, for example, has this to say about Web style:[8]

> Look to the Web not for embroidered prose, but for the sudden narrative, the dramatic story told in 150 words. Text must be complemented by clever interface design and clear graphics. Think brilliant ad copy, not long-form literature. Think pert, breezy pieces almost too ephemeral for print. Think turned-up volume – cut lines that are looser, grabbier, more tabloidy. Think distinctive voice or attitude.

This, as an empirical statement about Web pages, represents only a limited amount of what is actually 'out there'; but as a prescription for good practice it is widely followed. With many screens immediately displaying up to 30 functional areas, any initial on-screen textual description of each area is inevitably going to be short – generally a 3–4 word heading or a brief description of 10–20 words. Main pages reflect this trend. For example, a sample of 100 news reports taken from Web-designed BBC, CBN, and ABC sites showed that paragraphs were extremely short, averaging 25 words, and usually consisting of a single sentence; only in one case did a paragraph reach 50 words. Even when specially designed sites had nothing to do with news (such as introductions to educational courses or chambers of commerce), the way their material was displayed took on some of the characteristics of a news-type presentation. On the other hand, sites which simply reproduce material originally written for a paper outlet (such as government reports, academic papers, electronic versions of newspaper articles) move well away from any notion of succinctness. By all accounts, they are more difficult to read, but daily experience suggests that they nonetheless constitute a large proportion of pages on the Web.

---

[8] Hale and Scanlon (1999: 5).

Certain defining properties of traditional written language (p. 25) are also fundamentally altered by the Web. In particular, its staticness is no longer obligatory, in that the software controlling a page may make the text move about the screen, appear and disappear, change colour and shape, or morph into animated characters. As the user moves the mouse-controlled arrow around a screen, the switch from arrow to hand will be accompanied by the arrival of new text. A mouse-click will produce yet more new text. Some sites bring text on-screen as the user watches – for example, BBC News Online had (October 2000) a top-of-the-screen headline appear in the manner of a teleprinter, letter-by-letter. It is all a dynamic graphology, in which the range of visual contrastivity available for linguistic purposes is much increased, compared with traditional print. One of the immediate consequences of this is that new conventions have emerged as signals for certain types of functionality – for example, the use of colours and underlining to identify hypertext links (see below) and e-mail addresses, or to establish the distinct identity of different areas of the screen (main body, links, help, advertising banner, etc.). Web pages need to achieve coherence while making immediate impact; they need structure as well as detail; interactive areas need to be clear and practicable; words, pictures, and icons need to be harmonized. These are substantial communicative demands, and the increased use of colour is the main means of enabling them to be met. As Roger Pring puts it, in a discussion of Web legibility:[9]

> Control of the colour of text and background is the single most important issue, followed by an attempt to direct the browser's choice of size and style of typeface.

Whatever else the Web is, it is noticeably a colourful medium, and in this respect alone it is distinct from other Netspeak situations.

---

[9] Pring (1999: 14). It can be quite tricky, especially in relation to the choice of fonts, to ensure that WYSIWTS ['What You Send Is What They See'] (pp. 30–1).

Hypertext and interactivity

Probably the most important use of colour in a well-designed Web site is to identify the *hypertext* links – the jumps that users can make if they want to move from one page or site to another. The hypertext link is the most fundamental structural property of the Web, without which the medium would not exist. It has parallels in some of the conventions of traditional written text – especially in the use of the footnote number or the bibliographical citation, which enables a reader to move from one place in a text to another – but nothing in traditional written language remotely resembles the dynamic flexibility of the Web. At the same time, it has been pointed out that the Web, as it currently exists, is a long way from exploiting the full intertextuality which the term *hypertext* implies. As Michele Jackson points out, true hypertext 'entails the *complete* and *automatic* interlocking of text, so that all documents are coexistent, with none existing in a prior or primary relation to any other'.[10] This is certainly not the case in today's Web, where there is no central databank of all documents, and where a link between one site and another is often not reciprocated. There is no reason why it should be: the sites are under different ownership, autonomous, and displaying structures that are totally independent of each other. One site's designer may incorporate links to other sites, but there is no way in which the owners of those sites know that a link has been made to them (though the obligation to seek permission seems to be growing) and no obligation on them to return the compliment. Nor does the existence of a link mean that it is achievable – as everyone knows who has encountered the mortuarial black type informing them that a connection could not be made. Some servers refuse access; some sites refuse access. Owners may remove pages from their site, or close a site down, without telling anyone else – what is sometimes called 'link rot'. They may change its location or its name. Whatever the cause, the result is a 'dead link' – a navigation link to nowhere.

[10] Jackson (1997). See also Bolter (1991).

As Tim Berners-Lee points out,[11] a link does not imply any endorsements: 'Free speech in hypertext implies the "right to link", which is the very basic building unit for the whole Web.' The link is simply a mechanism to enable hypertext to come into being. And, as with all tools, it has to be used wisely if it is to be used well – which in the first instance means in moderation. As William of Occam might have said, 'Links should not be multiplied beyond necessity.' Because virtually any piece of text can be a link, the risk is to overuse the device – both internally (within a page, or between pages at the same site) and externally (between sites). But just as one can over-footnote a traditional text, so one can over-link a Web page. There is no algorithm for guiding Web authors or designers as to the relevance or informativeness of a link. The designer is in the unhappy position of those unsung heroes, the book indexers, who try to anticipate all the possible information-retrieval questions future readers of a book will make. However, page designers are much worse off, as the 'book' of which their particular document is a tiny part is the whole Web. One does one's best.

From the Web user's point of view, the links are provided by the system. When someone else's e-mail arrives on our screen, we can, if we wish, edit it – add to it, subtract from it, or change it in some way. This is not possible with the copy of the page which arrives on our computer from our server. We, as readers, cannot alter a Web site: only the site owner can do that. The owner has total control over what we may see and what may be accessed, and also what links we may follow. As Web users, only three courses of action are totally under our control: the initial choice of a particular site address; scrolling through a document once we have accessed it; and cutting and pasting from it. Although we may choose to follow a hypertext link that a designer has provided us, the decision over what those links should be is not ours. As Jackson says:[12]

> the presence of a link reflects a communicative choice made by the designer. A link, therefore, is strategic. The possible variations for

---

[11] Berners-Lee (1999: 151).   [12] Jackson (1997: 8).

structure are shaped by communicative ends, rather than
technological means.

We, as users, cannot add our own links. The best we can do is send
a message to the owner suggesting an extra link. It is then entirely
up to the owner whether to accept the suggestion.

But for any of this to happen, interactivity needs to be built into
the system. This is the only way in which the Berners-Lee dream
can be fully realized:[13] 'The Web is more a social creation than
a technical one... to help people work together'. Genuine working together presupposes a mutuality of communicative access,
between site designers and site users. At present, in many cases,
the situation is asymmetrical: we, as Web users, can reach their
knowledge, but they cannot reach ours (or, at least, our questions
and reactions). The authors of *Wired Style* issue page-designers
with a blunt warning: 'On the Web, you forget your audience at
your peril.'[14] Fortunately, the warning seems to be being heeded. A
distinctive feature of an increasing number of Web pages is their
interactive character, as shown by the Contact Us, E-mail Us, Join
Our List, Help Questions, FAQs, Chat, and other screen boxes. The
Web is no longer only a purveyor of information. It has become
a communicative tool, which will vastly grow as it becomes a part
of interactive television. Doubtless, the trend is being much reinforced by the e-commerce driver, with its 'subscribe now', 'book
here', 'e-auction', 'stop me and buy one' character. Web owners
have come to realize that, as soon as someone enters a site, there
is a greater chance of them staying there if the site incorporates an
e-mail option, or offers a discussion forum.

Evolution and management

Because the linguistic character of the Web is in the hands of its site
owners, the interesting question arises of what is going to happen
as its constituency develops. Anyone may now publish pages on

[13] Berners-Lee (1999: 133).   [14] Hale and Scanlon (1999: 7).

the Web, and professional designers have been scathing about the untutored typographical hotchpotches which have been the result, and have issued warnings about the need for care. Roger Pring, for example:[15]

> Web screens may blossom with movies and be garnished with sound tracks but, for the moment, type is the primary vehicle for information and persuasion. Its appearance on screen is more crucial than ever. Intense competition for the user's attention means that words must attract, inform (and maybe seduce) as quickly as possible. Flawless delivery of the message to the screen is the goal. The road to success is very broad, but the surface rather uneven.

The uneven surface is apparent on many current Web pages. Page compilers often fail to respect the need for lines to be relatively short, or fail to appreciate the value of columns. They may overuse colour and type size, or underuse the variations which are available. And they can transfer the habits of typing on paper, forgetting that the HTML conventions ('Hypertext Markup Language', which instructs the computer about how to lay out text) may be different.[16] To take just one example, a simple carriage return is enough to mark a paragraph ending on the paper page, but on screen this would not result in a new paragraph: to guarantee that, the HTML <P> needs to be inserted into the text at the appropriate point. Erratic lineation, obscured paragraph divisions, misplaced headings, and other such errors are the outcome. For the linguist, this complicates the task enormously, making it difficult to draw conclusions about the linguistic nature of the medium. The situation resembles that found in language learning, where learners pass through a stage of 'interlanguage', which is neither one language nor the other.[17] Many Web pages are, typographically speaking, in an 'in between' state.

---

[15] Pring (1999: 6). He also points out (p. 8) that designers for print have had only some 15 years' experience of dealing with language in a computer-mediated environment.

[16] For a convenient guide to HTML tagging, see <http://www.willcam.com/cmat/html/crossref.html>.

[17] For interlanguage, see Selinker (1972).

There are other linguistic consequences of Web innocence, when
we consider that people are producing content for a potentially
worldwide readership. How does one learn to write for potential
millions, with clarity and (bearing in mind the international audience) cultural sensitivity? The point is routinely recognized in
chatgroups (chapter 5). Usenet help manners, for example, has
this to say:[18]

> Keep Usenet's worldwide nature in mind when you post articles.
> Even those who can read your language may have a culture wildly
> different from yours. When your words are read, they might not
> mean what you think they mean.

The point is even more powerful when we consider the vastly greater
range of subject-matter communicated via the Web. But the Web
presents us with a rather different problem. Its language is under
no central control. On the Web there are no powerful moderators
(p. 133). Individual servers may attempt to ban certain types of
site, but huge amounts of uncensored language slip through. There
are several sites where the aim is, indeed, contrary to conventional
standards of politeness and decency, or where the intention is to
give people the opportunity to rant about anything which has upset them.[19] Conventional language may be subverted in order to
evade the stratagems servers use to exclude pornographic material:
a Web address may use a juxtaposition of interesting and innocu-
ous words, and only upon arrival at the site does one realize that
the content is not what was conveyed by their dictionary meaning. The debate continues over the many social and legal issues
raised by these situations – laws of obscenity and libel, matters of
security and policing, questions of freedom of speech – all made
more difficult by the many variations in practice which exist between countries. The Internet, as has often been pointed out, is no
respecter of national boundaries.

Issues associated with textual copyright have particular linguistic
consequences. Although we are unable to alter someone else's Web

---

[18] 'What is Usenet?' <http://www.faqs.org/faqs/usenet/what-is/part1>.
[19] An example is <www.angry.net>.

pages directly, it is perfectly possible to download a document to our own computer, change the text, then upload the new document to a Web site we have created for the purpose. In this way, it is relatively easy for people to steal the work of others, or to adapt that work in unsuspected ways. There is a widespread opinion that 'content is free', fuelled by the many Web pages where this is indeed the case. But freedom needs to be supplemented with responsibility, and this is often lacking. Examples of forgery abound. Texts are sent to a site purporting to be by a particular person, when they are not. I know from personal experience that not all the 'I am the author' remarks in some book sites are actually by the author. And there have been several reported instances when a literary author's work has been interfered with. This does not seem to be stopping the number of authors ready to put their work directly onto the Web, however.

Most traditional printed texts have a single author – or, if more than one author is involved, they have been authorized by a single person, such as a script editor or a committee secretary. Several pairs of eyes may scrutinize a document, before it is released, to ensure that consistency and quality is maintained. Even individually authored material does not escape, as publishers provide copy-editors and proof-readers to eradicate unintended idiosyncrasy and implement house style. It is in fact extremely unusual to find written language which has not been edited in some way – which is one reason why chatgroup and virtual worlds material is so interesting (p. 170). But on the Web, these checks and balances are often not present.[20] There are multi-authored pages, where the style shifts unexpectedly from one part of a page to another. The more interactive a site becomes, the more likely it will contain language from different dialect backgrounds and operating at different stylistic levels – variations in formality are particularly common.

---

[20] The lack of editorial quality control in many Web sites appals people brought up in the rigorous climate of traditional publishing. A licensed edition of the electronic text of the *Cambridge Biographical Encyclopedia*, which I edit, to one Web site was reproduced there with no in-house editing at all – even to the extent of reproducing on-screen the printer codes and page cross-references from the printed book, some of which were to sections in the printed book that the Web site decided not to include. This is one story out of dozens.

Because reactions to an interactive site are easy to make, they are often made. The linguistic character of a site thus becomes increasingly eclectic. People have more power to influence the language of the Web than in any other medium, because they operate on both sides of the communication divide, reception and production. They not only read a text, they can add to it. The distinction between creator and receiver thus becomes blurred. The nearest we could get to this, in traditional writing, was to add our opinions to the margin of a book or to underline or highlight passages. We can do this now routinely with interactive pages, with our efforts given an identical typography to that used in the original text. It is a stylistician's nightmare.

A nightmare, moreover, made worse by the time-sink effect. A little while ago I was searching the Web for some data on the Bermudas. I received many hits, but the first few dozen were all advertisements for Bermuda shorts, which was not exactly what I had in mind. This is a familiar search-engine problem (p. 197), but what was noticeable about this particular result was the time-range displayed by the hits. The ads were monthly accounts of the range and prices dating back several years – April 1994, May 1994, and so on. Quite evidently, many owners do not delete their old Web pages; they leave them there. I do not know of any source which will tell me just how much of the Web is an information rubbish-dump of this kind. Unless data-management procedures alter to cope with it, the proportion must increase. And in due course, there will be an implication for anyone who wants to use the Web as a synchronic corpus, in order to make statements about its stylistic character. Let us jump forward fifty years. We call up an interactive site to which people have now been contributing for two generations. The contributions will reflect the language changes of the whole period, displaying words and idioms yet unknown, and perhaps even changes in spelling, grammar, and discourse patterns. Though some sites already date-stamp all contributions (e.g. Amazon's reader reactions), by no means all do so. In the worst-case scenario, we could encounter a single text created by an indefinite number of people at indefinite times over several years. Several competitors for the 'world's longest sentence ever' are already of this form.[21] While these are instances of language play, the implications for serious stylistic investigation are far-reaching. But handling the increasingly diachronic character of the Web, and coping with its chronological clutter, raises issues which go well beyond the linguistic.

The trouble with the notion of 'knowledge' is that it is all-inclusive. The price of Bermuda shorts in April 1994 counts as knowledge. So does A.N. Other's account of his break-up with his girlfriend, which may be found on his Web page. At the heart of knowledge management is therefore the task of evaluation. Judgements have to be made in terms of significance vs. triviality, with reference to a particular point of view, and criteria have to be introduced to enable a notion of relevance to be implemented. The common complaint nowadays is that we are being swamped by knowledge; such phrases as 'information overload' are everywhere. What use is it to me to be told that, if I search for 'linguistics' on my search engine, I have 86,764 hits? Part of Berners-Lee's vision was shared knowledge: 'the dream of people-to-people communication through shared knowledge must be possible for groups of all sizes'.[22] But unless the notion of sharing is subjected to some sort of assessment, the dream begins to take on nightmarish qualities. For Berners-Lee, another part of the dream is a 'semantic web ... capable of analysing all the data on the Web – the content, links and transactions between people and computers'. This is a stirring vision, which will keep generations of semanticists yet unborn in jobs. But no semantic or pragmatic theory yet devised is capable of carrying out the kind of sophisticated relevance analysis which would be required.

---

[21] For example, the 'Amazing Run-on Sentence Page' at
<http://www.users.zetnet.co.uk/bywater/ee.res09.htm>.
[22] Berners-Lee (1999: 169); also for the next quotation. Several sites now provide guidance in Web page evaluation, especially from a scholarly point of view, such as the Internet Detective: <http://www.sosig.ac.uk/desire/internet-detective.html>.

Even the most basic semantic criteria are missing from the heavily frequency-dominated information retrieval techniques currently used by search engines. All such engines incorporate an element of encyclopedic classification into their procedure, but this is only a small part of the answer to the question of how to implement relevance. Any search-engine assistant needs to supplement its encyclopedic perspective by a semantic one. The typical problem can be illustrated by the word *depression*, which if typed into the search box of a search engine will produce a mixed bag of hits in which its senses within psychiatry, geography, and economics are not distinguished (nor, of course, less widespread uses, such as in glassware and literature). The experience of trawling through a load of irrelevant hits before finding one which relates to the context of our enquiry is universal. The solution is obvious: to give the user the choice of which context to select.[23] The user is asked on screen: 'Do you mean *depression* (economics) or *depression* (psychiatry) or *depression* (geography)...?' Once the choice is made, the software then searches for only those hits relevant to the selection. The procedure sounds simple, but it is not, for the notion of context has to be formalized and the results incorporated into the software. But what is the semantic basis of a domain such as economics or psychiatry, or of any of their relevant sub-domains? Which lexical items are the 'key' ones to be searched for, and how are they organized? The task goes well beyond scrutinizing the items listed in a dictionary or thesaurus. These can provide a starting-point, but the alphabetical organization of a dictionary and the uncontrolled conceptual clustering of a thesaurus lack the kind of sharp semantic focus required. In linguistics, several notions have been developed to provide such a focus – such as the recognition of lexemes (as opposed to words), semantic fields, sense relations, and the componential analysis of lexical meanings.[24] They are not unproblematic, but they do have considerable potential for application in such computer-mediated situations as Web-searching

---

[23] This is the procedure used in the *ALFIE* ['A Lexical Filter Internet Enquirer'] project: see Crystal (1997d).
[24] For semantic fields see Crystal (1997a: 104).

and automatic document classification, once software is adapted to cope.[25]

The lack of even an elementary semantics also bedevils those software systems which attempt to evaluate the content of Web sites (*censorware*), replacing parts of words by X's, filtering out pages, or blocking access to sites which contain 'dangerous' words.[26] Thus, in one report, a student was barred from his high school's Web site from the school library because the software objected to his word *high*. A woman named Hilary Anne was not allowed to register the username *hilaryanne* with a particular e-mail company because it contained the word *aryan*. Sites which fight against pornography can be banned because they contain words like *pornography*. In 2000, Digital Freedom Network held a 'Foil the Filters' contest to demonstrate the unreliability of censorware. Their Silicon Eye Award ('for finding objectionable content where only a computer would look') was given to someone who wanted to register an account with a site which would not accept the name *Heather* because it contained the phrase *eat her*! Honourable mentions were given to another enquirer who could not access a biotechnology site because its name (*accessexcellence.org*) contained the word *sex*. Doubtless residents of *Essex* and *Sussex*, people called *Cockburn* and *Babcock*, or anyone who uses *Dick* as their first name, encounter such problems routinely. Other examples of words which have been banned include *cucumbers* (because it contains *cum*), *Matsushita* (*shit*), *analysis* (*anal*), *class* (*ass*), and *speech* (*pee*). More puzzlingly, among the words which some cyberware systems have blocked are *golden*, *mate*, and *scoop*. The linguistic naivety which lies behind such decision-making beggars belief.

---

[25] This is no small problem either. My initial semantic investigation of the keywords corresponding to the encyclopedia classes for the ALFIE project (fn. 23) produced over a hundred keywords for each class. This proved impossible for search-engine software to implement, so the number of keywords was reduced to an arbitrary 40. Even then, some applications could not cope with such a number. But working with large clusters of lexical items is a *sine qua non* of any semantic approach to Web-searching. A large question-mark therefore hangs over the semantic approach to the Web envisioned by Berners-Lee, at least until such time as much more powerful processing options become available.

[26] The examples in this paragraph all come from the Digital Freedom Network site: http://dfn.org/focus/censor/contest.htm>.

The linguistic limitations of word-processing and search-engine software affect our ability to find what is on the Web in several ways, and eventually must surely influence our intuitions about the nature of our language. So do the attempts to control usage in areas other than the politically correct. Which writers have not felt angry at the way pedants in the software companies have attempted to interfere with their style, sending a warning when their sentences go beyond a certain length, or when they use *which* instead of *that* (or vice versa), or *-ise* instead of *-ize* (or vice versa), or dare to split an infinitive? The advice can be switched off, of course; but many people do not bother to switch it off, or do not know how to. Sometimes they do not want to switch it off, as something of value is lost thereby. The software controlling the page I am currently typing, for example, inserts a red wavy line underneath anything which is misspelled, according to the dictionary it uses. I find this helpful, because I am no perfect typist. On the other hand it has just underlined *scrutinizing* and *formalized*, in the previous paragraph (though, curiously, not *organized*). The red lines are a constant irritant, and it takes a real effort of will not to yield to them and go for the software-recommended form. Whether others resist this insidious threat to linguistic variety I do not know. My feeling is that a large number of valuable stylistic distinctions are being endangered by this repeated encounter with the programmer's prescriptive usage preferences. Online dictionaries and grammars are likely to influence usage much more than their traditional Fowlerian counterparts ever did. It would be good to see a greater descriptive realism emerge, paying attention to the sociolinguistic and stylistic complexity which exists in a language, but at present the recommendations are arbitrary, oversimplified, and depressingly purist in spirit (p. 74).[27]

---

[27] Dorner (1992) illustrates from various offerings. She comments on the nature of the software writer's problem: 'Software that upbraids a writer too often is irritating and saps the confidence of inexperienced writers: software that fails to deal with one of the matters that can expose a writer to public scorn is unreliable and saps the confidence of experienced writers' (p. 30).

I am therefore pleased to see the arrival of satire, as a means of drawing attention to the problem. Bob Hirschfeld's newspaper article, 'Taking liberties: the pluperfect',[28] is one such contribution. In it he describes the deadly Strunkenwhite virus which returns e-mail messages to their senders if they contain grammatical or spelling errors. He explains:

> The virus is causing something akin to panic throughout corporate America, which has become used to the typos, misspellings, missing words and mangled syntax so acceptable in cyberspace. The CEO of LoseItAll.com, an Internet startup, said the virus has rendered him helpless. 'Each time I tried to send one particular e-mail this morning, I got back this error message: "Your dependent clause preceding your independent clause must be set off by commas, but one must not precede the conjunction." I threw my laptop across the room.'

His article concludes:

> 'We just can't imagine what kind of devious mind would want to tamper with e-mails to create this burden on communications', said an FBI agent who insisted on speaking via the telephone out of concern that trying to e-mail his comments could leave him tied up for hours.

It is good to see some artists coming on board. Turner prize nominee Tomoko Takahashi has a Web project he devised to object to the way software is imposing a 'standardised corporate language on to our writing' while 'subtly altering its meaning'. He calls it Word Perhect.[29]

Some degree of normalization is unavoidable in automatic information retrieval (IR), as US librarian and information scientist Terrence Brookes comments:[30]

> Although IR searchers are said to be 'searching a database' or 'searching for documents', these metaphors obscure the reality of

---

[28] *Washington Post*, 2 May 1999, B05.
[29] Seen at the online gallery <http://www.chisenhale.org.uk/ch2>.
[30] Brookes (1998: 732), from which some of the following examples are taken.

the more mundane task of matching query term to index term. In an IR system hosting unrestricted text, the task of matching one string of characters to another string of characters would be very difficult unless there was a normalizing algorithm that processed both the document text and the query text.

But for every normalization decision that has negligible conse-quences for linguistic meaning (such as standardizing the amount of blank space between paragraphs), there are several which result in the loss of important linguistic detail. If careful attention is not paid to punctuation, hyphenation, capitalization, and special sym-bols (such as &, /, *, $) valuable discriminating information can be lost. When contrasts from these areas are ignored in searching, as is often the case, all kinds of anomalies appear, and it is extremely dif-ficult to obtain consistency. Software designers underestimate the amount of variation there is in the orthographic system, the per-vasive nature of language change, and the influence context has in deciding whether an orthographic feature is obligatory or optional. For example, there are contexts where the ignoring of an apostro-phe in a search is inconsequential (e.g. in *St Paul's Cathedral*, where the apostrophe is often omitted in general usage anyway), but in other contexts it can be highly confusing. Proper names can be disrupted – *John O'Reilly* is not *John Oreilly* or *John O Reilly* (a ma-jor problem for such languages as French and Italian, where forms such as *d'* and *l'* are common). Hyphens can be critical unifiers, as in *CD-ROM* and *X-ray*. Similar problems arise when slashes and dashes are used to separate words or parts of words within an expression, as in many chemical names. Disallowing the amper-sand makes it hard to find such firms as *AT&T* or *P&O*, whether solid or spaced; no hits may be returned, or the *P...O* string is swamped by other *P O* hits, where the ampersand has nothing to do with their identity. When more than one of these conventions are involved in the same search, the extent to which the search-engines simplify the true complexity of a language's orthography is quickly appreciated. Brookes[31] points out that a string such as

31 Brookes (1998).

Brother-in-Law O'Toole would be normalized in different ways by different IR systems. And it gets worse, if O'Toole turns out to be the author of a particular version of a software program, as in *Brother-in-Law O'Toole's 'Q & A' System/Version 1.0*. Few of us would know what to expect of any software system processing this search request.

The stop words recognized by different systems pose a special problem. These usually comprise a list of the grammatical words which are so frequent and contain so little semantic content that the search mechanism ignores them. The trouble is that these words often form an obligatory part of something which does have semantic content (such as the title of a novel or film) or are homographic with content words – in which case they become irretrievable. For example, the Dutch firm for which the ALFIE project (see fn. 23) was undertaken was called *AND* (the initials of its founders); as *and* would be on any stop-list, a search engine which is not case-sensitive would make this string virtually impossible to find among the welter of hits in which the word *and* is prominent. The *AND* case is not unique, as anyone knows who has tried searching for the discipline of *IT* – let alone for the Stephen King novel, *It.* Several forms which are grammatical in one context become content items in another, such as *a* in *Vitamin A, A-team*, and the Andy Warhol novel *a*, or *who* in *Doctor Who*, as well as the polysemy involved in such words as *will* and *may* (cf. *May*). Finding US states by abbreviation, under these circumstances, can be tricky: there is no problem with such states as KY (Kentucky) and TX (Texas), but it would be unwise to try searching for Indiana (IN), Maine (ME), or Oregon (OR), or even for Ohio (OH) and Oklahoma (OK). Cross-linguistic differences add further complications: those computers which block *an* and *or* in English exclude the words for 'year' and 'gold' in French (as well as a significant part of English heraldry, where the term *or* is crucial). C. L. Borgman comments:[32]

---

[32] Borgman (1996: 499); see also Borgman (1986).

> As the non-English-speaking world comes online and preserves their full character sets in their online catalogs and other retrieval systems, matching filing order, keyboard input, and display, will become ever more complex.

And it is precisely this world which is now coming online, in ever-increasing numbers.

Languages on the Web

The Web is an eclectic medium, and this is seen also in its multilinguistic inclusiveness. Not only does it offer a home to all linguistic styles within a language; it offers a home to all languages – once their communities have a functioning computer technology. This has been the most notable change since the Web began. It was originally a totally English medium – as was the Internet as a whole, given its US origins.[33] But with the Internet's globalization, the presence of other languages has steadily risen. In the mid-1990s, a widely quoted figure was that just over 80% of the Net was in English. This was supported by a 1997 survey by Babel, a joint initiative of the Internet Society and Alis Technologies, the first major study of language distribution on the Internet.[34] This study used a random number generator to find 8,000 computers hosting an HTTP server; and a program then subjected a selection of pages to an automatic language identification, using software which could recognize 17 languages. Of 3,239 home pages found, the language distribution (after correction for various types of possible error) was as shown in Table 7.1. The gap between English and the other languages is notable, and supports the widespread impression, frequently reported in newspaper headlines, that the language of the Internet 'is' English. 'World, Wide, Web: 3 English Words' was the

---

[33] See Crystal (1997c). Jim Erickson (1998) sums it up in a story from Al Gore reporting the remark of the eight-year-old son of Kyrgyzstan's President Akayev, who told his father that he had to learn English. When asked why, the child apparently replied: 'Because the computer speaks English'.
[34] <www.isoc.org:8030/palmares.en.html>. For Babel's project on internationalizing the Internet, see <http://babel.alis.com:8080/>.

Table 7.1 Language distribution on the Web (see fn. 34)

Ranking	Language	Number of pages	Corrected percentage
1	English	2,722	82.3
2	German	147	4.0
3	Japanese	101	1.6
4	French	59	1.5
5	Spanish	38	1.1
6	Swedish	35	0.6
7	Italian	31	0.8
8	Portuguese	21	0.7
9	Dutch	20	0.4
10	Norwegian	19	0.3
11	Finnish	14	0.3
12	Czech	11	0.3
13	Danish	9	0.3
14	Russian	8	0.1
15	Malay	4	0.1
	none or unknown (correction)		5.6
Total		3,239	100

headline of one piece in *The New York Times*,[35] and the article went on to comment: 'if you want to take full advantage of the Internet there is only one real way to do it: learn English'. The writer did acknowledge the arrival of other languages:

> As the Web grows the number of people on it who speak French, say, or Russian will become more varied and that variety will be expressed on the Web. That is why it is a fundamentally democratic technology.

However, he concluded:

> But it won't necessarily happen soon.

The evidence is growing that this conclusion was wrong. The estimates for languages other than English have steadily risen since

---

[35] Specter (1996).

then, with some commentators predicting that before long the Web (and the Internet as a whole) will be predominantly non-English, as communications infrastructure develops in Europe, Asia, Africa, and South America. A Global Reach survey[36] estimated that people with Internet access in non-English-speaking countries increased from 7 million to 136 million between 1995 and 2000. In 1998, the total number of newly created non-English Web sites passed that for newly created English Web sites, with Spanish, Japanese, German, and French the chief players.[37] Alta Vista had six European sites in early 2000, and were predicting that by 2002 less than 50% of the Web would be in English.[38] Graddol predicted an even lower figure in due course, 40%.[39] In certain parts of the world, the local language is already dominant. According to Japanese Internet author Yoshi Mikami, 90% of Web pages in Japan are now in Japanese.[40] A report published in October 2000 by Jupiter Media Matrix[41] suggested that the greatest growth in online households over the first half of the '00s is going to be outside the USA. A Nua Internet Survey the previous month[42] estimated that about 378 million people were online worldwide: of these, 161 million were in North America and 106 million in Europe. What is interesting is that 90 million were in Asia and the Pacific, a total that is likely to pass Europe's soon, given the population growth differential between those two parts of the world. The 15 million in Latin America and the tiny 3 million in Africa show the potential for growth in those areas one day.

The Web is increasingly reflecting the distribution of language presence in the real world, and there is a steadily growing set

---

[36] <http://www.euromktg.com/eng/GR>.   [37] Lebert (1999).
[38] Session on 'Search Engines' in Search Engine Strategies 2000, 27 April, May Fair Inter-Continental, London.
[39] Graddol (1998: 51). Only 32% of European Web surfers consult the Web in English, according to data reported in Lebert (1999).
[40] Interviewed in Lebert (1999). Mikami is the author of 'The languages of the world by computers and the Internet', a site which includes information on a wide range of languages, including data on their writing system, character set, and keyboard. See <http://www.threeweb.ad.jp/logos>.
[41] <http://www.jupitermediamatrix.com>.   [42] <http://www.nua.ie/surveys>.

of sites which provide the evidence.[43] They range from individual businesses doing their best to present a multilingual identity to major sites collecting data on many languages. Under the former heading we encounter several newspapers, such as the Belgian daily, *Le Soir*, which is represented by six languages: French, Dutch, English, German, Italian, and Spanish. Under the latter heading we find such sites as the University of Oregon Font Archive, providing 112 fonts in their archives for over 40 languages – including, in a nicely light-hearted addendum, Morse, Klingon, Romulan, and Tolkien (Cirth, Elvish, etc.). The same centre's Interactive Language Resources Guide provides data on 115 languages.[44] A World Language Resources site lists products for 728 languages.[45] Some sites focus on certain parts of the world: an African resource list covers several local languages; Yoruba, for example, is illustrated by some 5,000 words, along with proverbs, naming patterns, and greetings.[46] Another site deals with no less than 87 European minority languages.[47] Some sites are very small in content, but extensive in range: one gives the Lord's Prayer in nearly 500 languages.[48] Nobody has yet worked out just how many languages have obtained a modicum of presence on the Web. I started to work my way down the *Ethnologue* listing of the world's languages,[49] and stopped when I reached 1,000. It was not difficult to find evidence of a Net presence for the vast majority of the more frequently used languages, and for a large number of minority languages too, especially in

---

[43] The trend now extends beyond the Web to other Internet situations, where there are signs of slow progress towards an increasing multilingualism. Chatgroups and MUDs are steadily coming online in different languages: for example, Internet Relay Chat was listing 20 languages in late 2000. The list is at <http://www.irchelp.org/irchelp/misc/foreign.html>. Geoff Nunberg (personal communication) had by 1996 found some 60 Usenet groups wholly or partly using other languages.

[44] <http://babel.uoregon.edu/YLC/guides.html>. Examples of other resource sites are <http://www.itp.berkeley.edu/~thorne/HumanResources.html>, <http:www.call.gov/resource/language/language.htm>, the dictionary list at <http://www.yourdictionary.com>, the Human Languages Page at <http://www.june29.com/HLP>, and the Languages on the Web site at <http://www.languages-on-the-web.com>, which provides parallel translations of 55 languages.

[45] <http://secure.worldlanguage.com>.   [46] <http://www.africaservice.com>.

[47] <http://www.smo.uhi.ac.uk/saoghal/mion-chanain/Failte-en.html>.

[48] <http://www.christusrex.org>.   [49] *Ethnologue* is at <http://www.sil.org>.

those technologically developed parts of the world which happen
to contain large numbers of minority or endangered languages,
such as the USA, Canada, and Australia. I would guess that about a
quarter of the world's languages have some sort of Internet presence
now.

How much use is made of these sites is, of course, a different
matter. Until a critical mass of Internet penetration in a country
builds up, and a corresponding mass of content exists in the local
language, the motivation to switch from English-language sites will
be limited to those for whom issues of identity outweigh issues of
information. The notion of 'critical mass' is recognized in Metcalfe's
Law (named after Ethernet inventor, Robert M. Metcalfe): networks
increase in functionality by the square of the number of nodes they
contain. In other words, a single language site is useless, because
the owner has nobody to link to; two provides a minimal commu-
nicativity; and so on. The future is also very much dependent on
the levels of English-speaking ability in individual countries, and
the likelihood of further growth in those levels.[50] Code-mixing is
also found in many interactive Internet situations, though not so
much as yet on the Web.[51] Technological progress (see chapter 8)
will also radically alter the situation. There is no doubt that low-
cost Internet use is going to grow, all over the world, as wireless
networking puts the Internet within reach of people in developing
nations who will use access devices powered by solar cells or clock-
work generators. Global mobile phones will have dish-on-a-chip
transceivers built into them, with communication up and down via
LEO ['low earth orbit'] satellite.[52] All of this must have an impact
on language presence.

In the above examples, we are encountering language presence
in a real sense. These are not sites which only analyse or talk about
languages, from the point of view of linguistics or some other

---

[50] See Vehovar, Batagelj, and Lozar (1999), for a discussion of this situation in relation to
Slovenian.
[51] Code-switching is noted by both Li Longyan (2000: 34) and Li Lan (2000: 28), both with
Chinese English. See also p. 166.
[52] See the account in Cotton and Garrett (1999: 14ff.).

academic subject; they are sites which allow us to see languages as they are. In many cases, the total Web presence, in terms of number of pages, is quite small. The crucial point is that the languages are out there, even if represented by only a sprinkling of sites. It is the ideal medium for minority languages, given the relative cheapness and ease of creating a Web page, compared with the cost and difficulty of obtaining a newspaper page, or a programme or advertisement on radio or television. On the other hand, developing a significant cyber-presence is not easy. As Ned Thomas comments, in an editorial for *Contact*, reflecting on the reduced dominance of English on the Net (p. 216):[53]

> It is not the case... that all languages will be marginalized on the Net by English. On the contrary, there will be a great demand for multilingual Web sites, for multilingual data retrieval, for machine translation, for voice recognition systems to be multilingual.... The danger for minority languages – and indeed for all small languages – is that they will be left outside the inner circle of languages for which it is commercially viable to develop voice recognition and machine translation systems. Typically, such systems depend on the analysis of large bodies of language which can be expensive to develop and which can take time to develop.

The interviews conducted by Marie Lebert for her study indicate that those in the business are fairly unanimous about the future multilinguality of the Internet in general, and the Web in particular.[54] Take this comment, from Marcel Grangier, head of the Section française des Services linguistiques centraux (SLC-f) ['French Section of the Central Linguistic Services'] of the Swiss Federal Administration:

> Multilingualism on the Internet can be seen as a happy and above all irreversible inevitability. In this perspective we have to make fun of the wet blankets who only speak to complain about the supremacy of English. This supremacy is not wrong in itself, inasmuch as it is the result of mainly statistical facts (more PCs per

---

[53] Ned Thomas (2000). *Contact* is the bulletin for the European Bureau of Lesser Used Languages.
[54] This and the following quotation are from Lebert (1999).

inhabitant, more English-speaking people, etc.). The counter-attack is not to 'fight against English' and even less to whine about it, but to increase sites in other languages. As a translation service, we also recommend the multilingualism of websites.

Tyler Chambers, creator of various Web language projects, agrees:

> the future of the Internet is even more multilingualism and cross-cultural exploration and understanding than we've already seen.

The point seems to be uncontentious among those who shaped the Web. Tim Berners-Lee, for example:[55]

> The Web must allow equal access to those in different economic and political situations; those who have physical or cognitive disabilities; those of different cultures; and those who use different languages with different characters that read in different directions across a page.

The problem is a practical one, but a great deal has been done since the mid-1990s.[56] First, the ASCII character set was extended, so that non-English accents and diacritics could be included, but its 8-byte restriction meant that only a maximum of 256 characters could be handled – a tiny number compared with the array of letter-shapes in Arabic, Hindi, Chinese, Korean, and the many other languages in the world which do not use the Latin alphabet.[57] The UNICODE system represents each character with 16 bytes, allowing over 65,000 characters; but the implementation of this system is still in its infancy.[58] The Web consortium now has an internationalization activity looking specifically at different alphabets, so that operating systems can support a page in any alphabet. And Berners-Lee looks forward to the day when the linking of meanings, within and between languages, is possible through the use of 'inference

---

[55] Berners-Lee (1999: 178).
[56] As reviewed, for example, by Bourbonnais and Yergeau (1996).
[57] For the world's writing systems, see Daniels and Bright (1996).
[58] See the Unicode site at <http://www.unicode.org>; also the review of fonts and special characters in Condron (2000b).

languages' which 'will make all the data in the world look like one huge database'.[59]

A great deal has to be done before this day dawns. There needs to be immense progress in Internet linguistics, especially in semantics and pragmatics, and also in graphology and typography. There is an enormous gap to be filled in comparative lexicography: most of the English technical terms used on the Web have still not been translated into other languages, and a great deal of varying usage exists, with English loanwords and local variants uncertainly co-existing.[60] On the positive side, there has been an enormous growth of interest in translation issues and procedures during the past decade. And localization (the adaptation of a product to suit a target language and culture) is the buzz-word in many circles. There seems little doubt that the character of the Web is going to be increasingly multilingual, and that the issues discussed in the first half of this chapter are going to require revision in the light of what has been said in the second. But I have as yet found no comparative research into the way different languages approach the same problems on their respective Web sites. Nor is it clear what happens linguistically when Internet technology is used in new areas of application, and when new technological developments influence the language to move in different directions. What is clear is that the linguistic future of the Web, and of the Internet as a whole, is closely bound up with these applications and future developments. They therefore provide the topic of the final chapter.

---

[59] Berners-Lee (1999: 200–1).
[60] See, for example, the Multilingual Glossary of Internet Terminology project at <http://www.netglos.com>.

8   *The linguistic future of the Internet*

It seems to be a standard convention for books dealing with digital technology to begin or end by warning their readers that everything they contain is going to be soon out of date; and a linguistic perspective on the subject is no exception. Any attempt to characterize the language of the Internet, whether as a whole or with reference to one of its constituent situations, immediately runs up against the transience of the technology. The different arenas of communication described in earlier chapters will not remain for long as they are, given that the technological developments upon which they rely are constantly evolving, putting users under constant pressure to adapt their language to the demands of new contexts, and giving them fresh opportunities to interact in novel ways. The readiness with which people do adapt language to meet the needs of new situations, which is at the heart of linguistic evolution – and which the central chapters of this book clearly demonstrate – is going to be fully exploited in the next few decades, with the emergence of yet more sophisticated forms of digitally mediated communication. Nor is the population using it any more stable: it is unusual to see a disclaimer in a bibliography of the kind used on p. 243, for example, but there is simply no guarantee that any of the URLs [uniform resource locators] listed in my footnotes and bibliography will still exist by the time this book appears. They may have become 'dead links' (p. 202).[1]

The Internet has been the focus of this book, within which I have looked at five situations – e-mail, synchronous and asynchronous chatgroups, virtual worlds, and the World Wide Web. In each case,

---

[1] 'There's a curse, a curse so potent and vile that writers dare not give it a name, which guarantees that as soon as you include a reference to a time-honored resource in your book, that resource vanishes' (Ihnatko, 1997: v).

I have found clear signs of the emergence of a distinctive variety of language, with characteristics closely related to the properties of its technological context as well as to the intentions, activities, and (to some extent) personalities of the users. But the Net is only a part of the world of computer-mediated language. Many new technologies are anticipated, which will integrate the Internet with other communication situations, and these will provide the matrix within which further language varieties will develop. We have already seen this happen with broadcasting technology: radio brought a new kind of language, which quickly yielded several sub-varieties (commentary, news, weather . . .); then television added a further dimension, which similarly evolved sub-varieties. How many computer-mediated varieties of language will eventually emerge, it is difficult to say; but we can be sure of one thing – it will be far greater than the five tentatively identified in this book. As Bob Cotton and Malcolm Garrett say, in the title of their review of the future of media and global expert systems, 'You ain't seen nothing yet'.[2]

Immediate innovation is anticipated in each of the three traditional domains of communication: production, transmission, and reception. Cotton and Garrett, somewhat analogously, describe the future in terms of major developments in delivery systems, processing power, and access devices. All of these will have an impact on the kind of language we use. The heart of the matter seems to be the immense increase in bandwidth, already seen in ISDN, cable, and optical fibre technologies, which will permit many channels to be simultaneously available within a single signal, and thus allow hitherto separate communication modalities to be integrated. The two main modes, sound and vision, have already begun to be linked in this way; and there is in principle no reason why other modes (tactile, olfactory, gustatory) should not also be incorporated. The various established media elements are already becoming increasingly integrated, in a frame of reference neatly captured by the

---

[2] Cotton and Garrett (1999); see also Atwell (1999). Futurological implications are also the theme of Gilder (2000), whose notion of the *telecosm* captures a world 'enabled and defined by new communications technology'.

phrase *streaming media*. It would appear that the aim is to make anything speedily available with anything – Web with sound and video, personal digital assistants with Web access, television with Internet access, Internet with television access, radio programmes with pictures, and so on. Cotton and Garrett illustrate some of the combinations:[3]

> expect to see digital cameras incorporating a personal organiser, stylus handwriting recognition, audio voice recording and internet access (e-mail and messaging, and JPEG image transfer). Or a basic PDA (personal digital assistant) that becomes a stills camera, digital radio, web browser, fax machine, mobile phone, television set, video camcorder, voice memo-recorder on demand – whenever the user plugs in the appropriate smartcard or (eventually) presses the appropriate button.

New terms are already evolving to describe the novel combinations of function, such as *teleputer*. Some domains, such as holography, have yet to develop their communicative nomenclature.

From a linguistic point of view, the developments are of two broad kinds: those which will affect the nature of language use within an individual speech community; and those which bring different languages together. Under the former heading, there will be linguistic implications when speech is added to already existing visual modalities, as in Internet telephony, with the microphone and loudspeakers giving the Net the functionality of a phone. In due course, we will be able to interact with systems through speech – already possible in a limited way – with speech recognition (at the sender's end) making it unnecessary to type messages into a system, and speech synthesis (at the receiver's end) providing an alternative to graphic communication. Then there is the complementary effect, with vision being added to already existing speech modalities (both synchronous and asynchronous), as in the case of the personal videophone, videoconferencing using mobile phones, and video extensions to e-mail and chat situations. Here we shall

---

[3] Cotton and Garrett (1999: 14). JPEG refers to Joint Photographic Experts Group, the standard method for the electronic transmission of photographs.

experience real-time smooth visibility of the person(s) we are talking to – and also, in some applications, the option of seeing ourselves as well – thus making irrelevant the communicative inadequacies described in earlier chapters. Of course, whether these technologies will be welcomed or implemented by, for example, the members of those synchronous chatgroups where anonymity and fantasy are the essence of the interaction, remains to be seen.

The developments which will bring languages together take me away from the theme of this book, but they should at least be mentioned for the sake of completeness. Here we are talking about the provision of automatic translation of increasing quality via multilingual browsers. It will still take some decades for translation devices to leave behind their errorful and pidgin-like character, and routinely achieve a language level with high-quality grammatical, semantic, and discourse content; but once available, it will be routinely accessible through the Internet. We can also envisage the translating telephone, where we speak into a phone, and the software carries out the required speech recognition, translation, and speech synthesis, enabling the listeners to hear our speech in their own language. It is only a short step from here to Douglas Adams' 'Babel fish', inserted into the ear to enable the same thing to happen in face-to-face communication.[4] The implications of such technologies on languages have yet to be fully appreciated. Plainly the arrival of automatic translation will act as a natural force counteracting the currently accelerating trend towards the use of English (or any other language) as a global lingua franca. But there are more fundamental implications, for, in a world where it is possible to translate automatically from any one language into any other, we have to face up to the issue of whether people will be bothered to learn foreign languages at all. Such a world is, of course, a very long way off. Only a tiny number of languages are seen to be commercially viable prospects for automatic translation research, and few of the world's languages have attracted linguistic research of

---

[4] Adams (1979: ch. 6).

the magnitude required to make machine translation viable. The issue is, accordingly, only of theoretical interest – for now.

Most of the technological developments in the above paragraphs are, fortunately, not so apocalyptic in their implications; but every one does raise a linguistic issue of some kind. Interactivity is one of the key themes. The more integration there is, the more it will need to be managed. We need to think about the design of interactive screens, and the development of a simple and unambiguous command structure which will handle both linear and interactive media. How linguistically smart will 'smart software' actually be? The psychophysical limitations of the technology have to be anticipated: just how much manageable information is it possible to receive on a wristwatch television, or on the screen of a mobile phone? Each technical context will present its own linguistic constraints and opportunities, whether it be 'interactive digital television' (DTV), 'interactive video-on-demand', 'interactive movies', or any other development. For example, what language demands will be made on us when we decide to be involved in the last of these – real-time computer-generated scenarios, in which we would find ourselves interacting with film-stars in predesigned cinematic settings? [5] Or, in cases where speech synthesis is going to present our persona to the rest of the world, whether in our own language or in some other, what type of accent will we choose to use? A new kind of anonymity will then be possible, as we display ourselves in a phonetic guise of our own choosing (within the set allowed by the software). Accent being such a sensitive issue, I can foresee all the old issues of appropriateness and correctness, so beloved by correspondents to the BBC, taking on a new computer-mediated lease of life.

The following example illustrates how a new technology has immediate linguistic consequences. During the 1990s, the mobile phone industry developed its *short message service* (SMS), often referred to as *texting*. This has seen a remarkable growth, with

---

[5] The possibility was illustrated in the 'a, b, and c' episode of *The Prisoner* ITC television series of the 1960s, where the character played by Patrick McGoohan is electronically introduced into a film dream scenario where he interacts with the characters.

some 8 billion messages sent worldwide in August 2000, 15 billion in December, and a steady lowering of the age of phone users – two-thirds of 14- to 16-year-olds have their own phone, and 10- to 11-year-olds are the fastest growing market. It is a cheaper medium than conventional voice calling, and a more private medium, in that users can communicate without their conversation aurally disturbing other people they happen to be with. A Mori/Lycos UK survey published in September 2000 showed that 81% of mobile phone users between the ages of 15 and 24 were using their phone for sending text messages, typically to co-ordinate their social lives, to engage in language play, to flirt, or just to send a 'thinking of you' message. Apparently, 37% of all messagers have used the service to tell someone they love them. At the same time, reports suggest that the service is being used for other purposes, such as sexual harassment, school bullying, political rumour-mongering, and interaction between drug dealers and clients.

The challenge of the small screen size and its limited character space (about 160 characters), as well as the small keypad, has motivated the evolution of an even more abbreviated language than emerged in chatgroups and virtual worlds (see also p. 84). Some of the same abbreviations appear, either because of their 'obvious' rebus-like potential (e.g. *NE1*, *2day*, *B4*, *C U l8r* ['later'], and *Z* ['said']) or because the generally youthful population of users were familiar with Netspeak shorthand in its other situations (e.g. *Msg* ['message'], *BRB* ['be right back']). Basic smileys (p. 36) are also used. Capital letters can be given syllabic values, as in *thN* ['then'] and *nEd* ['need']. But the medium has motivated some new forms (e.g. *c%l* ['cool']) and its own range of direct-address items, such as *F2T* ['free to talk?'], *Mob* ['mobile'], *PCM* ['please call me'], *MMYT* ['Mail me your thoughts'], and *RUOK* ['are you OK?']. Multi-word sentences and sequences of response utterances, especially of a stereotyped kind, can be reduced to a sequence of initial letters: *SWDYT* ['So what do you think?'], *BCBC* ['Beggars can't be choosers'], *BTDT* ['Been there, done that'], *YYSSW* ['Yeah, yeah, sure, sure, whatever'], *HHOJ* ['Ha, ha, only joking']. Users seem to be aware of the information value of consonants as opposed to vowels, judging by such vowel-less items as *TXT* ['text'] and *XLNT* ['excellent']. The process saves a great deal of time and energy (given the awkwardness of selecting letters on the small keypad), and in those companies which still charge by the character (as opposed to the whole message), there is an economic value in abbreviation, too. In a creation such as *ru2cnmel8r* ['Are you two seeing me later?'], less than half the characters of the full form of the sentence are used. Even more ingenious coded abbreviations have been devised, especially among those for whom argot is a desirable safeguard against unwelcome surveillance.[6]

What is not clear is just how limiting this technology is, as a text messaging system. There must be a serious limit to the amount of information which can be conveyed using abbreviation, and a real risk of ambiguity as soon as people try to go beyond a stock set of social phrases. These constraints will become increasingly apparent as people try to adapt the technology to grander designs, such as Internet access. While it is possible in principle[7] to send e-mails and download Web pages onto a WAP ['Wireless Application Protocol'] phone screen or the display of our personal digital assistant, several questions are still not answered (or even asked, it sometimes appears), such as: what do we lose, informationally speaking, when a graphically elaborate text is reduced to such a scale? To what extent will perceptual constraints affect our ability to process linguistic contrastivity? What kind of linguistic 'translation' needs to take place in order to ensure that the sentence structures used on the small screen are manageable and intelligible? It seems inevitable that sentence length will tend to be short, and that certain types of complex sentence structure (involving relative clauses, for instance) will be avoided. If the loss or distortion of information is going to be great, might this not have an effect on the desirability of the

---

[6] The first small dictionaries of abbreviations began to appear in 2000, compiled by Motorola, BT Cellnet (Genie), and others; for example, some 250 forms are listed in the Genie SMS DXNRE ['dictionary']. As with all dictionaries of 'new words', it is likely that only a small number of these neologisms will stand the test of time.

[7] 'In principle', because current WAP phones cannot access many Web sites, since they operate on WML ['Wireless Markup Language'], whereas the current language of the Web is HTML (see p. 205). The arrival of XML ['Extensible Markup Language'] should remove this difficulty.

technology? Great claims have been made for its use in accessing e-mail, booking tickets, receiving news, gambling, playing games, and so on, but – to take just one example – how many text games will it be possible to play? Having explored this possibility myself, on behalf of an electronic publishing firm, the answers are not promising, with rather simple-minded multiple-choice games pushing the system to its limits. Doubtless, as the technology develops, a whole new domain of restricted language will emerge, as people adapt their messages to fit the screen, and make use of new software options.[8] But as I write, some commentators are already casting doubts on the long-term future of WAP, despite its strengths. Ironically, because abbreviation saves time and money, the linguistic innovations brought about by this technology are likely to outlast its demise.

Applied Internet linguistics

A further dimension to the linguistic variety promoted by the new technologies relates to the content they carry. As with traditional written expression, the medium will influence the general character of the language to be used – whether it is information, education, entertainment, edutainment, advertising, buying and selling, on-screen guides, teletext services, or any other domain. Within these broad categories, subject-related domains (science, religion, law, etc.) will doubtless evolve computer-mediated varieties along similar lines to those which emerged in traditional speech and writing. I would also expect to see more specialized varieties, as organizations develop intranet systems and use them for their individual purposes, such as conferences, brainstorming, voting, and in-house editing. And I would expect to see a huge increase in the range of 'applied' varieties, as different professions gain more confidence in computer-mediated technology, and start to develop its potential for their individual purposes. The Internet has already begun to be used in this way.

---

[8] For example, a typical phone is able to predict likely words from the keystrokes entered, using a stored list of 10,000 or more pre-programmed words.

The various language professions have begun to take strides of varying length, with respect to the different Internet situations, the field of foreign language teaching taking the first and longest ones (as has traditionally been the case in applied linguistics). Language pathologists, literacy specialists, mother-tongue teachers, and others have begun to sense the possibilities of the Internet as a medium for motivating their populations (patients, reluctant readers, etc.), and as a way of facilitating some of their clinical, remedial, or educational tasks, at least with reference to reading and writing.[9] But it is in relation to foreign-language pedagogy that the most searching discussions have taken place, along with some innovative and effective practices relating to both teaching and learning. This domain has long been involved in computer-assisted language learning (CALL), but the Internet has provided a fresh dimension. Mark Warschauer and Deborah Healey, in a state-of-the-art review in 1998, sum it up in this way:[10]

> It is the rise of computer-mediated communication and the Internet, more than anything else, which has reshaped the uses of computers for language learning at the end of the 20th century (Eastment 1996). With the advent of the Internet, the computer – both in society and in the classroom – has been transformed from a tool for information processing and display to a tool for information processing and communication. For the first time, learners of a language can now communicate inexpensively and quickly with other learners or speakers of the target language all over the world.

The reference is to David Eastment, who carried out a survey on English-language teaching (ELT) in relation to the Internet, on behalf of the British Council in 1996,[11] and who was in 'no

---

[9] A typical forward-looking statement in the field of speech and language pathology and audiology is Masterson, Wynne, Kuster, and Stierwalt (1999). For references to educational Web-based language projects generally, see Atwell (1999); and for projects in creative writing, see Dorner (2000). For writing composition, see the papers in the special issue (8:1) of the journal *Written Communication* (1991). A wide range of topics is covered in the journal *Literary and Linguistic Computing*.

[10] Warschauer and Healey (1998: 63).

[11] Eastment (1999: 1), the published version of a survey originally carried out for the British Council's English 2000 project. See also Dudeney (2000).

doubt that the Internet ... will eventually transform the way that the teaching and learning of English, and the business of ELT is conducted'.

Each of the five Netspeak situations reviewed in this book has relevance. E-mail, to begin with, is a convenient medium which gives students the experience of authentic writing tasks, in relation to fellow-students, teachers, and native-speaker contacts.[12] It is now widely incorporated into language teaching – in those parts of the world where Internet access is routine – for a broad range of purposes, such as 'domestic' exchanges on everyday topics, teacher feedback on points of usage, exercises in business correspondence, and collaborative research projects. It is even possible to have the words of a text given an automatic grammatical parsing, using an e-mail connection.[13] Additional textual and graphic material can be sent through the use of attachments. An interesting example of the way the medium has been adapted for a specific teaching purpose is the 'language learning in tandem' approach, in which people with different languages work together in pairs. Each participant sends messages in the other person's language, and provides feedback on problems of usage as they occur. The procedure also gives the participants the chance to learn about each other's character and culture, and exchange knowledge about their professional lives. David Little and Helmut Brammerts summarize the aims of the approach in this way:[14]

> to create, in the international computer network, the Internet, the technical, organizational and didactic requirements for students of the participating institutions – and eventually even more universities – to work together across national boundaries in order to learn languages from one another and to learn more about one another's culture by learning in tandem.

---

[12] See Kelm (1995) and Tella (1992), which also contains reference to two earlier projects (Reports 95 and 99).
[13] <amalgam-tagger@scs.leeds.ac.uk>.
[14] Little and Brammerts (1996: 19). The International E-Mail Tandem Network, with several European universities participating, was set up to take forward this method of working. Follow-up studies include Appel (1999) and Little, Ushioda, Appel, Moran, O'Rourke, and Schwienhorst (1999).

The use of e-mail in this way certainly puts traditional methods of contact in the shade. I recall in 1960, after a multinational work experience in Europe, attempting to work in tandem with an Algerian Arab friend – my English in exchange for his Arabic. It lasted only a few weeks, simply because of the impracticability of the only method then available to us – exchange by slow and expensive letter. If e-mail had existed then . . .

Both of the main types of chatgroup interaction are used in foreign-language teaching. Asynchronous situations, such as mailing lists and newsgroups, have been found to facilitate teacher-level discussion of issues, opportunities for student contact, and teacher–student interaction, the latter settings soon taking on the characteristics of a virtual classroom. The asynchronous context gives students time to read, understand, and respond, without the pressures of real-time interaction. But synchronous interaction is also being used, both as a straightforward chatgroup and as a virtual world. One chat procedure uses split-screen techniques, in which a message from a student typed onto the bottom half of the screen is seen by any other students involved in the exercise on the top half of their screens, with messages listed in the order in which they are received. While this procedure can take place in a local environment, the Internet widens the options considerably.[15] The educational benefits already noted in chapter 5, where all the students were native speakers, are enhanced in a foreign-language-teaching context, with students participating more evenly, and teachers exercising a less dominant role. Logs of interactions can be saved for later study – an extremely useful option for learners. The greater imaginative content and authenticity of a virtual world, which can be tailored to meet students' interests, can also be highly motivating. However, the constraining effects of multi-person interaction on language, such as shorter sentence length and uncertain turn-taking, have yet to be fully investigated. Lively and authentic MUDs may be,

---

[15] An example of a programme used for local area networks is Daedalus Interchange. For a discussion with reference to virtual worlds, see Pinto (1996).

and an excellent medium for promoting rapid responses, but their utterances represent only a small part of the grammatical repertoire of a language.

Finally, the Web offers an unprecedented array of opportunities for both students and teachers. Whatever complaints there may have been in the past, over the lack of availability of 'authentic materials', there must now be a general satisfaction that so much genuine written data is readily available, with spoken data on the horizon (see above). (Indeed, the pedagogical problem is now the opposite – to evaluate and grade what is available, so that students are not overwhelmed.) Another benefit is that the Web can put learners in contact with up-to-date information about a language, especially through the use of online dictionaries, usage guides, and suchlike – though at present these are in limited supply, with problems of access fees and copyright still awaiting solution in many instances. Web sites can provide a greater variety of materials, attractively packaged, such as newspaper articles, quizzes, exercises, self-assessment tasks, and other forms. As a publishing medium, moreover, the Web offers unprecedented opportunities to students, for both individual and collaborative work.[16] David Eastment estimated that (in 1999) there were a thousand ELT sites devoted to language learning activities, resources, and materials.[17] At the same time, he was firm about the need for caution:

> A few ELT sites are worthwhile; but at the moment, they are few and far between, and the learner, whether in class or studying alone, would be better advised to concentrate on conventional ELT materials. . . . At the time of writing, it is clear that a shelf of EFL workbooks and coursebooks would offer far more in terms of exercises, activities and ideas than the whole of the World Wide Web.

The situation will change, but only after there has been much more progress in the adaptation of materials, to the screen and in teacher training. Eastment puts it this way:[18]

---

[16] See Bowers (1995).   [17] Eastment (1999: 23–4).   [18] Eastment (1999: 28).

Conventional CALL was difficult enough for many teachers. The Web, for all its advantages, can be even more harrowing. What do you do when the site around which you had planned your session suddenly disappears? How can you keep your students learning when the whole Internet slows to a crawl? How can you keep control during an IRC [Internet Relay Chat] session? And what is the best way of handling a student who covertly calls up the Playboy site?

Teachers, he suggests, need to learn search-engine skills, ways of evaluating Web pages, techniques for manipulating and creating their own Web materials, and methods of integrating Web activities with the rest of their teaching. And he adds a further point: 'Teachers need to learn new languages' – by which he does not mean new foreign languages, but the 'language of the Internet' – an essential first step of familiarization with procedures and nomenclature.

The use of the Internet in foreign-language teaching may be in its infancy, but it is plainly here to stay. Yet it already presents teachers with fresh challenges. The difficulties noted in chapter 2, arising out of the nature of the medium in conversation, apply with greater force to foreign learners – the lack of intonational cues, facial expressions, and so on. Also, teachers have to work out ways of handling a new kind of difficulty – new, at least, in the order of magnitude that it presents – namely, the fact that so much of the native-speaker usage in chatgroups and virtual worlds is non-standard, often ludic and highly deviant. The tolerance of typographical error, and the relaxation of the rules of spelling, punctuation, and capitalization (p. 87), are not in themselves novelties to learners, for the same flexibility doubtless exists in their own mother-tongue Internet use. But foreign learners lack the intuitive sense of the boundary between standard and non-standard, or a sense of just how deviant a chatgroup usage might be, and by dint of exposure to repeated instances they may well end up misusing a construction, idiom, or other form. The bending and breaking of rules, which is a hallmark of ludic linguistic behaviour,[19] always

---

[19] Crystal (1998: ch. 1).

presents a problem to those who have not yet developed a confident command of the rules *per se*. Ironically, learners can sometimes give the impression that they are more fluent than they actually are, in that their errors can superficially resemble the deviant forms flamboyantly manifested by chatgroup users.

Increasing the richness of language

Writers on the Internet struggle to find ways of expressing its unprecedented impact. Here is John Naughton, continuing the visionary theme with which I introduced my Preface:[20]

> A force of unimaginable power – a Leviathan ... – is loose in our world, and we are as yet barely aware of it. It is already changing the way we communicate, work, trade, entertain and learn; soon it will transform the ways we live and earn. Perhaps one day it will even change the way we think. It will undermine established industries and create new ones. It challenges traditional notions of sovereignty, makes a mockery of national frontiers and continental barriers and ignores cultural sensitivities. It accelerates the rate of technological change to the point where even those who are supposed to be riding the crest of the wave begin to complain of 'change fatigue'.

Language being such a sensitive index of social change, it would be surprising indeed if such a radically innovative phenomenon did not have a corresponding impact on the way we communicate. And so it can be argued. Language is at the heart of the Internet, for Net activity is interactivity. 'The Net is really a system which links together a vast number of computers *and the people who use them*.'[21] These are Naughton's words, and his italics. The Internet is not just a technological fact; it is a social fact, as Berners-Lee has insisted (p. vii); and its chief stock-in-trade is language.

What kind of impact might we expect a 'force of unimaginable power' to make on language? We have seen, in the central chapters

---

[20] Naughton (1999: 45).   [21] Naughton (1999: 40).

of this book, a range of intriguingly new and still evolving linguistic varieties, characterized by sets of specific adaptations, in graphology, grammar, semantics, and discourse, to the properties of the technology and the needs of the user. They suggest an answer to the second of the two questions I raised in chapter 1 (p. 9): is the Internet emerging as a homogenous linguistic medium or is it a collection of distinct dialects? The latter, surely, is the case. Although there are a few properties which different Internet situations seem to share, these do not in aggregate make a very strong case for a view of Netspeak as a variety. But if Netspeak is not a variety, what is it? Is there anything at all to be said, if we step back from the detail of these situations, and 'take a view' about Internet language as a whole? The first question I asked on p. viii was whether the 'electronic revolution' was bringing about a linguistic revolution. The evidence suggests that it is. The phenomenon of Netspeak is going to 'change the way we think' about language in a fundamental way, because it is a linguistic singularity – a genuine new medium.

At various places in this book, linguists, stylists, editors, and other observers have groped for analogies to express what they find in Internet language, and have failed. The kind of language which is on the Internet in its different situations, though displaying some similarities with other forms of communication, is fundamentally different from them. Comparisons with note-taking, letter-writing, amateur radio, citizens'-band radio, and all the other communicative acts mentioned in earlier chapters prove to be singularly unilluminating. For Netspeak is something completely new. It is neither 'spoken writing' nor 'written speech'. As I argued in chapter 2, it is something fundamentally different from both writing and speech, as traditionally understood. It is, in short, a fourth medium. In language studies, we are used to discussing issues in terms of 'speech vs. writing vs. signing'. From now on we must add a further dimension to comparative enquiry: 'spoken language vs. written language vs. sign language vs. computer-mediated language'.[22] Netspeak is a

---

[22] A contrast is intended here with 'computer-mediated communication', which includes the whole range of communicative expression (pictures, music, etc.), whether linguistically

development of millennial significance. A new medium of linguistic communication does not arrive very often, in the history of the race.

As a new linguistic medium, Netspeak will doubtless grow in its sociolinguistic and stylistic complexity to be comparable to that already known in traditional speech and writing.[23] But it is too soon to be certain about the form these new varieties will take. Even the ones identified in this book are somewhat tentative, in view of the difficulties of researching them. Studies of Netspeak are in their earliest stages. Part of the difficulty is finding extensive samples of usable data, relating to each of the Internet situations. We saw in earlier chapters how there is still a great deal of sensitivity over using logs of chatgroups and virtual worlds, and the issue of e-mail sampling has hardly been addressed. Uncertain copyright and privacy issues embattle the Web. Even when good data samples are obtained, there are immense problems over displaying their discourse structure, given the number of participants involved and the difficulties of monitoring turn-taking.[24] Each situation also presents problems arising out of the transitional nature of the medium: Netspeak is still in an early stage of its evolution, and generalizations are difficult to make. I am under no illusion, therefore, that this book can only provide a somewhat blurred snapshot of how things appeared at this particular point in time.[25]

Another reason for the difficulty in predicting Internet language development is the existence of so many conflicting trends and pressures. The Net is an immensely empowering, individualistic, creative medium, as can be seen from the numerous experimental ways in which people use it. Writers are exploring new ways of

structured or not. Herring uses the phrase 'text-based CMC' (Herring, 1996a: 1); Collot and Belmore (1996) use 'electronic language'.

[23] A conclusion also of Collot and Belmore (1996: 27).

[24] An interesting attempt to display chatgroup conversational structure is Donath, Karahalios, and Viégas (1999). They use a system of chat circles, which grow in size depending on how much text there is. The postings are shown for a few seconds, and then gradually fade – as if in real-life conversation, where the focus is on the words of the person who spoke last. They introduce a 'zone of hearing' which mimics the way a participant stays with one conversation or switches between different conversations.

[25] For other linguistic snapshots, and a similar plea for empirical research, see the introduction and papers in Herring (1996a).

using the Web, such as by publishing work there in instalments, collaborating in creative writing, and allowing users to influence the direction in which a story goes.[26] Editors are producing collaborative critical editions of texts and oeuvres.[27] Digital artists are exploiting the graphic properties of the medium to produce pictorial and pictographic works of 'ASCII art'.[28] There is evidence of a fresh interest in the visual properties of letters and other symbols, and in exploiting the potential of the software to present typographical variation. The creativity can be seen even in very restricted linguistic domains of Net activity, such as naming. The apparently straightforward issue of e-addresses has proved to be a world of considerable complexity, because the enormous expansion of the Net, and the limited number of 'ordinary words' available for names, has forced individuals as well as companies to be highly creative in their naming practices (p. 159).[29] The creativity, moreover, is moving in unexpected directions. With so much emphasis on the way the Net promotes global interaction and shared knowledge, it comes as a surprise to note that increasing numbers of Net-users do *not* want to interact globally or share information. On the contrary, they want to protect their knowledge, and their privacy. We have already devised barriers to stop undesired interruptions in the senior communication services – ex-directory telephone numbers, for example. Attention is now being paid to developing similar protective measures in Netspeak, such as filters for e-mail spam (p. 53) and increasingly sophisticated measures of encryption. This too has its linguistic dimension.

As I said in my Preface, I wrote this book because I wanted to find out about the Internet and its effect on language, and could

---

[26] See the hypertext journal of creative writing, *Kairos* <http://english.ttu.edu/kairos>; also Deegan (2000: 7), Sutherland (1997).

[27] For example, of *Beowulf, Canterbury tales*, Wittgenstein: see Deegan (2000: 8).

[28] Several other artistic projects have explored new cyber-uses of language. For example, Nick Crowe's 'New Medium' (2000) is a series of fifteen glass panels functioning as memorial sites, each with a hand-engraved loving message to a deceased person. Alicia Felberbaum's 'Textures of memory: the poetics of cloth' (2000) uses weaving to reflect the evolving language of the Internet.

[29] See Koizumi (2000), who advises companies looking for a name to avoid diacritics, long names, and trendy contractions and spellings (cf. p. 22).

find none already written. It has proved to be an exploratory, programmatic work, in no way definitive. It suggests material for a thousand theses.[30] But the sheer scale of the present Internet, let alone its future telecosmic incarnations, has convinced me that we are on the brink of the biggest language revolution ever. Whereas in the past we have had speech, then writing, and throughout the 20th century debated the relationship between the two, now we are faced with a new medium, and one which could be bigger than either of its predecessors. What I have been calling Netspeak will become part of a much larger computer-mediated language, which in the digitally designed enhanced-bandwidth environment of the future could be the community's linguistic norm. Whereas, at the moment, face-to-face communication ranks as primary, in any account of the linguistic potentialities of humankind, in the future it may not be so. In a statistical sense, we may one day communicate with each other far more via computer mediation than in direct interaction. The effects on what counts as 'normal' language acquisition could be similarly profound. The social implications of this are so mind-boggling that this linguist, for the moment, can only ruminate ineffectively about them. Perhaps here there are grounds for real concern.

But with respect to the kinds of neurosis expressed at the beginning of chapter 1, I do not feel concern. I do not see the Internet being the death of languages, but the reverse (p. 219). I view each of the Netspeak situations as an area of huge potential enrichment for individual languages. I cannot say anything systematic about what is happening to languages other than English, but casual observation of non-English sites suggests that other languages are evolving in the computer-mediated setting in analogous ways.[31] The English experience, as illustrated in earlier chapters, and despite the still emerging nature of the language in each case, is one of remarkable

---

[30] To take just one field: the acquisition of Netspeak. How do people – adults and children alike – go about acquiring proficiency, or even competence, in the situations I have described? Longitudinal and comparative studies are conspicuous by their absence. A comparative perspective (between novice users of IRC and young children using the phone) does however motivate Gillen and Goddard (2000).

[31] Both French and English data are included in Werry (1996).

diversity and creativity. There is no indication, in any of the areas
I have examined, of Netspeak replacing or threatening already existing varieties. On the contrary, the arrival of new, informal, even
bizarre forms of language extends the range of our sensitivity to
linguistic contrasts.[32] Formal language, and other kinds of informal
language, are seen in a new light, by virtue of the existence of Netspeak. An analogy with clothing helps make this point. I remember
once owning a very formal shirt and another I used for informal
occasions. Then I was given a grotesque creation that I was assured
was the latest cool trend in informality; and certainly, the effect was
to make my previously informal shirt look really somewhat staid.
The new shirt had not destroyed my sense of the value of a formal
vs. informal contrast in dress behaviour; it simply extended it. I was
sartorially enriched, with more options available to me. I see the
arrival of Netspeak as similarly enriching the range of communicative options available to us. And the Internet is going to record this
linguistic diversity more fully and accurately than was ever possible
before.

What is truly remarkable is that so many people have learned
so quickly to adapt their language to meet the demands of the
new situations, and to exploit the potential of the new medium
so creatively to form new areas of expression. It has all happened
within a few decades. The human linguistic faculty seems to be in
good shape, I conclude. The arrival of Netspeak is showing us *homo
loquens* at its best.

[32] The point is beginning to be recognized. John Cumming (1995: 7) quotes a US columnist,
Jon Carroll: 'E-mail and computer conferencing is teaching an entire generation about the
flexibility and utility of prose.' Li Lan (2000: 55) answers his question, 'email: a challenge
to Standard English?' in the negative: 'E-mail style may not therefore directly challenge
Standard English, but seems likely to extend it in a variety of ways.'

References

URLs here and in the footnotes were correct at the time of going to press (February 2001), but are subject to change.

Adams, Douglas. 1979. *The hitch-hiker's guide to the galaxy.* London: Pan.

Adams, Lin, Lori Toomey, and Elizabeth Churchill. 1999. Distributed research teams: meeting asynchronously in virtual space. *Journal of Computer-Mediated Communication* 4(4).
<http://www.ascusc.org/jcmc/vol4/issue4/adams.html>.

Aijmer, Karin, and Bengt Altenberg (eds.). 1991. *English corpus linguistics.* London: Longman.

Angell, David, and Brent Heslop. 1994. *The elements of e-mail style.* New York: Addison-Wesley.

Appel, Marie Christine. 1999. *Tandem language learning by e-mail: some basic principles and a case study.* Centre for Language and Communication Studies Occasional Paper 54. Dublin: Trinity College.

Atwell, Eric. 1999. *The language machine.* London: British Council.

Baron, Naomi S. 1984. Computer Mediated Communication as a force in language change. *Visible Language* 18, 118–41.

1998a. Writing in the age of email: the impact of ideology versus technology. *Visible Language* 32, 35–53.

1998b. Letters by phone or speech by other means: the linguistics of email. *Language and Communication* 18, 133–70.

2000. *Alphabet to email.* London: Routledge.

Bateson, Gregory. 1972. *Steps to an ecology of mind.* New York: Ballentine.

Bauer, Laurie. 1983. *English word-formation.* Cambridge: Cambridge University Press.

Baym, Nancy K. 1993. Interpreting soap operas and creating community: inside a computer-mediated fan culture. *Journal of Folklore Research* 30(2/3), 143–76.

1995. The performance of humor in computer-mediated communication. *Journal of Computer-Mediated Communication* 1(2).
<http://www.ascusc.org/jcmc/vol1/issue2/baym.html>.

Bechar-Israeli, Haya. 1996. From <Bonehead> to <cLoNehEAd>: nicknames, play, and identity on Internet Relay Chat. *Journal of Computer-Mediated Communication* 1(2). <http://www.ascusc.org/jcmc/vol1/issue2/bechar.html>.

Berners-Lee, Tim. 1999. *Weaving the Web.* London: Orion Business Books.

Biber, Douglas. 1988. *Variation across speech and writing.* Cambridge: Cambridge University Press.

Biber, Douglas, Stig Johansson, Geoffrey Leech, Susan Conrad, and Edward Finegan. 1999. *Longman grammar of spoken and written English.* Harlow: Longman.

Bolter, Jay David (ed.). 1991. *The writing space: the computer, hypertext and the history of writing.* Hillsdale, NJ: Erlbaum.

Borgman, Christine L. 1986. Why are online catalogues hard to use? Lessons learned from information-retrieval studies. *Journal of the American Society for Information Science* 37, 387–400.

   1996. Why are online catalogues still hard to use? *Journal of the American Society for Information Science* 47, 493–503.

Bourbonnais, Jean, and François Yergeau. 1996. Languages on the Internet. <http://www.isoc.org/inet96/proceedings/a5/a5_3.htm>.

Bowers, R. 1995. Web publishing for students of EST. In Mark Warschauer (ed.), *Virtual connections: online activities and projects for networking language learners.* Honolulu: University of Hawaii.

Branwyn, Gareth. 1997. *Jargon watch.* San Francisco: HardWired.

Brookes, Terrence A. 1998. Orthography as a fundamental impediment to online information retrieval. *Journal of the American Society for Information Science,* 49(8), 731–41.

Bruckman, Amy. 1993. Gender swapping on the Internet. Proceedings of INET. <http://www.cc.gatech.edu/fac/Amy.Bruckman/papers/index.html>.

Butcher, Judith. 1992. *Copy-editing,* 3rd edn. Cambridge: Cambridge University Press.

Cherny, Lynn. 1999. *Conversation and community: chat in a virtual world.* Stanford, CA: CSLI Publications.

Coates, Jennifer. 1993. *Women, men and language,* 2nd edn. London: Longman.

Collot, Milena, and Nancy Belmore. 1993. Electronic language: a new variety of English. In Jan Aarts, Pieter de Haan, and Nelleke Oostdijk (eds.), *English language corpora: design, analysis and explanation.* Amsterdam: Rodopi.

   1996. Electronic language: a new variety of English. In Herring (ed.), 13–28.

Condron, Frances. 2000a. Starting points on the Internet. In Condron, Fraser, and Sutherland (eds.), 13–18.

2000b. Fonts and special characters. In Condron, Fraser, and Sutherland (eds.), 233–5.

Condron, Frances, Michael Fraser, and Stuart Sutherland (eds.). 2000. *CTI* [=Computers in Teaching Initiative] *textual studies: guide to digital resources for the humanities.* Oxford: University of Oxford, Humanities Computing Unit.

Connery, Brian A. 1996. Authority and egalitarian rhetoric in the virtual coffeehouse. In Porter (ed.), 161–79.

Cotton, Bob, and Malcolm Garrett. 1999. *You ain't seen nothing yet: the future of media and the global expert system.* London: Institute of Contemporary Arts.

Cowan, Andrew. 1997. History of MUDs. <http://www.mudconnect.com/mud_intro.html>.

Crystal, David. 1969. *Prosodic systems and intonation in English.* Cambridge: Cambridge University Press.

1984. *Who cares about English usage?* Harmondsworth: Penguin.

1995. *The Cambridge encyclopedia of the English language.* Cambridge: Cambridge University Press.

1997a. *The Cambridge encyclopedia of language,* 2nd edn. Cambridge: Cambridge University Press.

1997b. *Dictionary of linguistics and phonetics,* 4th edn. Oxford: Blackwell.

1997c. *English as a global language.* Cambridge: Cambridge University Press.

1997d. A Lexical Filter Internet Enquirer (ALFIE). White paper for AND Classification Data, Rotterdam and Oxford.

1998. *Language play.* Harmondsworth: Penguin.

1999. Language BLANK literature: from conjunction to preposition. *English Today,* 15, 13–21.

Crystal, David, and Derek Davy. 1969. *Investigating English style.* London: Longman.

1976. *Advanced conversational English.* London: Longman.

Crystal, David, and Randolph Quirk. 1964. *Systems of prosodic and para-linguistic features in English.* The Hague: Mouton.

Cumming, John D. 1995. The Internet and the English language. *English Today* 11(1), 3–8.

Daniels, Peter T., and William Bright (eds.). 1996. *The world's writing systems.* Oxford: Oxford University Press.

Danielson, Peter. 1996. Pseudonyms, mailbots, and virtual letterheads: the evolution of computer-mediated ethics. In Charles Ess (ed.),

Philosophical perspectives on computer-mediated communication (Albany, NY: State University of New York Press), 67–94.

Davis, Boyd H., and Jeutonne P. Brewer. 1997. *Electronic discourse: linguistic individuals in virtual space.* Albany, NY: State University of New York Press.

Deegan, Marilyn. 2000. Introduction. In Condron, Fraser, and Sutherland (eds.), 1–12.

Dery, Mark. 1993. Flame wars. *Southern Atlantic Quarterly* 92, 559–68.
   (ed.) 1997. *Flame wars: the discourse of cyberculture.* Durham: Duke University Press.

Dibbell, Julian. 1997. A rape in cyberspace. In Dery (ed.), 237–61.

Donath, Judith, Karrie Karahalios, and Fernanda Viégas. 1999. Visualizing conversation. *Journal of Computer-Mediated Communication* 4(4).
   <http://www.ascusc.org/jcmc/vol4/issue4/donath.html>.

Dorner, Jane. 1992. Virtual English. *English Today* 32, 29–34.
   2000. *The Internet: a writer's guide.* London: A. and C. Black.

Dudeney, Gavin. 2000. *The Internet and the language classroom.* Cambridge: Cambridge University Press.

Dunbar, Robin. 1996. *Grooming, gossip, and the evolution of language.* London: Faber and Faber.

Durusau, Patrick. 1996. *High places in cyberspace.* Atlanta: Scholars Press.

Eastment, David. 1999. *The Internet and ELT.* Oxford: Summertown Publishing.

Economist, The. 1996. Language and electronics: the coming global tongue. 21 December, 37.

Elmer-Dewitt, Philip. 1994. Bards of the Internet. *Time,* 4 July, 66–7.

Erickson, Jim. 1998. Cyberspeak: the death of diversity. *Asiaweek,* 3 July, 15.

Erickson, Thomas. 1999. Persistent conversation: an introduction. *Journal of Computer-Mediated Communication* 4(4).
   <http://www.ascusc.org/jcmc/vol4/issue4/ericksonintro.html>.

Ferrara, K., H. Brunner, and G. Whittemore. 1991. Interactive written discourse as an emergent register. *Written Communication* 8(1), 8–34.

Flynn, Nancy, and Tom Flynn. 1998. *Writing effective e-mail.* Menlo Park, CA: Crisp Publications.

Foster, Derek. 1996. Community and identity in the electronic village. In Porter (ed.), 23–37.

Gains, J. 1998. Electronic mail – a new style of communication or just a new medium: an investigation into the text features of email. *English for Specific Purposes* 18(1), 81–101.

Gilder, George. 2000. *Telecosm: how infinite bandwidth will revolutionize our world.* New York: Free Press.

Giles, Howard, Justine Coupland, and Nikolas Coupland (eds.). 1991. *Contexts of accommodation.* Cambridge: Cambridge University Press.

Gillen, Julia, and Angela Goddard. 2000. Medium management for beginners: the discursive practices of undergraduate and mature novice users of internet relay chat, compared with those of young children using the telephone. Paper presented at the International Association for Dialogue Analysis, Bologna.

Goffman, E. 1959. *The presentation of self in everyday life.* Garden City, NY: Doubleday.

Goodman, Robert F., and Aaron Ben Ze'ev (eds.). 1994. *Good gossip.* Kansas: University Press of Kansas.

Graddol, David. 1998. *The future of English?* London: The British Council.

Grice, H. P. 1975. Logic and conversation. In Peter Cole and Jerry L. Morgan (eds.), *Syntax and semantics 3: speech acts.* New York: Academic Press, 41–58.

Gurak, Laura J. 1997. *Persuasion and privacy in cyberspace.* New Haven: Yale University Press.

Hahn, Harley. 1999. Harley Hahn's guide to Muds. <http://www.harley.com/muds>.

Hale, Constance, and Jessie Scanlon. 1999. *Wired style: principles of English usage in the digital age.* New York: Broadway Books.

Hall, Edward T. 1959. *The silent language.* New York: Doubleday.

Halliday, Michael. 1978. *Language as social semiotic.* London: Arnold.

Hatch, Evelyn. 1992. *Discourse and language education.* Cambridge: Cambridge University Press.

Herring, Susan C. (ed.). 1996a. *Computer-mediated communication: linguistic, social and cross-cultural perspectives.* Amsterdam: Benjamins.

1996b. Two variants of an electronic message scheme. In Herring (ed.), 81–106.

1999. Interactional coherence in CMC. *Journal of Computer-Mediated Communication* 4(4). <http://www.ascusc.org/jcmc/vol4/issue4/herring.html>.

Ihnatko, Andy. 1997. *Cyberspeak: an online dictionary.* New York: Random House.

Iro, Mizuko. 1996. Virtually embodied: the reality of fantasy in a multiuser dungeon. In Porter (ed.), 87–109.

Jackson, Michele H. 1997. Assessing the structure of communication on the World Wide Web. *Journal of Computer-Mediated Communication* 3(1). <http://www.ascusc.org/jcmc/vol3/issue1/jackson.html>.

Johansson, Stig. 1991. Times change, and so do corpora. In Aijmer and Altenberg (eds.), 305–14.

Keegan, Martin. 1997. MUD tree. <http://camelot.cyburbia.net.au/~martin/cgi-bin/mud_tree.cgi>.

Kelm, O. 1995. E-mail discussion groups in foreign language education: grammar follow-up. In Mark Warschauer (ed.), *Telecollaboration in foreign language learning*. Honolulu: University of Hawaii.

Knowles, Elizabeth. 1997. *The Oxford dictionary of new words*. Oxford: Oxford University Press.

Koizumi, Yuiko. 2000. What shall we name the product? *Language International* 12(2), 26–7.

Lakoff, Robin. 1975. *Language and women's place*. New York: Harper.

Lamb, Linda, and Jerry D. Peek. 1995. *Using email effectively*. Sebastopol, CA: O'Reilly and Associates.

Lawrence, Steve, and C. Lee Giles. 1999. Accessibility of information on the Web. *Nature* 400(6740), 107–9.

Lebert, Marie-France. 1999. *Le multilinguisme sur le Web*. <http://www.ceveil.qc.ca/multi0.htm>. In English at <http://www.ceveil.qc.ca/multieng2.htm>.

Levinson, Stephen C. 1983. *Pragmatics*. Cambridge: Cambridge University Press.

Li Lan. 2000. Email: a challenge to Standard English? *English Today* 64, 23–9, 55.

Li Yongyan. 2000. Surfing emails. *English Today* 64, 30–4, 55.

Little, David, and Helmut Brammerts. 1996. *A guide to language learning in tandem via the Internet*. Centre for Language and Communication Studies Occasional Paper 46. Dublin: Trinity College.

Little, David, Ema Ushioda, Marie Christine Appel, John Moran, Breffni O'Rourke, and Klaus Schwienhorst. 1999. *Evaluating tandem language learning by e-mail: report on a bilateral project*. Centre for Language and Communication Studies Occasional Paper 55. Dublin: Trinity College.

Mabry, Edward A. 1997. Framing flames: the structure of argumentative messages on the net. *Journal of Computer-Mediated Communication* 2(4). <http://www.ascusc.org/jcmc/vol2/issue4/mabry.html>.

McCormick, N. B., and J. W. McCormick. 1992. Computer friends and foes: content of undergraduates' electronic mail. *Computers in Human Behavior* 8, 379–405.

McLaughlin, M. L., K. K. Osborne, and C. B. Smith. 1994. Standards of conduct on Usenet. In Steven G. Jones (ed.), *Cybersociety: computer-mediated communication and community*. Thousand Oaks, CA: Sage, 90–111.

McLuhan, Marshall. 1962. *The Gutenberg galaxy: the making of typographic man.* London: Routledge and Kegan Paul.

Malinowski, Bronislaw. 1923. The problem of meaning in primitive languages. Supplement I to C. K. Ogden and I. A. Richards, *The meaning of meaning* (London: Routledge and Kegan Paul), 296–336.

Marvin, Lee-Ellen. 1996. Spoof, spam, lurk and lag: the aesthetics of text-based virtual realities. *Journal of Computer-Mediated Communication* 1(2). <http://www.ascusc.org/jcmc/vol1/issue2/marvin.html>.

Masterson, Julie J., Michael K. Wynne, Judith M. Kuster, and Julie A. G. Stierwall. 1999. New and emerging technologies: going where we've never gone before. *ASHA* [= American Speech–Language–Hearing Association], May/June, 16–20.

Maynor, Nancy. 1994. The language of electronic mail: written speech? In Michael B. Montgomery and Greta D. Little (eds.), *Centennial usage studies.* Tuscaloosa: University of Alabama Press, 48–54.

Millard, William B. 1996. I flamed Freud: a case study in teletextual incendiarism. In Porter (ed.), 145–59.

Miller, George A. 1969. *The psychology of communication.* Baltimore: Penguin.

Milroy, James, and Lesley Milroy. 1991. *Authority in language,* 2nd edn. London: Routledge.

Murray, Denise E. 1989. When the medium determines turns: turn-taking in computer conversation. In Hywel Coleman (ed.), *Working with language: a multidisciplinary consideration of language use in work contexts.* Berlin: Mouton de Gruyter.

Naughton, John. 1999. *A brief history of the future: the origins of the Internet.* London: Weidenfeld and Nicolson.

Paccagnella, Luciano. 1997. Getting the seats of your pants dirty: strategies for ethnographic research on virtual communication. *Journal of Computer-Mediated Communication* 3(1). <http//www.ascusc.org/jcmc/vol3/issue1/paccagnella.html>.

Paolillo, John. 1999. The virtual speech community: social network and language variation on IRC. *Journal of Computer-Mediated Communication* 4(4). <http://www.ascusc.org/jcmc/vol4/issue4/paolillo.html>.

Peters, Pam. 1998. Langscape: surveying contemporary English usage. *English Today* 53, 3–5.

Pinto, D. 1996. What does 'schMOOze' mean? Non-native speaker interactions on the Internet. In Mark Warschauer (ed.), *Telecollaboration in foreign language learning.* Honolulu: University of Hawaii.

Porter, David. 1996a. Introduction. In Porter (ed.), xi–xviii.

(ed.). 1996b. *Internet culture*. New York and London: Routledge.

Pring, Roger. 1999. *www.type: effective typographic design for the world wide web*. London: Weidenfeld and Nicolson.

Pullum, Geoffrey K., and James D. McCawley (eds.). 1991. *The great Eskimo vocabulary hoax*. Chicago: University of Chicago Press.

Quirk, Randolph, Sidney Greenbaum, Geoffrey Leech, and Jan Svartvik. 1985. *A comprehensive grammar of the English language*. London: Longman.

Rheingold, Howard. 1993. *The virtual community: homesteading on the electronic frontier*. New York: HarperCollins.

Sanderson, David. 1993. *Smileys*. O'Reilly and Associates.

Sebeok, Thomas A., Alfred S. Hayes, and Mary Catherine Bateson (eds.). 1964. *Approaches to semiotics*. The Hague: Mouton.

Selinker, L. 1972. Interlanguage. *International Review of Applied Linguistics* 10, 201–31.

Shea, Virginia. 1994. *Netiquette*. Albion Books.

Slater, Lydia. 2000. Quite e-vil: the mobile phone whisperers. *The Sunday Times*, 30 January, 10.

Specter, Michael. 1996. World, Wide, Web: 3 English Words. *The New York Times*, 14 April, 4–5.

Standage, Tom. 1999. *The Victorian Internet*. New Haven: Phoenix Press.

Stivale, Charles J. 1996. Spam: heteroglossia and harassment in cyberspace. In Porter (ed.), 133–44.

Stubbs, Michael. 1983. *Discourse analysis*. Oxford: Blackwell.

Sutherland, Kathryn (ed.). 1997. *Electronic text: investigations in method and theory*. Oxford: Clarendon Press.

Tannen, Deborah. 1990. *You just don't understand: women and men in conversation*. New York: Morrow.

Tannen, Deborah, and Muriel Saville-Troike (eds.). 1985. *Perspectives on silence*. Norwood, NJ: Ablex.

Tella, Seppo. 1992. *Boys, girls and e-mail: a case study in Finnish senior secondary schools*. Research Report 110. University of Helsinki: Department of Teacher Education.

Thomas, David. 2000. Modern netiquette. *Daily Mail*, 17 July, 11.

Thomas, Ned. 2000. How much IT can minority languages afford? Editorial, *Contact* 16(3), 2.

Thompson, P. A. and D. Ahn. 1992. To be or not to be: an exploration of E-prime, copula deletion and flaming in electronic mail. *Et Cetera: A Review of General Semantics* 49, 146–64.

Twyman, Michael. 1982. The graphic presentation of language. *Information Design Journal* 3, 1–22.

Vehovar, Vasja, Zenel Batagelj, and Katja Lozar. 1999. Language as a barrier. Internet Society Proceedings.
<http://www.isoc.org/inet2000/cdproceedings/inet99/3i/3i_3.htm>.

Wallace, Patricia. 1999. *The psychology of the Internet.* Cambridge: Cambridge University Press.

Walther, J. B. 1996. Computer-Mediated Communication: impersonal, interpersonal and hyperpersonal interaction. *Communication Research* 23(1), 3–43.

Warschauer, Mark, and Deborah Healey. 1998. Computers and language learning: an overview. *Language Teaching* 31(2), 57–71.

Werry, Christopher C. 1996. Linguistic and interactional features of Internet Relay Chat. In Herring (ed.), 47–63.

Wilbur, Shawn T. 1996. An archaeology of cyberspaces: virtuality, community, identity. In Porter (ed.), 5–22.

Witmer, Diane F., and Sandra Lee Katzman. 1997. On-line smiles: does gender make a difference in the use of graphic accents? *Journal of Computer-Mediated Communication* 2(4).
<http://www.ascusc.org/jcmc/vol2/issue4/witmer1.html>.

Yates, Simeon J. 1996. Oral and written linguistic aspects of computer conferencing: a corpus based study. In Herring (ed.), 30–46.

Index of authors

The alphabetical order of this index is letter-by-letter.

Index of topics

The alphabetical arrangement of this index is word-by-word.

inconsistency, 75
indention, 115
Independent, The, 72–3
indexes, 45, 203
  to chat messages, 134, 137
indirect speech, 187
inference languages, 222–3
infixation, 83
informality, 40–1, 64, 77, 101–2, 107, 111,
  122, 127–8, 242
information
  exchange, 168
  overload, 209
  retrieval, 203, 210–11, 213–15
  superhighway, 3
  value of letters, 229–30
informativeness, 49, 203
initialisms, 103, 156
institutional e-mails, 100–1, 103, 110, 114
instructional language, 181
intelligibility, 2, 7, 17, 110–13, 230
interactive
  television, 204
  Web pages, 207–8
  written discourse, 17, 25
Interactive Language Resources Guide, 219
interactivity, 9, 14, 18, 24, 29, 40, 72, 109,
  220, 226, 228, 237
  chatgroups, 153–4, 168–70
  multiparty, 153–4
  non-linear, 136
  virtual worlds, 172, 175, 187
  Web, 202–4
intercaps, 87–8
interest (in subject-matter), 7
interjections, 164
interlanguage, 205
International E-Mail Tandem Network,
  233
Internet
  addiction, 4–5
  addresses, 240
  capitalization, 3
  characterization, 2–3
  globalization, 216
  identity, 62–94
  linguistic future, 216–42
  linguistics, 231–7
  nature of the medium, 24–61, 166, 198,
    236–9
  penetrating a country, 220

  situations, 6–17
  speech used, 9, 226
Internet Corporation for Assigned Names
  and Numbers, 20
Internet Detective, 209
Internet Protocol, 13
Internet Relay Chat, 11, 129, 151–2,
  154–67, 177, 219, 236, 241
Internet Society, 94, 216
interpersonal
  community, 169
  component, 144
interrupted linearity, 196
interruptions, 145, 152–3, 158, 184
intertextuality, 202
interviews, 125, 135
intonation, 34, 38, 236
intranets, 3, 231
inverted pyramid style, 109–10
IRC *see* Internet Relay Chat
IRCnet, 152
irony, 36, 91, 127, 182
irreverence, 75
ISDN, 225
isocybes, 189
isoglosses, 189
it, use of, 147
Italian, 19, 21, 214, 217, 219
italics, 76, 87, 110

Japanese (language), 217, 218
Japanese attitudes to silence, 32
Japanese Patent Bureau, 22
jargon, 25, 67–70, 75, 81, 83–4, 89, 147,
  165, 189
  translation, 223
Jargon File, 67–70
Jargon watch, 67–8
Joint Photographic Experts Group,
  226
*Journal of Computer-Mediated
  Communication*, viii
journalism, 122, 157
JPEG, 226
junk-mail, 10, 54, 77, 97, 99, 103
Jupiter Media Matrix, 218

k-as emphatic prefix, 88–9
Kairos, 240
keyboard properties, 24–5
keypads, 229–30

-*speak*, 17–18
speech
  characteristics, 25–8
  community, 6
  compared to Netspeak, 41–8
  pathology, 232
  recognition, 226–7
  synthesis, 226–8
  technology, 9, 226
  vs writing, 24–48, 238
speech acts, 29
speed
  of e-mails, 111, 127
  of speech, 34, 40
spelling, 2, 195, 198
  American, 88
  checkers, 67
  exaggerated, 34, 88, 185
  guidelines, 74–5, 108
  mistakes, 45, 111–12, 123,
    186, 212
  non-standard, 88–9, 147, 164–6,
    236, 240
  simplification, 75
spontaneity, 40, 111, 127, 148
spoofing, 52, 175
spying, 53
stereotyping, 229
stop words, 215
stream-of-consciousness, 125, 182
streaming media, 225–6
stress (prosodic), 34
Strunkenwhite virus, 213
student conference, 135–8, 141, 143, 145,
    149–50
style manuals, 57, 62–81, 235
  for e-mail, 97, 104–12, 127–8
stylistics, 7–9, 28–9, 64, 124, 128, 147, 198,
    208, 212, 239
subcultural literacy, 75
subject line (in e-mails), 95, 97–8, 140
  as part of the message, 99
suffixes
  in domain names, 20
  in Netspeak, 83–4
suits, 68–9
Sunday Times, The, 1
Surfing, 168
Survey of English Usage, 192–3
Swedish, 21, 217
Swiss Federal Administration, 221

symbols, graphic, 89–90, 124, 214
synchronic vs diachronic nature of the
    Web, 208–9
synchronous vs asynchronous situations,
    11–12, 129, 141, 167, 226
  in language teaching, 234–5
  see also chatgroups

tab character, 110
taboos, 186
Talk facility (Unix), 151–2
tandem learning, 233–4
TCI/IP, 13
technobabble, 2
technology *see* communications
    technology
teenage usage, 88, 124, 166
teleconferencing, 30
telecosm, 225
telegram, 125
telegraph, 2, 125
telephone, 2, 30, 32, 41, 50, 125–6, 162
  ex-directory, 240
  Internet, 226
  tag, 125–6
  translating, 227
  word prediction, 231
teleprinter, 30, 201
teleputer, 226
television, 226, 228
  interactive, 204, 228
  wristwatch, 228
tenses, 181, 191
terminology *see* jargon
text, 6
  games, 231
  graphic types of, 196–7
texting *see* short messaging service
text-messaging *see* short messaging service
textual
  component, 144
  conversation, 25
  records, 169
thesaurus, 210
thinking (in MUDs), 180
thought-bubble, 180
threads, 34, 45, 58
  in chatgroups, 137–40, 142
  in e-mails, 98, 120–1
  in virtual worlds, 183
  losing, 137